Gems TV
Guide to Gems and Jewellery 2006
Revised and Expanded Edition

By Gems TV

In the UK watch Gems TV 24 hours a day on Sky Guide 646, ntl channel 177 and Telewest channel 755

Welcome to Gems TV.

Our dedicated team of over 1,300 craftsmen and jewellers design and create an exclusive range of stunning jewellery.

Whether you are a collector of gemstones or a lover of colourful jewellery, you can now cut out the middlemen by buying direct from one of the world's largest gemstone suppliers.

Gems TV specialises in sourcing only the most beautiful gemstones from the four corners of the globe and setting them in gorgeous handcrafted jewellery, making these stunning creations available direct to you.

In Europe visit our website www.GemsTV.com

You can also watch Gems TV2 24 hours a day on Sky Guide 660, ntl channel 179 and Telewest channel 756

In America & Asia visit our website: www.Thaigem.com

GUIDE TO GEMS & JEWELLERY

This book has been written to provide information on gems and jewellery to hobbyists, collectors and, of course, to those who wear jewellery. Neither the publisher nor the authors will be held liable or responsible to any person or entity with respect to loss or damage as a result of the information supplied in this book, whether caused or said to be caused by a direct or indirect result of its contents.

For further information and the latest updates on the colourful world of gemstones, please visit www.GemsTV.com

Please direct enquiries to either:

Gems TV (UK)
PO Box 12916
Redditch
B97 9BT

Gems TV (Thailand)
Thaigem Building
23/999 Yannaviroch Road
Chanthaburi, Thailand 22000

Published by Gems TV (UK) Ltd
Printed in the UK

First Printed 2006
Copyright © 2006 Gems TV

ISBN-13: 978-0-9551491-1-5
ISBN-10: 0-9551491-1-8

CONTENTS

FOREWORD 6

A-Z OF GEMS CONTENTS 7

A-Z OF GEMS 8

OTHER GEMSTONES 155

WHAT IS A GEM?..................................156

GEM FORMATION.................................158

GEM CRYSTAL PROPERTIES 164

FIRE, LUSTRE & BRILLIANCE..............170

MINING TECHNIQUES 173

FACETING & GEM CUTS 177

GEMSTONE TREATMENTS 189

THE GEM SUPPLY CHAIN...................191

CARAT WEIGHT EXPLAINED 192

JEWELLERY DESIGN 193

JEWELLERY MAKING 175

JEWELLERY SETTINGS..........................203

PRECIOUS METALS 207

HALLMARKING 210

TOP 9 TIPS 212

JEWELLERY VALUATIONS....................215

BIRTHSTONE GEMS 218

ANNIVERSARY GEMS 221

ZODIAC GEMS......................................222

USEFUL CONTACTS 223

INDEX 224

FOREWORD

Since antiquity, kings and queens and the rich and famous have all worn coloured gemstone jewellery. Their rarity and beauty is such that throughout the ages, they have been believed to hold mystical and spiritual powers. History books are full of stories and adventures that feature gems and even the Bible makes numerous references to them.

During the 20th Century, as a result of clever marketing campaigns, Diamonds have become the most renowned gemstone. While nobody doubts the attraction of their brilliance (even though several other coloured gems have a higher refractive index) or their durability (Diamonds are the hardest of all gemstones), in the folklore and legends of centuries gone by, it is the coloured gemstone and not the Diamond that has dominated. Presenting over 490 gem types sourced from over 40 countries, Gems TV is proud to continue this tradition. In this guide, and of course live on Gems TV, you'll discover a dazzling array of coloured gemstones well suited to every pocket and every taste.

Throughout history, many legends have arisen regarding the esoteric and metaphysical properties of gemstones and even today, belief in their powers continues to be widespread. In the A to Z section of this book you will find details on both folklore and gemology. When you read about the beliefs of spiritual healers, please remember that little scientific evidence has been found to substantiate these beliefs. If this area of gem lore interests you, there are numerous books on the subject and a quick search on the Internet will yield thousands of results.

With hundreds of different gem types on offer at Gems TV, 365 days a year, this guide is intended to give you a background into those gems that we feel will form the backbone of our collection throughout 2006. However, the one thing that you can be sure about Mother Nature, is that nothing can be taken for granted. We therefore cannot guarantee the availability of all gems featured in this guide, but likewise I am confident that we will be able to bring you many additional gems that to date we have yet to feature.

"Happy gem hunting!"

Don Kogen, the Gem Hunter

Our A-Z of Gems provides an invaluable insight to the legends, colours and diversity of the wonderful world of gemstones.

A-Z OF GEMS CONTENTS

8	AGATE
9	ALEXANDRITE
13	AMBER
15	AMETHYST
18	AMETRINE
20	AMMOLITE
21	ANDALUSITE
22	APATITE
23	AQUAMARINE
26	AVENTURINE
27	BERYL
28	BIXBITE
29	CASSITERITE
30	CHALCEDONY
31	CHRYSOBERYL
32	CHRYSOCOLLA
33	CHRYSOPRASE
34	CITRINE
35	CORNELIAN
36	DANBURITE
37	DIAMOND
44	DIASPORE
45	DIOPSIDE
48	EMERALD
54	FIRE BERYL™
55	FLUORITE
56	GARNET
64	GREEN AMETHYST (PRASIOLITE)
65	HELIODOR
67	HERDERITE
68	HIDDENITE
69	IDOCRASE
70	IOLITE
72	JADE (NEPHRITE)
73	JASPER
75	KORNERUPINE
76	KUNZITE
78	KYANITE
79	LABRADORITE
80	LAPIS LAZULI
82	MALACHITE
83	MOONSTONE
84	MORGANITE
85	MOTHER OF PEARL
88	OBSIDIAN
89	ONYX
90	OPAL
95	PEARL
101	PERIDOT
103	PEZZOTTAITE
104	PYRITE (MARCASITE)
105	QUARTZ
107	RHODOCHROSITE
108	RUBY
112	SAPPHIRE
121	SCAPOLITE
122	SILLIMANITE
123	SODALITE
124	SPHENE
125	SPINEL
128	SUNSTONE
131	TANOLITE™
132	TANZANITE
137	TEKTITE (MOLDAVITE)
139	TIGER'S EYE
140	TOPAZ
144	TOURMALINE
150	TURQUOISE
152	UNAKITE
153	ZIRCON

As several gems are sometimes referred to by different names, if you cannot find what you are looking for in the A to Z section, please use the index on page 224.

AGATE

Agate is the banded form of Chalcedony (also spelt Calcedony, it is the catch all term for cryptocrystalline Quartz) and its name was derived from the site of its discovery, the river Achates (now Dirillo) in southwest Sicily. You will often find beautifully flowing patterns within Agate, which are caused by the presence of iron and manganese.

Legends and lore

Said by the ancients to render the wearer invisible, Agate has been admired by humanity for thousands of years. Its beauty and durability have prompted humankind to use it for both practical and ornamental purposes. Valued by the ancient Sumerians and Egyptians who used it for amulets, receptacles, and ornamental pieces, Agate is one of the oldest known gems. In Roman times, Agate intaglio (a gem carved in negative relief) signet rings were particularly popular.

Black Agate set in sterling silver

Agate is mentioned in the Bible as being one of the "stones of fire" (Ezekiel 28:13-16) that were given to Moses and set in the breastplate of Aaron (Exodus 28:15-30). A variety of Agate, Sardonyx is one of the twelve gemstones set in the foundations of the city walls of Jerusalem (Revelations 21:19). As compiled by Andreas, Bishop of Caesurae, one of the earliest writers to tie the Apostles with the symbolism of the twelve gems of Jerusalem, Sardonyx represents the Apostle James.

A beautiful example of Fire Agate set in 9k gold with a traditional cabochon cut

Agate was especially valued during medieval times when one of the more outlandish uses was to bind an Agate to each horn of an ox to ensure a good harvest. The danger here is that your Agated beasts of burden may then become invisible and a little hard to find!

Agate is believed to cure insomnia, ensure pleasant dreams, protect against danger, and promote strength and healing.

A 3ct Moss Agate with an unusual 6 Claw setting

Just the facts

The main conditions necessary for Agate formation are the presence of silica from devitrified volcanic ash, water from rainfall or ground sources, manganese, iron and other mineral oxides that form the white, red, blue, grey, brown or black bands.

Agate comes in many different forms ranging from transparent to opaque. Varieties include Blue Agate, Blue Lace Agate, Crazy Lace Agate, Green Agate, Indian Agate, Moss Agate, Fire Agate, Tree Agate, Onyx, Sardonyx and Wood Agate.

AGATE:	Mentioned in the Bible
Locations:	Brazil, India, South Africa
Colours Found:	Various
Typical Cuts:	Cabochon, Ornamental
Family:	Chalcedony
Hardness:	6.50 - 7.00
Refractive Index:	1.53 - 1.54
Relative Density:	2.55 - 2.64

ALEXANDRITE

Known in Russia as the "gem of the tsars", colour change Alexandrite is truly a miraculous gemstone. Often described as "Emerald by day" and "Ruby by night", when viewed under sunlight, Alexandrite appears teal to forest green, but when seen by candlelight, it appears violet, crimson red, raspberry, purple or orange.

Scant availability, remarkable colour change, excellent durability and a sparkling "adamantine" or Diamond-like lustre, makes Alexandrite a "must have" for any true jewellery connoisseur. A rare variety of Chrysoberyl, Alexandrite ranks alongside Tanzanite and Padparadscha Sapphire as one of the world's most coveted gemstones.

Legends and lore

Early one chilly October morning in 1830 a Russian peasant, Maxim Stefanovitch Koshevnikov, was making his way through the silver birch forests along the banks of the Tokovaya River. Tripping on the exposed roots of a large tree felled by a storm, he discovered some gemstones. Quickly identified as Emeralds, by 1831 this deposit in Russia's Ural Mountains was being mined.

The Tokovaya Emerald mines also yielded other gemstones, including a new one that had the strange ability to change colour. When viewed under sunlight, rich green colours appeared but when seen by candlelight it displayed red hues. The gem was named "Alexandrite" after the young Tsarevitch, who was crowned Tsar Alexander II in 1855. Legend has it that Alexandrite was discovered by Emerald miners on his birthday, April 23, 1830, the year the Russian heir apparent came of age. However, Vitaliy Repej, a Ukrainian Alexandrite specialist, believes that Alexandrite was actually discovered on April 3, 1834 by the Tsar's famous Finnish mineralogist Dr. Nils Nordenskjold and wasn't officially called Alexandrite until 1842.

Its birthday aside, this new gem created a sensation - everyone wanted an Alexandrite! But this was certainly no fun for the miners. Following the sparse Alexandrite veins through pegmatite rock with hand dug trenches, open pits and small tunnels, mining was very primitive to say the least. Imagine working through long winters plagued by biting cold and blinding snowdrifts. Summer brought no respite, just great swarms of gnats, mosquitoes and gadflies.

The fortuity of the discovery of Alexandrite on the

Unusual drop earrings with fine Russian Alexandrite

An exceptionally rare Russian Alexandrite in 18k gold

The beautiful simplicity of this solitaire pendant displays a pear shape Alexandrite to excellent effect

Alexandrite in different lighting conditions

ALEXANDRITE

A bracelet by Gems TV with one of the rarest gems - Alexandrite

Fine Alexandrite complemented by Diamonds and 18k gold

Fashionable yet timeless - drop earrings in white gold and Alexandrite

Don Kogen, the Gem Hunter says:

"Without doubt, Alexandrite along with Tanzanite are two of the most glorious gems that we set into jewellery. During my 15 years travelling the world sourcing gems, the relationships I have built to source these gems are the very best."

future Tsar's birthday was considered manifold as the colours displayed by this unusual gem can mirror the Imperial Russian military colours of red and green. Possessing dual nationalistic connotations, Alexandrite quickly gained popularity in Russia, where it was believed to bring good luck.

Because of its two colours, in Russia it is also believed to invite loneliness if you only wear one piece of Alexandrite jewellery.

Alexandrite is believed by crystal healers to strengthen the wearer's intuition in critical situations. Some also attribute Alexandrite with the ability to aid creativity and inspire imagination.

Just the facts

In gemmology, it is correct to call any Chrysoberyl that changes colour Alexandrite. The nomenclature is not dependent on the colours of the change. However, Alexandrite's colour change is dependant on pure light sources (pure candescent light to pure incandescent light, for example sunlight to candlelight).

Interestingly, the colour change effect is not unique to Alexandrite. Many gem types display colour change, such as Sapphire and Garnet. However, the degree of colour change exhibited by Alexandrite is the most extreme encountered in natural gems.

Similar to Emeralds, inclusions are a common feature in Alexandrite. Far from being flaws, inclusions record a gem's natural relationship with the earth. Given the prevalence of synthetic Alexandrite, they are also a fascinating hallmark of authenticity that helps us distinguish real gems from artificial impostors.

Arguably, one of the best uses of Alexandrite is in earrings and pendants. In this position, the vibrancy of Alexandrite's colour change is easily noticed. Alexandrite rings are also popular, as it is a very tough gem with a hardness that is only transcended by Rubies, Sapphires or Diamonds.

Because of this gem's scarcity, Alexandrite is found in a wide variety of shapes and sizes faceted to maximise the carat weight and beauty of each individual crystal.

Coveted for their beautiful and mysterious optical effects, when you look at a Cat's Eye Alexandrite you can see a single band of light on its surface. Technically known as "chatoyancy", this intriguing phenomenon is unique to the world of gemstones. It is caused by minerals reflecting a band of light back to the eye like a mirror. Cat's Eye Alexandrite makes particularly stunning signet rings and is a powerful display of a unique sense of style.

While beautiful Alexandrite is available from other locales, amongst Alexandrite connoisseurs, Russian Alexandrite maintains an historical pedigree that is highly coveted. In 1898 Edwin Streeter wrote in Precious Stones & Gems: "The wonderful Alexandrite is an Emerald by day and an Amethyst at night. Its market value is extremely variable, and sometimes as much as £20 per carat is paid for a fine stone". Today, the same Russian Alexandrite is worth many thousands of pounds!

Although the Tokovaya deposit closed only after a few decades, limited mining resumed in 1995. To date, very little mining of Russian Alexandrite is taking place. In December 2005, Coloured Stone reported that "there have been unconfirmed reports of new activity in this area, but no significant amount of material has hit the market yet". While it is a country rich in gemstones, since the fall of the Soviet Union much of Russia's gems have not been mined due to both economic conditions and outdated mining practices. Interesting, both De Beers (a famed Diamond consortium) and Russian geologists are currently surveying Russian Diamond reserves and an offshoot of this exploration may be the discovery of new Alexandrite deposits. Regardless, very little Russian Alexandrite is available and those lucky enough to own one truly are custodians of a gem from a bygone era.

While it wasn't until 1996 that the tribal peoples of Andhra Pradesh unearthed the first hints of Alexandrite in the Araku Valley, since its discovery Indian Alexandrite has endured a history as turbulent as Imperial Russia. From much needed mining regulation in 1999, to the destruction of coastal mines during the 2004 Tsunami, Indian Alexandrite has certainly had its ups and downs. Displaying teal apple greens with changes ranging from orange raspberries to grape, the first Alexandrite ever featured on Gems TV was from Vishnakahaputnam in Andhra Pradesh, India. Always on the hunt for this stunning gem, we recently encountered Indian Alexandrite from a new locale whose rich colours are reminiscent of Alexandrite from the original Russian deposit. Today, Indian Alexandrite primarily hails from Narsipattnanm, 100 kilometres inland from the first discovery in Vishnakahaputnam. It is characterized by an intense

ALEXANDRITE

A contemporary ring by Gems TV in white gold and Alexandrite

Simple but effective earrings in white gold and Alexandrite

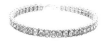

A tennis bracelet encrusted with rare Russian Alexandrite

An example of Alexandrite from India

ALEXANDRITE

Showing fine chatoyancy - Alexandrite Cat's Eye

Six perfectly colour matched Cat's Eye Alexandrite gems

Cat's Eye Alexandrite

green with an incredible colour change that ranges from vibrant Amethyst, to Ruby red and reddish purple. Formed hundreds of millions of years ago during the Palaeozoic era, it is believed that the pegmatite rocks found at the location of Alexandrite's discovery in the Urals in Russia and at Narsipattnanm are the same. Mining Indian Alexandrite is a dangerous business and the tribal miners risk life and limb tunnelling muddy soil to a depth of 30 metres to find rocks rich with tiny clusters of Alexandrite.

While gems from the famous Brazilian state of Minas Gerais have enchanted the world for over 100 years, good quality Alexandrite was only discovered in 1987. As with other mines containing pegmatite rocks, Brazilian Alexandrite is found in rugged areas that can be difficult to access. Usually mined using primitive hand tools, one of the most famous exceptions is the Hematitia mine, whose beautiful Alexandrite is now regrettably depleted. Although the majority of Brazilian Alexandrite is heavily included or translucent, a tiny amount of better quality gems have been unearthed. In 2004, a new pocket of Brazilian Alexandrite was discovered, yielding blue green Alexandrite that changed to a delightful raspberry red.

Mines in Madagascar, Tanzania and Mozambique, have been producing good quality Alexandrite for several years. African Alexandrite is typically located in wet regions near rivers and mined by digging through river beds by hand to unearth the Alexandrite rich pegmatite rock.

For approximately 90 years Russia and Sri Lanka were the only know sources of Alexandrite. Obtained from alluvial gravels (in contrast to most other deposits that are mined from host pegmatite rock), Sri Lankan Alexandrite is characterized by a fine Sapphire green colour in daylight with a change to columbine red, similar to purplish red Spinel, in incandescent light.

Steve Bennett, Gems TV MD says:

"I wear my Alexandrite Cat's Eye ring nearly every day. There is something magical and mystical about it. At times, the optical illusion of the chatoyancy within the gem will even appear as if it is winking at you - simply fascinating!

With so much history surrounding Alexandrite, I often launch into a massive story about the gemstone when asked about my ring. And because of its rarity and deep green colour, when alone and quietly sitting and admiring it, the feeling I experience is one of calmness."

ALEXANDRITE:	June's birthstone
Locations:	Brazil, Madagascar, India, Russia, Tanzania
Colours Found:	Teal to forest green changing to violet, crimson red, raspberry, purple or orange
Typical Cuts:	Brilliant, Heart, Marquise, Oval
Family:	Chrysoberyl
Hardness:	8.50
Refractive Index:	1.74 - 1.75
Relative Density:	3.71

AMBER

Amber is the ancient and fossilised resin of long dead trees that grew in forests millions of years ago. Over the eons, chemical and physical changes occurred, fossilizing the resin to produce the Amber we know today.

Research indicates that Amber ranges from about 2 million to 360 million years in age although most gem quality Amber ranges from 5 million to 50 million years.

Amber is a unique gem. On top of its beauty, Amber bequeaths man valuable scientific data through its ability to act as a window on the past. Its unique ability to preserve the organic tissues of prehistoric life forms is valued by both gem collectors and scientists..

Legends and lore

In classical times, Amber was used medicinally and was also believed to offer a magical light for the deceased as they progressed through the underworld. Given this association, Amber was once believed to provide magicians and sorcerers with special powers.

Other attributes associated with Amber include love, strength, luck, healing, protection and the ability to calm stressed nerves.

Just the facts

When you rub Amber, static electricity is generated. In fact, the word electricity is derived from the ancient Greek word for Amber, "elektron" or "sun made". Although a fossilised plant resin that generally consists of organic carbon, hydrogen and oxygen structures, the composition varies depending on the type of parental plant species.

The organic inclusions commonly found in Amber include plant debris, small animals and a variety of pre-historic insects. These ancient creatures are predominantly extinct ancestors of today's cockroaches, ants, termites, caddis flies, centipedes, crickets, scorpions and millipedes. These preserved life forms were trapped by fresh sticky resin that oozed from coniferous trees millions of years ago. Preserved in the Amber, the insects are visible in almost perfect condition, showing the position they were in when they were entombed millions of years ago.

The most valued variety of Amber for manufacturing jewellery and decorative objects is Baltic Amber. Occurring in yellow, golden and brown colours, Baltic Amber is also known as Succinite after its parent tree

A simple and eyecatching design containing this amazing prehistoric gem

Nine pieces of stunning Baltic Amber

A regal design with radiant Amber results in this majestic necklace

Amber

13

AMBER

This contemporary necklace contains 16 inches of beautiful Amber

A simple and eyecatching design containing this amazing pre-historic gem

Contemporary style and ancient beauty

pinus succinfera that was common in the tertiary period, some 50 million years ago. At present, the primary source of Baltic Amber is the various deposits around the Russian port of Kaliningrad, the old German enclave of Koenigsberg. Incredibly light, Amber is occasionally buoyant in salt water and is sometimes transported long distances by the sea, having been found as far away as the beaches of England and Scotland. It's from this ability it gains one of its common names, "Seastone". Important secondary sources include the Dominican Republic and Mexico.

Since the Jurassic Park movies, interest in insect and animal included Amber has exploded, making it highly collectable. In regard to the film Jurassic Park, the alleged source of the dinosaur DNA was Dominican Amber. However Dominican Amber is thought to be about 25 million years too young to truly contain dinosaur DNA, making the plot slightly inaccurate. However, other Amber sources from around the world could potentially contain the genetic material of these avian ancestors.

In 1994 a molecular biologist from California reported that he had extracted DNA from an insect sealed in Amber 120 to 130 million years ago. Dr. Raul Canu claimed the insect was trapped when dinosaurs ruled the earth; leading people to speculate that Michael Crichton's novel could one day become a scientific reality.

In 2005, 96% of Gems TV customers said their delivery arrived on time or earlier than they expected.[*]

AMBER:	Preserves pre-historic life forms
Locations:	Russia
Colours Found:	Golden yellow, pale yellow, deep cherry-red to dark brown
Typical Cuts:	Beads, Cabochon, Ornamental
Family:	Organics
Hardness:	2.00 - 3.00
Refractive Index:	1.54
Relative Density:	1.05 - 1.10

AMETHYST

*Oval cut Uruguayan
Amethyst*

AMETHYST

A modern designer ring in white gold and Amethyst

Contemporary drop earrings with Amethyst briolettes

Unusual and stunningly cut Amethyst in white gold

Rough Amethyst

Dionysus, known for his love of grape juice, was the Greek god of wine, however after a few goblets he became a little confrontational. One day in the forest with goblet in hand, the tipsy Dionysus took insult from a passing mortal that refused to show him respect. The incident provoked his wrath and Dionysus swore revenge on the next mortal that he saw…

Along came Amethyst, a beautiful young maiden on her way to pay tribute to the goddess Diana. Dionysus targeted Amethyst as the object of his revenge, and with the snap of his fingers, he summoned two ferocious tigers to devour the girl. As Dionysus sat back to enjoy the spectacle, Amethyst cried out to her goddess Diana. Seeing what was about to happen, Diana transformed Amethyst into a glimmering pure white Quartz statue thus protecting her from the ferocious tigers. Moved with guilt, Dionysus realised the ruthlessness of his actions and began to weep with sorrow. As the tears dripped into his goblet, Dionysus collapsed spilling the tear-tainted wine onto the statue of Amethyst. The white Quartz absorbed the wine's colour creating the coloured gem that we refer to today as Amethyst, the gemstone of the gods..

Legends and lore

With the mythology surrounding the origin of Amethyst, it is perhaps fitting that it was once considered a talisman to prevent drunkenness, which explains why wine goblets were once made from this gem. Indeed, it derives its name from the Greek word "amethustos", meaning "not drunk".

Amethyst's shades of purple have served as a symbol of royalty throughout history. Pharaohs, kings and queens, as well as leading lights in religious sects have long treasured it because of its rich, royal colour.

Interestingly, this fascination with the colour purple dates back to Roman times when Generals celebrating triumphs (and later Emperors who never fought a battle) got to wear a "toga picta" (a bright purple toga with gold embroidery).

Because Amethyst is thought to encourage celibacy and symbolise piety, it was a key feature in the decoration of Catholic churches in the Middle Ages. Amethyst was considered to be the "papal stone". Even today, Bishops still wear Amethyst rings.

The history of adornment can be traced back to the Minoan period in Greece (circa 2500 BC), where Amethyst has been found as polished cabochons set into gold rings. Popular in the 19th century, Amethyst was a favourite gem in art nouveau jewellery.

AMETHYST

Just the facts

Coloured by iron, Amethyst is a variety of macrocrystalline Quartz that occurs in transparent pastel roses to deep purples.

Like many other gemstones, the quality of Amethyst varies according to its source. Amethyst from the Americas can be found in large sizes as opposed to African Amethyst (typically mined in Madagascar), which is small but carries a higher saturation in colour. Dark, highly saturated, Amethyst is also found in Australia. The Siberian variety is deep purple with occasional red and blue flashes and commands the highest price. However, the most prolific origin is Brazil, and if we were to believe Dionysus' wine was indeed the source of its colour, Brazilian Amethyst would have been born from the finest vintages.

Deep rich colour of Uruguayan Amethyst in simple white gold earrings

First appearing in Europe in 1727, Brazilian Amethyst soon became highly fashionable and expensive. Amethyst was very popular in France and England during the 18th century and many affluent families invested large amounts of money in this gemstone. For example, a necklace of Amethysts was purchased at a very high price for Queen Charlotte (1744-1818), wife of George III of England.

The chief mining areas for Brazilian Amethyst are Minas Gerais, Bahia and Maraba. Neighbouring Uruguay offers spectacularly beautiful varieties of Amethyst that were only discovered a few years ago.

Perfectly cut square Amethyst pendant

Rose de France Amethyst (also known as Lavender Amethyst) is the name for Brazilian Amethyst of a pastel lilac pinkish hue. Rose de France Amethyst was a very popular Victorian gem and while Rose de France Amethyst frequently appears in antique jewellery, it is currently experiencing a revival in popularity as part of a general awakening to the beauty of pastel gems.

Perfectly matched Amethysts in a gold bracelet by Gems TV

What our Craftsmen say:

Miss Natthika Sangsot - Jeweller

"Gems TV offers one of the world's most extensive collections of Amethyst gemstones, including the world's best deep purple Amethyst with red flashes from Uruguay. This stunning gem is ideal for all kinds of jewellery including earrings, necklaces and rings."

AMETHYST:	February's birthstone
Locations:	Brazil, Kenya, Madagascar, Uruguay, Zambia
Colours Found:	Shades of purple
Typical Cuts:	Fancy, Oval
Family:	Quartz
Hardness:	7.00
Refractive Index:	1.54 - 1.55
Relative Density:	6.50

17

AMETRINE

*Cushion cut Ametrine
pendant showing the
two colours to
perfection*

AMETRINE

Ametrine is one of the world's most unusual gemstones in that it is actually two gems in one! Bi-colour Ametrine blends the golden sunburst of Citrine with the purple sunset of Amethyst.

Legends and lore

Ametrine is said to possess all the metaphysical benefits of both Amethyst and Citrine, as well its own unique properties. Ametrine is said to aid in meditation, relieve tension, disperse negativity and help to eliminate prejudice.

Just the facts

The unusual colour variation found in Ametrine is due to the presence of iron in different oxidation states within the crystalline structure. Exactly how this occurs is not fully understood.

The world's main source of Ametrine, the Bolivian Anahi mine became famous in the 17th century when a Spanish Conquistador received it as a dowry after marrying an Ayoreos princess named Anahi.

Ametrine has only been readily available to the consumer market since 1980 when material from the Anahi mine in Bolivia began to appear in larger quantities. Before this it was considered to be quite unusual and was also known as Amethyst-Citrine Quartz, Trystine or Golden Amethyst.

The colour split is usually highlighted by cutting the gem into long shapes ideal for rings, earrings and necklaces. Larger Ametrine gemstones make particularly enchanting pendants, perfect for evening wear.

A fine split in the colours and colour intensity are the most important aspects to consider when evaluating Ametrine.

Ametrine is an amazing gemstone with a split personality. When handcrafting Ametrine jewellery we always try to ensure that both the Amethyst and the Citrine are clearly visible to the naked eye.

Beautifully coloured Ametrine in gold by Gems TV

Four baguette cut Ametrines displayed in a beautifully unusual Bar setting

A Brazilian Ametrine pendant showing the amazing split colour quality of this rare and unusual gemstone

Ametrine

AMETRINE:	Bi-colour split
Locations:	Bolivia
Colours Found:	Golden & purple
Typical Cuts:	Baguette, Octagon
Family:	Quartz
Hardness:	7.00
Refractive Index:	1.54 - 1.55
Relative Density:	6.50

AMMOLITE

When used in jewellery, Ammolite is sometimes crafted into Quartz or Spinel doublets (gemstones consisting of two or more parts that have been artificially joined together to give the impression of a single gemstone) for additional strength.

Ammonite Fossil

Rarer than Diamond, Ammolite is the fossilised remains of a squid-like creature called an Ammonite that used jet propulsion to travel over 65 million years ago. From the Palaeozoic era to the end of the cretaceous era, Ammonites jetted around the world's oceans preying on smaller forms of marine life. For nearly 330 million years, they were abundant in all of the oceans until they suddenly became extinct, around the same time as the demise of the dinosaurs.

Ammolite is named after "ammon", the ancient Egyptian god of life and reproduction, because the shell of the Ammonite is similar in appearance to the ram-headed deity's horns. For a similar reason (along with a legend of prosperity), the Blackfoot Tribe of North America knows Ammolite as the "Buffalo Stone".

Legends and lore

The legend of Ammolite goes back to the Blackfoot tribe of North America. The story begins amidst a severely harsh winter with a blizzard wiping out all the Blackfoot Indians' food reserves. Upon seeing the devastation that befell the Blackfoot people, the Great Goddess sent a dream to an Indian princess. In the dream she directed the princess to a brilliantly coloured gemstone, telling her "take this stone back to your tribe, for its magic will bring with it a huge herd of buffalo that will sustain you through the winter". After days of perilous travel, she found the gem hidden in a cave. With sunlight dancing off of its rainbow coloured skin, it was truly magnificent. The next day everyone was woken up by the sound of stomping hooves. When coming outside, the tribe found that a herd of buffalo had returned to pasture nearby. The people rejoiced at their salvation and thanked the Goddess for her gift. Through the aid of Ammolite, the Blackfoot were able to survive and ever since Ammolite has been referred to as the "Buffalo Stone", signifying wealth and abundance.

Just the facts

Ammonite fossils are found on every continent but it is those found in and around Alberta, Canada that display the most vivid colours and are treasured as gems. In 1908 a member of the National Geological Survey team found mineralized fossils of Ammonite along the St. Mary's River in Alberta. It was not until 1981 that enough high quality Ammolite was discovered to make mining commercially viable. CIBJO (International Jewellery Confederation) officially recognized Ammolite as a gemstone in 1981.

AMMOLITE:	Also known as Buffalo Stone
Locations:	Canada, USA
Colours Found:	Various
Typical Cuts:	Cabochon
Family:	Organics
Hardness:	5.00 - 6.00
Refractive Index:	1.52 - 1.67
Relative Density:	2.80

ANDALUSITE

Andalusite, an aluminium silicate, derives its name from the site of its discovery, Almeria in the southern Spanish province of Andalusia.

While Andalusite's colour play has been compared to Alexandrite, this is technically incorrect as pleochroic (displaying different colours in different directions) gemstones like Andalusite feature all their colours at once, whereas Alexandrite only changes colour in different light sources.

Legends and lore

Some Andalusite crystals have carbonaceous inclusions, arranged so that in cross-section they form a dark cross. This variety is called "Chiastolite" (named after the Greek word for cross) and sometimes referred to in ancient texts as "Lapis Crucifer", meaning "Cross Stone" or "Macle". Chiastolite existed in schist's near the town of Santiago de Compostela, northwest Spain, and many amulets of the "Cross Stone" were once sold to pilgrims. Chiastolite is often mentioned as a gemstone of protection and was once used to thwart evil eye curses.

Simple and effective Andalusite pendant in white gold

Andalusite is considered by crystal healers to be a gemstone that enhances intellect, problem solving abilities and mental clarity. It is also mentioned as being conducive to the receipt of messages from the netherworld.

One of our popular designs in Andalusite and gold

Just the facts

Andalusite is a polymorph with two other minerals, Kyanite and Sillimanite. Andalusite typically occurs in thermally metamorphosed pelitic rocks, and in pelites that have been regionally metamorphosed under low-pressure conditions. It also occurs, together with Corundum, Tourmaline, Topaz and other minerals in some pegmatites.

Andalusite complemented by Diamonds.

When cutting most pleochroic gemstones (Iolite, Tanzanite, Kunzite etc.), lapidaries typically try to minimize the pleochroism and maximize the single most prominent colour. Interestingly, Andalusite is the opposite, as cutters try to orient the gem to get a pleasing mix of orange, brown, yellow, green and golden colours. When cut successfully, Andalusite looks unlike any other gemstone, displaying patterns of colour dancing around its facets.

Andalusite

ANDALUSITE:	Pleochroism
Locations:	Brazil, Mozambique, Sri Lanka
Colours Found:	Brown, green, orange, red & white
Typical Cuts:	Oval, Round Brilliant
Family:	Andalusite
Hardness:	4.50 - 7.00
Refractive Index:	1.71 - 1.73
Relative Density:	3.56 - 3.68

21

APATITE

While it sounds like its hungry, it's actually trying to fool you! The name Apatite comes from the Greek word "apatao", meaning "to deceive", as Apatite has often been confused with gems such as Paraiba Tourmaline, Peridot (Olivine) and Beryl.

Ironically, the phosphates in bones and teeth of all vertebrate animals are members of the Apatite group, so the hunger connection is quite appropriate after all.

Legends and lore

Apatite is said to enhance one's insight, learning abilities and creativity, and to give increased self-confidence. It also is said to help achieve deeper states of meditation. Using Apatite is said to facilitate the desired results when working with other crystals.

Apatite is also believed by crystal healers to be useful to help improve one's coordination, to strengthen muscles, help suppress hunger and to ease hypertension.

Just the facts

Apatite is actually three different minerals depending on the predominance of either fluorine, chlorine or the hydroxyl group: calcium (fluoro, chloro, hydroxyl) phosphate. These ions can freely substitute in the crystal lattice and all three are usually present in every specimen although some specimens are almost 100% pure in one group.

Gem quality Apatite is rare, particularly over 1 carat. The colour of Apatite is often due to the presence of rare earth elements. It comes in many colours, including green, yellow, blue, violet, and a yellow-green variety, originally mined in Spain, commonly called "Asparagus Stone" because of its similarity in colour to the vegetable. Cat's Eye Apatite is also known.

Recent finds of Apatite in Madagascar have added to the popularity of this gem. Exhibiting excellent saturation, Madagascan Apatite's colours range from neon green to neon blue.

Simple Apatite stud earrings in yellow gold

Apatite tennis bracelet by Gems TV - always a popular choice

A stunning Apatite pendant

Rough Apatite

Apatite

Fort Dauphin Apatite

APATITE:	Pleochroism
Locations:	Brazil, Kenya, Madagascar, Mozambique, Sri Lanka
Colours Found:	Blue, green, neon, violet, yellow & yellow-green
Typical Cuts:	Oval
Family:	Apatite
Hardness:	5.00
Refractive Index:	1.63 - 1.64
Relative Density:	3.10 - 3.30

AQUAMARINE

*Sixteen Brazilian
Aquamarines
perfectly colour
matched to create
this elegant bracelet*

AQUAMARINE

Stunningly simple - fine Aquamarine set in gold with Sapphire and Diamond

The deep colour of Santa Maria Aquamarine shown in this exclusive Gems TV design

One for the evening, Aquamarine in an elegant classic piece of neckwear

The beauty of Santa Maria Aquamarine in an equally beautiful setting

The sheer beauty of Aquamarine, with its wonderful colour and fantastic clarity, makes it popular with both the collector and the wearer of fine jewellery. It will come as no surprise that its name was derived from the Latin words for "water of the sea".

Blue, the world's most popular colour, is famous for its calming effect, and out of all the blues available none match the serenity found in Aquamarine. Aquamarine embodies all that is natural. Aquamarine, the sparkling birthstone for March, ranges from pastel blue to light green, its passive tones reminiscent of an invigorating sea breeze.

Legends and lore

Since antiquity, Aquamarine has been seen as a gemstone of great vision, its crystals often being used as eyes in the creation of sculpted statues that symbolize power and wisdom. According to legend, any man or woman that set eyes on these statues became a person of great wisdom harnessing the ability to see into the future. On occasions, these statues were placed in strategic positions near the coastline where they could calm the wrath of the god Poseidon, thus insuring the safe return of those on ships at sea.

Aquamarine has long been associated with its ability to capture oceanic energy. When amulets made of Aquamarine were worn, sailors believed that unmatched bravery would be instilled in their souls. These fisherman's friends accompanied their owners while out on the high seas, and in the event of a storm, were tossed overboard to placate Poseidon's anger. Interestingly, Thai culture contains a common belief that Aquamarine can ward off seasickness and prevent wearers from drowning. Because of its association with the sea, Aquamarine is considered to be a gemstone of purification and cleansing that washes the mind with fresh clear thoughts and promotes self-expression. Its calming effects make it a popular gemstone for those

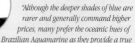

Don Kogen, the Gem Hunter says:

"Although the deeper shades of blue are rarer and generally command higher prices, many prefer the oceanic hues of Brazilian Aquamarine as they provide a true reflection of the sea. Either way, the gentle lustre and delicate tones of Aquamarine are a majestic contribution to any gemstone collection."

who practice meditation, as it is also believed to eradicate fears and phobias.

Just the facts

Aquamarine, symbolizing the near perfect clarity and transparency of the ocean, is the big sister of the Beryl family whose relatives also include Bixbite, Goshenite, Emerald, Heliodor and Morganite. Brazil has been the world's major supplier of Aquamarine for decades. The famous Marambaia area is one of the most important sources of fine Aquamarine in the world.

Today however, several African nations including Nigeria, Mozambique, Zambia and Madagascar provide an equal, if not greater supply of similarly beautiful examples. The different shades of Aquamarine are distinguished by their own names. "Santa Maria" is the name of the rare, intensely deep blue Aquamarine found in the Santa Maria de Itabira mines of Brazil. Very similar colours are also found in certain mines in Africa, especially in Mozambique, where they have come to be known as "Santa Maria Africana". Another Brazilian beauty is the deep blue "Espirito Santo", coming from the Brazilian state of Espirito Santo. Another beautifully coloured variety has taken its name from a 1954 Brazilian beauty queen, "Martha Rocha".

AQUAMARINE

The cool beauty of Aquamarine

One of the jewellery essentials, Aquamarine in an elegant bracelet

Aquamarine

AQUAMARINE:	March's birthstone
Locations:	Brazil, Madagascar, Mozambique, Namibia, Nigeria, Tanzania, Zambia
Colours Found:	Pastel blue to bluish green
Typical Cuts:	Various
Family:	Beryl
Hardness:	7.50 - 8.00
Refractive Index:	1.57 - 1.59
Relative Density:	2.68 - 2.80

AVENTURINE

Aventurine lends itself perfectly to gents jewellery as well as ladies

Unusual grey Adventurine in a 9k gold ladies ring

Blue Aventurine pendant in white gold

Aventurine's name is derived from an accident. During the 18th century, Venetian glass workers were preparing molten glass when copper filings accidentally fell into the batch producing glass with sparkles. The name Aventurine comes from the Italian "a ventura" which means "by chance". But make no mistake, Aventurine is certainly not glass, it is actually a much sought after member of the Chalcedony Quartz family.

Legends and lore

Aventurine has been used as a lucky talisman and is a popular gem for gamblers.

Legends say that it is an all-purpose healer, used to reduce stress, develop confidence, imagination and improve prosperity. An ancient legend from Tibet tells of its use to help nearsightedness and to improve the wearer's creativity.

Many crystal healers believe that Aventurine has the capacity to calm a troubled spirit, balance emotions and bring an inner peace. It is also believed to enhance leadership qualities allowing the wearer to act decisively, with strong intuitive power.

Just the facts

Aventurine is a Chalcedony that contains small inclusions of one of several shiny minerals which give the gem a glistening effect. The glistening effect of Aventurine is known as "aventurescence". The colour of the aventurescence depends on the mineral included in the gem. Mica inclusions give the gem a yellow or silver glitter or sheen. Goethite and Hematite inclusions give the gem a red or grey glitter or sheen. Fuschite inclusions give the gem a green sheen.

Aventurine ranges in colour from green, peach, brown, blue and creamy green. If a colour is not stated with the word Aventurine, it is usually assumed to be green. In the past, Green Aventurine has been miscalled "Indian Jade".

AVENTURINE:	Aventurescence
Locations:	Brazil, India, USA
Colours Found:	Blue, brown, creamy green, green & peach
Typical Cuts:	Beads, Cabochon, Ornamental
Family:	Quartz
Hardness:	6.50
Refractive Index:	1.54
Relative Density:	2.59 - 2.61

Aventurine

BERYL

The name Beryl is from the ancient Greek "Beryllos" for the precious blue-green colour of sea water. This was originally applied to all green gemstones, but later used only for Beryl. Some scholars believe the word Beryl is related to the ancient trading city of Belur or perhaps came from the word Pearl known as "Velurya" in old Hindi and "Vaidurya" in Sanskrit.

Beryl is, when absolutely pure, totally devoid of colour. Small amounts of metallic elements can be present in the crystal structure, giving rise to many colour variations. Aquamarine (page 24), Bixbite (page 28), Emerald (page 48), Fire Beryl™ - Goshenite (page 54) and Heliodor (page 65) are all members of the Beryl family and more information can be found on individual members of the Beryl family throughout this guide.

Just the facts

Gemstone colour varieties that belong to Beryl with specific names are listed below. All other colours of Beryl being simply referred to by their colour (e.g. Yellow Beryl):

Stunning clarity in this Trilliant cut Beryl pendant

Aquamarine	Pale green to blue
Bixbite	Red
Emerald	Green
Fire Beryl™ (Goshenite)	Colourless
Heliodor	Pale yellow to yellowish-orange
Morganite	Pale pink to salmon coloured

Marquise cut Yellow Beryl in this feminine piece

Beryl is famous for their perfect, six-sided prismatic hexagon crystals that usually occur individually. These are often enormous and some 8 meter, well-crystallized examples are known to have existed.

All Beryl varieties can be faceted into various gem cuts, and some Beryl displays phenomena including asterism (star effect), chatoyancy (cat's eye effect) and an unusual effect in Emerald called trapichism.

Yellow Beryl and Diamond in a classic cluster combination

BERYL:	Perfect 6-sided prismatic hexagon crystals
Locations:	Afghanistan, Brazil, Colombia, Madagascar, Mozambique, Nigeria, Pakistan, South Africa, Zambia
Colours Found:	Various
Typical Cuts:	Various
Family:	Beryl
Hardness:	7.50 - 8.00
Refractive Index:	1.56 - 1.61
Relative Density:	2.60 - 2.90

Beryl

27

BIXBITE

Bixbite is the red variety of Beryl. Named after the mineral collector Maynard Bixby, Bixbite was discovered at the turn of the 20th century at the Thomas Range, Utah.

Bixbite is commonly called Red Emerald and occasionally referred to as American Emerald.

Just the facts

Very scarce, Bixbite is only known to occur in a few areas of the western USA, possibly one location in Mexico and possibly in Brazil. Bixbite suitable for faceting is extremely rare and is typically small in size (under 0.5 carat). The average size is 0.15 carats and the largest recorded Bixbite weighed 7 carats.

The "traditional" deposit for Bixbite, the Wah Wah Mountains, Utah has presently ceased operation. The last operators had to completely restore the site when they passed on their option. Apparently, anyone wishing to go back and re-open the mine will spend millions just removing overburden. There may still be lots of Bixbite in the ground at the location but its extraction hasn't proved to be economically viable.

Like Emeralds, inclusions in Bixbite are common, especially in specimens over 1 carat. However, its rarity and novelty for gemstone collectors has always been the primary factor.

Contemporary design with Bixbite in this 9k gold pendant

Bixbite

BIXBITE:	Commonly known as Red Emerald
Locations:	USA
Colours Found:	Red
Typical Cuts:	Various
Family:	Beryl
Hardness:	7.50 - 8.00
Refractive Index:	1.57 - 1.60
Relative Density:	2.66 - 2.70

What our Craftsmen say:

Mrs.Chatchada Sutiphum - Polishing

"This is a gem that gets all of the girls talking here in Thailand. It is simply one of the most feminine of colours and often has a beauty that can mesmerise."

We cut out all the middlemen, which means lower prices for you.

GemsTV

28

Cassiterite's name comes from the Phoenician word for tin "cassiterid" (the Greek equivalent is "kassiteros"), which referred generically to the islands of England and Ireland. In fact, around the 6th century BC, Carthage (the greatest Phoenician colony) tried to create a tin monopoly by importing tin ores directly from the original areas of extraction, the "tin islands" (Cassiterid Islands), known today as England.

Just the facts

The primary ore of tin, most sources of Cassiterite today are not primary deposits but alluvial deposits containing weathered grains.

Cassiterite has been an important tin ore for eons and is still the greatest source of tin today. During the Bronze Age it was added to molten copper to form bronze. Some of the oldest Cassiterite mines, such as those in Cornwall, England have been worked since 2000 BC and are now exhausted. But this multifunctional ore is much more than just an industrial mineral, some rare specimens of Cassiterite are definitely gem quality: rare, beautiful and durable.

To discover the beauty of this gem, the rough material needs polishing. Once this is completed, Cassiterite displays a high lustre which, in combination with its multiple crystal faces, produces stunning brilliance.

Cassiterite is usually black, reddish brown and yellow in colour and gems larger than 1 carat are exceedingly rare. If you are looking for a gem with a historic connection to England to proudly adorn your body, Cassiterite must surely be a first choice.

CASSITERITE

Stylishly designed 18k gold pendant with Cassiterite

The classic simplicity of this solitaire ring shows the beauty of Cassiterite

Beautifully cut Trilliant Cassiterite 18k gold pendant

Cassiterite

CASSITERITE:	Greatest source of tin
Locations:	Bolivia, China, Indonesia, Malaysia, Mexico, Namibia, Russia, Spain
Colours Found:	Black, reddish brown & yellow
Typical Cuts:	Various
Family:	Rutile
Hardness:	6.00 - 7.00
Refractive Index:	2.00
Relative Density:	6.60 - 7.00

CHALCEDONY

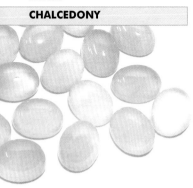

Chalcedony's (also spelt Calcedony) name is derived from Chalcedon or Calchedon, an ancient port of Bithynia, near present day Istanbul, Turkey. It has a waxy lustre and appears in a great variety of colours including blue, white, buff, tan, green, red, grey, black, yellow or brown. Different coloured varieties of Chalcedony have individual names.

Agate	White, red, blue, grey, brown or black bands
Bloodstone	Green with red spots
Chalcedony	Blue to brownish blue
Chrysoprase	Apple green
Cornelian	Orange to red
Flint	Dull grey to black
Jasper	Red, yellow, brown or green (generally has spots)
Sard	Light to dark brown

A striking 8.6ct icy Blue Chalcedony gem sits regally on the delicate shoulders of this ring

This stylishly simple pendant shows the versatility of Chalcedony gemstones

Chalcedony

Legends and lore

The Romans prized Chalcedony as seals, and in the New Testament (Revelations 21:19) Chalcedony is one of the twelve gemstones set in the foundations of the city walls of Jerusalem. As compiled by Andreas, Bishop of Caesurae, one of the earliest writers to tie the Apostles with the symbolism of the twelve gems of Jerusalem, Chalcedony represented the Apostle St. Andrew.

Chalcedony was used during the Renaissance as a magic amulet to promote health and safety.

Chalcedony is one of the gemstones used in commesso or Florentine mosaic. Developed in Florence in the late 16th century, commesso is a technique of fashioning pictures with thin, cut-to-shape pieces of brightly coloured gems.

Just the facts

Quartz gemstones are commonly separated into two groups based on the size of their individual crystals. The macrocrystalline Quartz (large crystal) group includes many popular gemstones such as Amethyst, Ametrine, Citrine and Green Amethyst (Prasiolite). Cryptocrystalline Quartz includes species whose individual crystals are too small to be easily distinguished. Apart from being a variety within the group, Chalcedony is also a catch all term to describe cryptocrystalline Quartz and includes many gems that have been coveted since antiquity.

Normally faceted as a cabochon it is often used to great effect in both necklaces and bracelets.

CHALCEDONY:	Waxy lustre
Locations:	Brazil, India, Madagascar, Mexico, South Africa, Tanzania, USA
Colours Found:	Blue, black, brown, buff, green, grey, red, tan, white & yellow
Typical Cuts:	Cabochon
Family:	Quartz
Hardness:	6.50
Refractive Index:	1.54
Relative Density:	2.58 - 2.64

CHRYSOBERYL

The gem of springtime, youth and innocence, the name Chrysoberyl is derived from the Greek words for golden "chryso" and green gemstone "Beryl".

Its rarest variety Alexandrite (the colour change variety of Chrysoberyl), is quite well known, although the number of people who have heard of Alexandrite is probably 100 times greater than the number who have ever seen one, and 1,000 times greater than the number who have ever owned one.

Legends and lore

Said to bring peace of mind and increase self-confidence, Chrysoberyl also promotes kindness, generosity, benevolence, hope, optimism, renewal, new beginnings, compassion and forgiveness.

Just the facts

When cut, Chrysoberyl is an extremely brilliant gem, ideal for everyday wear and is rapidly gaining in popularity.

The stunning Magara Chrysoberyl in an elegant piece of 18k jewellery

Displaying attractive golden lemons, limes, greens, oranges and chocolates, together with an extreme brilliance, Chrysoberyl is exceptionally tough, making it ideal for everyday wear. The colour in yellow Chrysoberyl is due to iron trace elements.

Cat's Eye Chrysoberyl is a translucent gem ranging in colour from a honey yellow or honey chocolate to yellowish green to apple green. It is known for its reflected light effect called chatoyancy (cat's eye). This is achieved by cutting gems that have small, parallel "silk" inclusions into cabochons. As the gem is rotated, it exhibits a distinct, silvery white line across its dome that seems to open and close like a cat's eye.

Magara Chrysoberyl with Diamonds - designed and made by master craftsmen at Gems TV

Exceptional quality Chrysoberyl has recently been an unearthed in Magara, Tanzania, a region made famous by Tanzanite and Tsavorite.

Chrysoberyl

CHRYSOBERYL:	Chatoyancy
Locations:	Brazil, India, Madagascar, Russia, Sri Lanka, Tanzania, Zambia, Zimbabwe
Colours Found:	Brown, yellow & yellowish-green
Typical Cuts:	Beads, Cabochon, Oval, Pear
Family:	Chrysoberyl
Hardness:	8.00 - 8.50
Refractive Index:	1.74 - 1.75
Relative Density:	3.50 - 3.80

CHRYSOCOLLA

**Want to learn more?
Log on to
www.GemsTV.com**

Chrysocolla

Chrysocolla is an attractive blue-green gemstone that provides a unique colour to the gem world. The name Chrysocolla first appears in the writings of Theophrastus (315 BC) and comes from the Greek words "chrysos" for gold and "kolla" for glue, because Chrysocolla resembles other materials used in soldering gold in ancient times.

Legends and lore

Crystal healers believe that Chrysocolla helps to bring out the best of one's creativity by calming and releasing fear and in expressing feelings both verbally and artistically. Chrysocolla is considered by some crystal practitioners to be a feminine lunar gemstone. Some people have said that Chrysocolla looks like the earth as seen from space. In combination with its feminine connections, some people believe it is useful in meditating for world peace. One popular approach is to hold Chrysocolla in your hand and visualize the peace and calm that emanates.

Just the facts

A hydrous copper silicate, Chrysocolla is a minor copper ore. Chrysocolla is often confused with Turquoise because of its colour. Chyrsocolla is perhaps more appropriately a mineraloid than a true mineral. Most of the time it is amorphous, meaning that it does not have a coherent crystalline structure. Chrysocolla forms as crusts, stalactites or stalagmites and in botryoidal grape-like shapes, as well as inclusions in other minerals. While Chrysocolla by itself is too soft for jewellery, when it appears as an inclusion in Quartz it is hard enough to polish as cabochons. Very rare, this form of Chrysocolla is often marketed as "Gem Silica" and is one of the most coveted Chalcedony Quartzes.

Chrysocolla is often cut as beautiful greenish-blue cabochons, and used for ornaments such as carvings and figurines. In the 1950's, USA lapidaries voted Chrysocolla Chalcedony Quartz the "most popular American gemstone".

CHRYSOCOLLA:	First appeared in writings 315BC
Locations:	Australia, South Africa
Colours Found:	Blue-green
Typical Cuts:	Cabochon
Family:	Chalcedony Quartz when used as a gem
Hardness:	2.00 - 4.00
Refractive Index:	1.54
Relative Density:	2.58 - 2.64

CHRYSOPRASE

Also colloquially know as Cat's Eye or Australian Jade, its name comes from the Greek words "chrysos" meaning golden and "prason" meaning leek, due to its colour similarities with the vegetable.

One of the most coveted varieties of Chalcedony Quartz, Chrysoprase is prized for its opalescent apple green colour and rarity.

Legends and lore

Chrysoprase was used by the Greeks, Romans and Egyptians in jewellery and other ornamental objects. In ancient Egyptian jewellery, Chrysoprase was often set together with Lapis Lazuli.

Chrysoprase is mentioned in the Bible as being one of the twelve gemstones set in the foundations of the city walls of Jerusalem (Revelations 21:19) and is the symbol of the Apostle St. Thaddeus.

Chrysoprase was very popular in the 14th century when the Holy Roman Emperor Charles IV used it to decorate chapels including the Chapel of Saint Wencelsas in Prague.

Chrysoprase was also a favourite gem of Frederick the Great of Prussia and Queen Anne of England.

Chrysoprase is believed by crystal healers to increase grace and inner equilibrium.

A simple but effective way of showing the beauty of the gem in this 9k gold and Chrysoprase ring

Just the facts

Chrysoprase can vary in colour from yellowish green to apple green and grass green depending on the levels of hydrated silicates and nickel oxides present in the gem.

Because of its semi-opaque green colour, Chrysoprase was often mistaken for Imperial Jade (Jadeite).

Other types of green Chalcedony include Prase (a very rare less vivid green Chalcedony found in Eastern Europe and Delaware & Pennsylvania, USA) and Mtorolite (a variety of green Chalcedony coloured by chromium found in Zimbabwe).

The ever popular Chrysoprase set in gold

Claw set simplicity for this beautiful piece of Chrysoprase

CHRYSOPRASE:	Mentioned in the Bible
Locations:	Australia, Brazil, Madagascar, Russia, South Africa, USA
Colours Found:	Apple green
Typical Cuts:	Beads, Cabochons, Cameo
Family:	Chalcedony
Hardness:	6.50
Refractive Index:	1.54
Relative Density:	2.58 - 2.64

CITRINE

Citrine is the yellow variety of macrocrystalline Quartz that takes its name from "citron", the French word for lemon. Citrine is a beautiful translucent gemstone and one of November's birthstones.

Legends and lore

Citrine was first used in jewellery in Greece during the Hellenistic period (end of the 4th to the end of the 1st century BC).

The first use of Citrine by the Romans was in intaglios (a gem carved in negative relief) and cabochons in the first centuries after the birth of Christ.

In antiquity, Citrine was believed to be the gemstone of happiness and used as a protective talisman against evil thoughts.

A fine example of bi-colour Citrine in 18k gold

Amongst its many historic medicinal uses, Citrine was believed to aid digestion, remove toxins from the body (Citrine was once commonly used as a charm against snakebites and other venomous reptiles) provide protection against the plague and bad skin, and to be useful in the treatment of depression, constipation and diabetes.

Crystal healers believe Citrine promotes creativity helps personal clarity and will eliminate self-destructive tendencies.

Unusual chequerboard faceting makes this Citrine pendant stunning

Just the facts

Citrine occurs naturally in proximity to Amethyst and is a related Quartz mineral. Citrine gets its yellow colour from the presence of iron.

Citrine ranges in colour from pastel lemon yellow to golden yellow to mandarin and "madeira" red, after the colour of the wine. Traditionally, the "madeira" shades were more coveted, but these days many people prefer Citrine's brighter lemon tones.

Briollette cut Lemon Citrine drop earrings by Gems TV

Most of the Citrine mined today comes from Uruguay, Brazil and many African nations. Citrine can also be found in the Ural Mountains of Russia, in Dauphine, France, and in Madagascar.

Citrine can be easily confused with Topaz and has even been called "Topaz Quartz".

CITRINE:	November's birthstone
Locations:	Brazil, Madagascar, Mozambique, Uruguay, Zambia
Colours Found:	Shades of yellow
Typical Cuts:	Various
Family:	Quartz
Hardness:	7.00
Refractive Index:	1.50
Relative Density:	2.60 - 2.70

Citrine

CORNELIAN

Also known as Sadoine or Mecca Stone and sometimes spelt Carnelian, the name is derived from the Latin world for flesh, "carne", due to its orangey red colour..

182ct of Round cut Sri Lankan Cornelian

Legends and lore

Cornelian has been an important gem in nearly every great civilization. From the royalty of Ur (the Mesopotamian capital of pre-biblical times), to Napoleon (he returned from his Egyptian campaign with a huge octagonal Cornelian) and Tibetan Buddhists, Cornelian has been revered for its healing, spiritual and creative qualities.

A deeply religious gem, Cornelian was used by the Egyptian goddess Isis to protect the dead on their journey through the afterlife.

Cornelian is mentioned in the Bible as being one of the "stones of fire" (Ezekiel 28:13-16) given to Moses for the breastplate of Aaron (Exodus 28:15-30) and is also one of the twelve gemstones set in the foundations of the city walls of Jerusalem (Revelations 21:19). It is the symbol of the Apostle Philip.

Popular in ancient Greece and Rome for intaglio (a gem carved in negative relief) signet rings, the Romans symbolically associated dark coloured Cornelian with men and light coloured Cornelian with women.

Muhammad's seal was an engraved Cornelian set in a silver ring.

To this day Buddhists in China, India and Tibet believe in the protective powers of Cornelian and often follow the Egyptian practice of setting the gem with Turquoise and Lapis Lazuli for enhanced power.

Just the facts

Cornelian is a translucent orange to red variety of Chalcedony. A uniformly coloured cryptocrystalline Quartz, its red tints are caused by iron oxide trace elements.

What our Craftsmen say:

Miss Alisa Klaban - Quality Assurance

"When our gem hunters are able to acquire Cornelian there is a rush of excitement in the design centre. Everyone at Gems TV loves working with this gem."

CORNELIAN:	Mentioned in the Bible
Locations:	Brazil, India, Madagascar, Sri Lanka, Uruguay
Colours Found:	Orange to red
Typical Cuts:	Beads, Cabochon, Cameo
Family:	Chalcedony
Hardness:	7.00
Refractive Index:	2.65 - 2.66
Relative Density:	1.543 - 1.554

DANBURITE

Danburite making an appearance in this popular design by Gems TV

Danburite and Chrome Tourmaline used to full effect in this ladies ring

Unusual but effective. Danburite and Amethyst

Danburite, discovered in 1839, is named after Danbury, Connecticut where it first was unearthed. Interestingly, the original deposits are now inaccessible as they lie under a major metropolitan area!

Danburite is a relatively new jewellery gemstone, but is rapidly growing in popularity.

An excellent and unique Diamond alternative, Danburite also has similarities with White Topaz.

Legends and lore

Danburite is believed by some to be an excellent healing tool and to help remove toxins from the body. Metaphysically, Danburite is believed to be a powerful intellectual activator, aiding with communication and relationships with others.

Just the facts

Danburite are rare crystals of calcium boron silicate, the best of which are usually found in Mexico. Danburite is also found in Japan, Madagascar, Switzerland, Germany and USA.

Although most Danburite is greyish and opaque, gem quality Danburite should possess a transparent to translucent clarity with a vitreous lustre. Fine Danburite is usually colourless or white but shades of yellow, pink and mahogany can also be found.

Visually, Danburite makes an excellent natural gemstone alternative to Diamonds, harmonizing with almost every complexion. Danburite is a durable gemstone and is stunningly beautiful when faceted and set in rings and pendants.

DANBURITE:	Natural Diamond alternative
Locations:	Madagascar, Mexico, USA
Colours Found:	Clear or white, but shades of yellow, pink & brown
Typical Cuts:	Fancy, Oval, Princess, Round, Trilliant
Family:	Danburite
Hardness:	7.00 - 7.50
Refractive Index:	1.63 - 1.64
Relative Density:	2.97 - 3.02

Don Kogen, the Gem Hunter says:

"Keep your eyes on this one, we are desperately hunting for more and believe it should become famous."

DIAMOND

The word Diamond comes from the Greek word "adamas" meaning unconquerable or invincible.

"Diamonds are forever", sang Shirley Bassey, while Marilyn insisted they were "a girl's best friend". Celebrated in song, over the last century, Diamond (April's birthstone) has become the most marketed of gemstones.

Legends and lore

The myths and facts associated with the Diamond transcend cultures and continents.

The world's first known reference to this gemstone comes from an Indian Sanskrit manuscript, the Arthsastra (which translates as The Lesson of Profit) written by Kautiliya, a minister to Chandragupta of the Mauryan Dynasty (322 BC – 185 BC).

Plato wrote about Diamonds as living beings, embodying celestial spirits.

Unusual two tone earrings in Diamond and 9k gold

Roman literature makes its first distinct mention of Diamonds only in the 1st century AD, in reference to the alluvial Diamonds found in India and Borneo.

The ancient Greeks and Romans believed they were tears of the Gods and splinters from falling stars. Cupids' arrows were supposed to be tipped with Diamonds, thus having a magic that nothing else can equal

The Hindus believed that they were created when bolts of lightning struck rocks. They even placed it in the eyes of some of their statues.

High impact piece using a solitaire White Diamond accented with more White Diamonds

Jewish high priests turned to Diamonds to decide the innocence or guilt of the accused. A Diamond held before a guilty person was supposed to dull and darken, while a Diamond held before an innocent glowed with increasing brilliance.

The Romans wore Diamonds because these were thought to possess broad magical powers over life's troubles, being able to give to the wearer strength, invincibility, bravery and courage during battle.

A very modern setting in white gold and Diamond

Kings of antiquity led the battles wearing heavy leather breastplates studded with Diamonds and other precious gems because it was believed that Diamonds possessed God given magical qualities and powers far beyond the understanding of humankind. Thus, warriors stayed clear of Kings and those who were fortunate enough to have the magical Diamonds in their breastplates.

A classic Diamond gent's ring by Gems TV

DIAMOND

White gold and White Diamonds by Gems TV

Beautiful Diamond ring in white gold

The ever popular Pink Sapphire - set here in 9k gold and Diamonds

The more regularly seen White Diamond set with rarely seen Blue Diamond

An act of Louis IX of France (1214 - 1270) established a sumptuary law reserving Diamonds for the King indicates the rarity and value of this gem.

Until the 14th century only Kings could wear Diamonds, because they stood for strength, courage and invincibility. Small numbers of Diamonds began appearing in the 14th century in European regalia and jewellery, set mainly as an accent point among Pearls. But the possession of extraordinarily large and noble Diamonds was always the privilege of royal houses and particularly rich families. As an example, the imperial crown of the Russian Tsarina Catherine the Second (1729 - 1796) was mounted with 4,936 sparkling Diamonds.

In the Middle Ages and the Renaissance, every ring set with a precious gem was not considered as much a piece of jewellery, but more as an amulet that bestowed magical powers upon its wearer. When set in gold and worn on the left side, it was believed that Diamonds held the power to drive away nightmares, to ward off devils, phantoms and soothe savage beasts. A house or garden touched at each corner with a Diamond was supposed to be protected from lightning, storms and blight. Diamonds were also supposed to impart virtue, generosity, as well as to calm the mentally ill and even to determine lawsuits in the wearer's favour.

Not only was it commonly believed that Diamonds could bring luck and success, but also that they could counter the effects of astrological events.

Just the facts

You may have heard about the 4 C's related to valuing gemstones and in particular, Diamonds. While other factors such as origin sometimes need to be taken into consideration when valuing coloured gemstones, below is a basic guide to the four C's that gemstone professionals and connoisseurs the world over rely on: cut, colour, clarity and carat weight.

Colour

Colourless and near-colourless Diamonds are rare, beautiful and highly prized amongst connoisseurs. To the untrained eye, most Diamonds look white. However, to the professional there are small differences in the degrees of whiteness seen.

DIAMOND

Cut

With round brilliant cut Diamonds accounting for over 80% of Diamond sales worldwide, ask a women "what shape is a Diamond?" and she'll probably say round. Despite this figure, there are many other beautiful Diamond cuts that warrant serious consideration. The eight most popular Diamond cuts are emerald cut, heart cut, marquise cut, oval cut, round brilliant cut, pear cut, princess cut and radiant cut.

Unlike coloured gemstones, Diamonds are cut, shaped and proportioned to a remarkably uniform ideal. In 1919, Marcel Tolkowsky published his opinions of what Diamond proportions result in the optimum balance of brilliance and fire.

Carat weight

As mentioned above, unlike other gemstones, Diamonds are cut to a uniform ideal for maximum brilliance (white light reflections), fire (flashes of colour) and scintillation (patterns of light and darkness). With this uniform cutting and proportions, we can very conveniently and accurately equate Diamond carat size with their millimetre size.

Stunning and rare - Blue Diamond accented with White Diamonds

Round Brilliant Cut Diamond	
1 mm	0.01 Ct.
2 mm	0.03 Ct.
3 mm	0.10 Ct.
4 mm	0.25 Ct.
5 mm	0.50 Ct.
6 mm	0.75 Ct.
6.5 mm	1.00 Ct.
7 mm	1.25 Ct.
7.5 mm	1.65 Ct.

A Blue Diamond solitaire accented with White Diamonds

18k gold bangle with perfectly matched Blue Diamonds

Clarity

Inclusions are tiny natural irregularities within the body of a Diamond. Nearly all gemstones contain some inclusions, however many are microscopic and can only be seen under magnification. While the prevalence and acceptability of inclusions varies from gemstone to gemstone, in general, if they do not interfere with the beauty of a gemstone, they are not only accepted but are also a fascinating hallmark of authenticity that records a gem's natural relationship with the earth.

Blue Diamond

DIAMOND

What is the GIA Diamond grading system ?

Developed by the GIA (Gemmological Institute of America), this system is now commonplace for the retailing of Diamonds across the globe and consists of a Diamond Clarity Scale and a Diamond Colour Scale.

GIA Diamond clarity scale

(FL) FLAWLESS: Shows no inclusions or blemishes of any sort under 10X magnification when observed by an experienced grader.

(IF) INTERNALLY FLAWLESS: Has no inclusions when examined by an experienced grader using 10X magnification, but will have some minor surface blemishes.

(VVS1 and VVS2) VERY VERY SLIGHTLY INCLUDED: Contains minute inclusions that are difficult even for experienced graders to see under 10X magnification.

(VS1 and VS2) VERY SLIGHTLY INCLUDED: Contains minute inclusions such as small crystals, clouds, or feathers when observed with effort under 10X magnification.

(SI1, SI2 and SI3) SLIGHTLY INCLUDED: Contains inclusions (clouds, included crystals, knots, cavities, and feathers) that are noticeable to an experienced grader under 10X magnification. The SI3 Diamond clarity grade was created because many in the Diamond industry felt that there was too wide a gap between SI2 and I1. After the EGL (European Gemmological Laboratory) started issuing certificates with the SI3 grade, the Rapaport Diamond Report (the definitive price guide for Diamonds) added SI3 to its price list.

Diamonds for the gent's by Gems TV

Pave set White Diamonds in this magnificent pendant

The classic cross pendant in Diamond - timeless and beautiful

Stunning dress ring using the classic combination of White Diamonds and white gold.

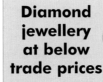

(I1, I2, I3) INCLUDED: Contains inclusions (possibly large feathers or large included crystals) that are obvious under 10X magnification.

(PK) PIQUE: Inclusions easily visible to the naked eye.

GIA Diamond colour scale

Prior to the introduction of the GIA grading system, the letters A, B and C were used to grade Diamonds. As the GIA wanted a fresh start, they decided to begin with the letter D.

D, E, F. These purest tints are rare and comparatively expensive. Their rare colour assigns them a higher market price.

G, H, I. Often offering much better value, to the untrained eye they seem the exact same colour as the more expensive D, E and F colours.

J, K, L. Discounted for their barely perceivable yellowish tints, Diamonds in this range offer excellent value.

M - Z. Further discounted for their more distinct yellow hues. Diamonds outside the normal colour range are called "fancy colours" and come in about any colour you can imagine (e.g. pink, red, green, purple, black, blue, yellow and more).

Pairs and suites

Pairs or suites of Diamonds matched for colour, clarity and cut are more highly valued per carat or per gem than single Diamonds of the same quality. Given the rarity of many Diamonds, a matching set is disproportionately hard to find and thus commands a higher per carat price than if each of the Diamonds from the suite were sold separately.

Coloured Diamonds

Most Coloured Diamonds found in jewellery today are normally treated. The process known as colour enhancement involves using clean Diamonds and modifying their colour with a combination of electron bombardment and heat using safe electron-accelerator technology. This enhancement exactly duplicates the "natural process" Coloured Diamonds undergo during their formation within the earth. All colour enhanced Diamonds sold by Gems TV are treated in the USA to certified international standards.

Unlike some other Diamond treatments, Colour Enhanced Diamonds are treated to fulfil preferences for vivid colour only; this colouring technique does not try

DIAMOND

Very contemporary ring in 9k gold with both White and Black Diamonds

One of Gems TV's exclusive and rare Black Diamond bracelets

The ever popular Black Diamond by Gems TV - In this case mixed with White Diamonds

Black Diamond

41

DIAMOND

to hide or dissipate flaws. The myriad of popular Diamond colours produced using this technology includes blue, green, red, orange, yellow, pink, purple and black. The real beauty and popularity of these Diamonds lies in the fact that they combine both the rich colour hues of coloured gems such as Rubies and Sapphires, with the unforgettable brilliance and sparkle of a Diamond. In other words, they virtually become "two gems in one".

A solitaire White Diamond

What are conflict Diamonds?

A conflict Diamond (also called a Blood Diamond) is a Diamond mined in a war zone and sold, usually clandestinely, in order to finance an insurgent or invading army's war efforts. The Kimberley Process is a global system to eradicate Conflict Diamonds and has two parts:

1. A government-regulated system adopted in 2000 by more than 40 countries, the United Nations, and the Diamond industry to control the export and import of rough Diamonds across borders. It requires that rough Diamonds mined after January 1, 2003 be shipped in tamper-resistant containers and accompanied by government-validated Kimberley Process Certificates. Only participating countries may legitimately export rough Diamonds and only to co-participating countries.

2. To strengthen the government program, the international Diamond and jewellery industry represented by the World Diamond Council (WDC) initiated and committed to a voluntary system of warranties. It requires that every time Diamonds (i.e. rough, polished or Diamond jewellery) change hands, the seller will affirm on the invoice that the Diamonds have been purchased through authorized channels not involved in funding conflict.

Gems TV is Kimberley Process compliant and our independent auditors verify our maintenance of warranties.

DIAMOND

The timeless gemstone of love in a contemporary twist on the half-eternity ring

A traditional Diamond solitaire of beautiful quality

White Diamond

Diamond rings at <u>less than</u> trade prices!

"Because we are both the manufacturer and the retailer, it is a fact that we often sell our Diamond jewellery direct to customers around the world at less than trade prices. We know this because we used to sell to the trade."

DIAMOND:	April's birthstone
Locations:	Africa
Colours Found:	Various
Typical Cuts:	Princess, Round Brilliant
Family:	Carbon
Hardness:	10.00
Refractive Index:	2.41
Relative Density:	3.50

DIASPORE

Diaspore

DIASPORE:	Can display colour change
Locations:	Turkey
Colours Found:	Brown, colour change, green, pink, red & yellow
Typical Cuts:	Antique Cushion, Marquise, Octagon, Oval, Pear, Round
Family:	Diaspore
Hardness:	6.50 - 7.00
Refractive Index:	1.70 - 1.75
Relative Density:	3.30 - 3.39

First discovered in Mramorskoi, Kossoibrod, the Ural Mountains, Russia in 1801, Diaspore is a relatively scarce gemstone that despite its beauty and suitability for jewellery is plagued by scant availability, particularly in better qualities. Not faceted until the 1970's, this beautiful gem has had its reputation tarnished by independent miners marketing poorly faceted low quality gems that do not maximize its colour change.

Also known as Empholite, Kayserite and Tanatarite, Diaspore has recently been branded Zultanite, in honour of the 36 sultans who founded the Ottoman Empire in Anatolia in the late 13th century.

Diaspore comes from the Greek word "Diaspora" meaning "to scatter" because it cracks when exposed to extreme heat..

Legends and lore

Some people believe Diaspore can assist in the development of psychic power, astral force, ambition, intellect, desire and emotions based on intellect and touch.

Just the facts

Diaspore is a transparent gem that comes in yellow, green, brown, pink or red and darker red with a higher Manganese content. Similar to Alexandrite, the colour change variety of Chrysoberyl, Diaspore can display the colour change effect. In daylight its colour appears greenish yellow to brownish green while in incandescent light (or at night) it is brownish pink to pink.

Diaspore possesses a perfect cleavage that makes it difficult to facet. As up to 90% of the rough can be lost during cutting, it is critical that the cutter orients the rough to minimize its perfect cleavage but not at the expense of incorrectly positioning the colour change.

Today, Diaspore is mined in Turkey in the Milas county of Mu la near the village of Selimiye. It first began appearing in the mid 1980's and while an article in Gems & Gemmology magazine (winter 1994) indicated that supplies were promising, this hasn't translated into the greater availability of good quality gems. While it was initially only collected by mineral enthusiasts and independent miners, at least one mine is now in operation. At a height of over 4,000 feet, this mine is 7 miles away from the nearest village and currently extracts Diaspore by hand, using chisels and pick-axes.

Diopside was named in 1800 from the Greek word "dis" meaning double and "opsis" meaning vision, in reference to the pleochroism (different colours are displayed when viewed from different angles) found in its prismatic form.

Legends and lore

Diopside is also called the "Crying Gemstone", because it is believed by crystal healers to heal trauma, by bringing forth cleansing tears.

Diopside is assumed to bring creativity to the wearer and is said to be related to love and commitment. Crystal healers believe that, when worn close to the chest (such as in a pendant), Diopside can benefit the heart, lungs and circulation.

Just the facts

Diopside is a calcium magnesium silicate found in metamorphosed impure limestone, meteorites and igneous basalts. Diopside has been previously named Schefferite, White Schefferite and Zinc-Schefferite.

Diopside is the magnesium rich member of the "monoclinic-pyroxene series" that occurs when ions (and magnesium) freely substitute each other.

Diopside crystals have a perfect cleavage in two directions, are often twinned and are short and columnar, but with an uneven fracture. Mineralogists easily recognize Diopside in the field by its crystals, its colour, its fracture, its cleavage and its white or white-green streak.

Diopside is typically white, blue, purple, brown, green, colourless and grey with a glassy lustre. The less common shades are yellowish brown and greenish brown.

Varieties of Diopside include "Russian Diopside" (a chromium-rich Diopside known for its deep green colour), "Violan" (a rare blue variety found in Italy), "Cat's Eye Diopside" (green with the effect due to inclusions of rutile needles), "Malacolite" (a white coloured variety), "Salaite" (an iron variety), "Dekalbite" (an iron free variety) and "Star Diopside" (a star with four rays).

Gem quality Diopside is mined in Siberia (Russia), Italy, Sri Lanka, Brazil, Madagascar, South Africa and Pakistan. Uzbekistan, located between Tajikistan and Turkmenistan, is becoming an important locality for a variety of Russian Diopside called Tashmarine. This

Elegant floral earrings in Chrome Diopside and 9k gold by Gems TV

A cluster of Chrome Diopside in yellow gold

Contemporary style - Two Russian Diopside set with White Topaz

Diopside

DIOPSIDE

A superb example of the beauty of Russian Diopside set with Diamonds

A trilogy of Russian Diopside in this white gold classic three stone ring

Diopside

DIOPSIDE:	Perfect cleavage in two directions
Locations:	Brazil, Colombia, India, Pakistan, Russia, Zambia, Zimbabwe
Colours Found:	Blue, brown, colourless, green, grey, purple & white
Typical Cuts:	Oval, Round
Family:	Pyroxene
Hardness:	5.00 - 6.00
Refractive Index:	1.66 - 1.72
Relative Density:	3.20 - 3.60

variety has a slightly lower chromium content than the Siberian material, a less saturated colour and can display grey or brown tones. India has the largest deposits of Cat's Eye or Star Diopside. The colour of African Diopside tends to be a more yellowish colour similar to Peridot.

Russian Diopside

Russian Diopside has a beautiful rich green colour, similar to that of the best Emeralds or the rarest Tsavorite Garnets.

Coloured by chromium, Russian Diopside is also known as Chrome Diopside and Imperial Diopside. While there is little historical information regarding this rare gem type, some claim it is beneficial for health, relationships, spirituality and financial success. Many people within the industry feel that Russian Diopside should be a birthstone for May.

One major reason Russian Diopside is relatively unknown is that it has only recently become available in sizable commercial quantities. Interestingly, a company recently trademarked the name "Vertelite" for Russian Diopside. The name was created from "verte" the Latin word for green and "lite" the Latin word for tone.

Russian Diopside displays strong birefringence and has a vitreous lustre. It is mostly available in small sizes, with large carat weights hard to find.

Russian Diopside is mostly mined in Yakutia, Siberia. Yakutia territory is located in the extreme north of Asia and is considered the coldest place in the northern hemisphere. Mining is limited due to cold winters lasting for nine months; hence this gem is seasonal and it has been difficult to maintain a steady supply.

Interestingly, Yakutia is also the source of 99% of all Russian Diamonds. Russian Diopside is a Diamond mine indicator mineral and is sometimes found as an inclusion inside Diamonds. The liberalisation of the economy of the former Soviet Union has made Russian Diopside more available than even before.

Star Diopside

Star Diopside is also known as "Black Star Diopside" because of its blackish colour. Asterism or the star effect is a reflection effect that appears as two or more intersecting bands of light cross the surface of a gem.

Star Diopside has four rays, two of which are straight, while the other two are not at right angles to the first pair.

DIOPSIDE

Star Diopside is mainly mined in India and is generally a black or blackish green colour.

Cat's Eye Diopside

A green variety of Diopside, chatoyancy or the cat's eye effect is a reflection effect that appears as a single bright band of light across the surface of a gemstone. Cat's Eye Diopside is mainly mined in India.

Violan

Violan is light blue to purple in colour due to the presence of large amounts of manganese. Violan is mined mainly in Italy.

Russian Diopside

EMERALD

Cabochon cut Cat's Eye Emerald accented with Diamond

Siberian Emerald shown in this amazing bracelet

Handcrafted earrings with Emerald and 9k yellow gold

For more than 4,000 years, the deep "green fire" of Emeralds has been treasured as a symbol of eternal spring and immortality.

Shrouded in myth and lore, the birthstone for May isn't just a beautiful gem, Emeralds are also ornaments of power and politics that have created legends and moulded world history.

Prized by Egyptians, Romans, Aztecs, crowned heads of Europe, and today, gem connoisseurs the world over, Emeralds, more than any other precious gemstone have sparked the eternal fires of our collective imagination.

Legends and lore

Spring is a time of growth and rejuvenation. Nothing reflects this more than the intense green shades of Emeralds, May's birthstone.

Emeralds are regarded by many cultures as a symbol of personal development. It was once thought that Emerald's possessed the power to soothe the soul and sharpen wit.

Some people believe that wearing an Emerald brings wisdom, growth and patience. And as any couple would agree, all of these qualities are essential for lasting love. This may explain why a gift of Emerald is considered symbolic of love and devotion. Emeralds are even believed to change colour upon infidelity!

Emeralds have long been thought to possess healing powers. While today we know that Emeralds are not a cure for all medical and psychological problems, many people still use Emeralds to sooth their eyes and bring them good health. In fact, green has long been considered a soothing colour and it is no coincidence that the "green room" in theatres and TV studios is supposed to relax a performer after the stress and eyestrain of studio and stage lights.

A truly ancient gemstone, there is archaeological evidence that the Babylonians may have been marketing Emeralds as early as 4000 BC.

The history of Egyptian Emeralds dates back over 4,000 years. Located in Egypt's eastern desert region, ancient miners braved extreme heat, scorpions and snakes to search for the "green fire". Interestingly, Greek miners once laboured in the Egyptian desert for Alexander the Great.

The ancient mines of Egypt were rediscovered in 1818 by the French explorer Caillaud. Finding the mine with the help of the Egyptian government, he noted that

Emeralds were probably mined there long after the Kings and Queens of Egypt ruled the land.

The Egyptians were known to engrave Emeralds with the symbol for foliage to represent eternal youth, burying these jewels with their dead.

Emeralds were said to be the favourite gem of Cleopatra. She often wore lavish Emerald jewellery and bestowed visiting dignitaries with large Emeralds carved with her likeness when they departed Egypt.

Egyptian Emeralds were first minded some 2,000 years before Cleopatra's birth. During her reign, Cleopatra claimed these Emerald mines as her own, as well as the world's oldest source of Peridot, the fog-wrapped, desert isle of Zeberget (St. John's Island). Zeberget Peridot has a uniquely Emerald-like colour, due to its high nickel content. This is probably why many of Cleopatra's "Emeralds" were later found to be Peridot.

The ancient Romans associated Emeralds with fertility and rebirth, dedicating it to Venus, their goddess of love and beauty. The Roman historian Pliny the Elder once said of Emerald's "nothing green is greener", and recorded that the Roman Emperor Nero, while presiding over gladiatorial fights, wore spectacles made of Emeralds. However, gemmologists now believe that this was highly unlikely as the ancient Egyptian Emerald produced crystals of insufficient size and clarity needed for such an instrument. Historians now believe that Fire Beryl™ was probably the gem used.

The legends and lore surrounding Emeralds would not be complete without recounting the infamous stories of the Conquistadors, Hernando Cortés, who started his campaign against the Aztecs in 1519, and Francisco Pizarro, who commenced his military operation against the Incas in 1526. When Hernando Cortés planted the Spanish flag on Aztec soil, he snatched from the berated Emperor Montezuma an enormous pyramid shaped Emerald, so big it could be seen from 100 yards away!

Just the facts

The neon green colour of Emeralds is unparalleled in the gem kingdom. Its beautiful green colour, combined with its rarity, makes Emeralds one of the world's most valuable gemstones. Interestingly, its name comes from the Greek word "smaragdos", meaning green gem.

Emeralds are a member of the Beryl family of minerals. Minute traces of chromium, vanadium and iron give Emeralds their famous "green fire". The green crystals grow slowly within metamorphic rocks and are

EMERALD

Stunning crossover ring in 9k with Emerald

White gold and Emerald make an impact in this classic pendant by Gems TV

EMERALD

A fine example of Columbian Emerald in 18k white gold

Colombian Emerald Claw set in white gold

Siberian Emerald

restricted in size by the host rock, making large Emeralds rare and costly.

Unlike other Beryl, Emeralds often contain inclusions and tiny fractures. These are commonly called "jardin", from the French word for "garden", because of their resemblance to foliage. For Emeralds, jardin is not looked on as a negative aspect as it would be for some other gem varieties, but instead are considered part of Emerald's character and can be used to assure the purchaser of a natural gemstone.

Although Emeralds are relatively hard and durable, it must be protected from harsh blows because the jardin found within make it susceptible to breaking. The famous "emerald cut" was developed specifically for this gem to reduce the amount of pressure exerted during cutting.

Transparent Emeralds are faceted in gem cuts for jewellery, while translucent material is cut and polished into cabochons and beads. Trapiche Emeralds are also cut into cabochons, making exquisite jewellery pieces.

A very small number of Emeralds display asterism and chatoyancy; these too are cut into cabochons.

When buying Emeralds the most important consideration is always colour, with clarity and quality of cut playing second fiddle. Nevertheless, the brightness of the gemstone (which is somewhat determined by the cutting and clarity) is also an important factor.

Traditionally, deep green is the most desired colour in Emeralds. Paler Emeralds are sometimes called "Green Beryl".

While we have generally not broken down the different features of gems from different locations, we felt that the Emerald was worthy of geographical analysis.

Colombian Emerald

Known for their vivid green colour, Colombian Emeralds are usually of exceptional quality. Colombia is by tradition and lore, the finest modern source for Emeralds.

With each comprised of many individual mines, there are three main areas of Emerald mining in Colombia; Muzo, Coscuez and Chivor.

Muzo Colombian Emerald

The famed Muzo mines lay 160km north of Bogota.

EMERALD

Emerald crystals from Muzo tend to have more saturated colour than either Coscuez or Chivor. They are considered some of the finest Emerald mines in the world.

A rare, prized form of Emerald, found only in the Muzo mining district of Colombia, Trapiche Emeralds are extremely unusual. Star-shaped rays that emanate from its centre in a hexagonal pattern characterize these Emeralds. These rays appear much like asterism, but unlike asterism, they are not caused by light reflection from tiny parallel inclusions, but by black carbon impurities that happen to form in the same pattern.

Coscuez Colombian Emerald

The Emerald crystals of Coscuez tend to exhibit a very wide range of colours but unfortunately also tend to be more included than those from Muzo. While Muzo and Coscuez are Colombia's most prolific Emerald producing locales, with the majority of Colombian Emeralds seen on the world market coming from these two areas, today Coscuez produces approximately sixty percent of Colombia's "green fire".

The elegant beauty of Majestic Emerald seen here accented with Diamonds

Chivor Colombian Emerald

Chivor Emeralds are best known for their bluish caste and generally have fewer inclusions and a lighter colour than either Coscuez or Muzo Emeralds. The Chivor mining area is the smallest area of the three and is separate from Muzo and Coscuez, which lay adjacent to each other.

Majestic Emerald set in 18k yellow gold to stunning effect

Brazilian Emerald

While Colombian Emeralds are known for their vivid green colour, Brazilian Emeralds are known for their variety of colour, ranging from light green to fine to medium dark blue green.

Emeralds were first discovered in Brazil about 500 years ago after the arrival of the Portuguese. However, it was only in 1963 when the first samples with commercial value were found in Bahia, close to the town of Paraiso du Norte in northern Brazil, effectively wiping out the notion that Brazil had no real "green fire" of its own.

Stunning pear shaped Majestic Emerald

Pakistani Emerald

While an extremely harsh climate prevents the mining of Emerald deposits at higher altitudes, at lower elevations in the Swat Valley of Pakistan lay the Gujar

Emeralds from Zambia faceted and strung as a necklace for Gems TV

EMERALD

Perfectly matched Siberian Emeralds in this 9k gold cluster ring

The rare and beautiful Siberian Emerald showing great clarity

Rough Emerald

EMERALD:	May's birthstone
Locations:	Brazil, Colombia, Pakistan, Siberia, Zambia, Zimbabwe
Colours Found:	Green
Typical Cuts:	Cushion, Emerald, Octagon, Oval, Round
Family:	Beryl
Hardness:	7.00 - 8.00
Refractive Index:	1.57 - 1.58
Relative Density:	2.67 - 2.78

Kili mine, and the ancient and historically significant Mingora mine. Gallo-Roman earrings featuring Mingora Emeralds have been discovered. Severe weather conditions restrict operations during winter, making the hand-dug output very limited. The Pakistani government tightly controls the mining of Emeralds from relatively new deposits discovered in 1960 in the Himalayan Mountains.

Siberian Emerald

Siberian Emerald is long prized for its breathtaking crystal clarity, green fire and forest green hues.

According to history, Siberian Emerald was discovered by a Russian peasant, Maxim Stefanovitch Koshevnikov, in 1830 in the roots of a tree that had been felled in a storm on the Tokovoya River near Ekaterinburg in Siberia's Ural Mountains. Despite this, rumours persist that Russia actually supplied Emeralds long before the Spaniards discovered the famous Colombian Emerald in the late 16th century. These legends even go as far as to suggest that the Scythian Emeralds mentioned by Pliny the Elder in his Historia Naturalis came from the Urals.

Rising to fame in the 19th century, the largest and best known source of Siberian Emerald is the Mariinsky (St. Mary's) mine. This mine was discovered in 1833 near the village of Malyshevo. The deposits were nationalized after World War I and Emerald mining soon ceased when Malyshevo became a military security zone. Siberian Emeralds almost entirely disappeared...

Thanks to Don "The Gem Hunter", Siberian Emerald is now back and we are delighted to offer an amazing selection exclusively to Gems TV customers! Siberian Emerald is mined in very rugged terrain - the area is wet, rocky and very mountainous, and less than half a percent of the rough crystals mined are suitable for faceting. As a result, Siberian Emeralds are a "must have" for any true Emerald connoisseur.

Zambian Emerald

Zambian Emeralds are of very high quality. Although Zambia has the world's second largest Emerald deposit, it is substantially underdeveloped and primarily restricted to artisanal mines near Kagem, Kitwe, Miku and Mufulira in remote northern Zambia. As basic hand tools are mainly used to mine Zambian Emerald, this limits supply, increasing their rarity and value. Zambian Emerald is extracted from talc-magnetite schist's Zambian miners call "paidas" (when it's unaltered) and "chikundula" (when it's weathered). They call small Emerald crystals that may be indicative of bigger crystals "ubulunga".

The Majestic Emerald's seen on Gems TV are from Zambia and are called "Majestic" because of their superior quality (colour and clarity). However, by calling an Emerald "Majestic" we are not suggesting that it is the best quality available anywhere, simply some of the best available at Gems TV.

Zambian Emerald

FIRE BERYL™ (GOSHENITE)

While most members of the Beryl family (commonly known as the "mother of gemstones") such as Emerald or Aquamarine are famous for their colours, Fire Beryl™ is the highly collectable clear variety that displays a Diamond-like fiery brilliance.

Legends and lore

The traditional gemmological name for this gemstone is Goshenite but at Gems TV we prefer our exclusive name Fire Beryl™. So named for its distinctive fiery brilliance, high lustre and colourless purity, its easy to see why Fire Beryl™ has long been compared with Diamonds. Naturally, at Gems TV our expert gem graders use years of skill and expertise to ensure that only the finest examples worthy of the name Fire Beryl™ are selected.

Oval cut Fire Beryl from Brazil with two White Diamonds

The name Goshenite is derived from the location of its first discovery, Goshen, Massachusetts, USA. Fire Beryl™ is also known as White Beryl or Lucid Beryl.

Fire Beryl™ is an enduringly popular gemstone and has been used in jewellery since antiquity. The ancient Greeks even used Fire Beryl™ as lenses in the first spectacles!

Brazilian Fire Beryl V-Claw set into yellow gold

Just the facts

Interestingly, pure Beryl is colourless, with traces of different metallic elements being responsible for this gem family's great colour range. Since Beryl's colour varieties are caused by metallic elements and pure Beryl is colourless, one could assume that Fire Beryl™ is Beryl in its most pure form. However, this is not technically correct as some metallic elements in natural Fire Beryl™ actually inhibit the colours that result from other metallic elements that may also be present.

Fire Beryl

FIRE BERYL:	Also known as White or Lucid Beryl
Locations:	Afghanistan, Brazil, Columbia, Pakistan, South Africa
Colours Found:	Colourless
Typical Cuts:	Octagon, Round, Square, Trilliant
Family:	Beryl
Hardness:	7.50 - 8.00
Refractive Index:	1.57 - 1.60
Relative Density:	2.60 - 2.80

FLUORITE

Deriving its name from the Latin word "fluere", meaning to flow (in reference to its low melting point), Fluorite is known as "the world's most colourful gemstone".

Fluorite, from which we get the word fluorescent, crosses the entire colour spectrum, from deep purple to crimson red, blue to green (Chrome Fluorite) and frosty orange to lemon yellow. Fluorite is one of the more famous fluorescent minerals. Many specimens strongly fluoresce, in a great variety of colours.

Legends and lore

According to crystal healers, Fluorite is a third-eye gem bringing rationality to intuitive qualities. It is believed to offer a stabilizing energy, facilitating order, balance and healing. Fluorite is also believed to be excellent for fostering clarity of mind, objectivity, concentration and meditation.

An impressive 18.7ct Colour Change Fluorite set in this regal looking pendant

Just the facts

Due to its glassy lustre Fluorite is highly coveted. Fluorite is the natural crystalline form of calcium fluoride and often forms beautiful cube-shaped crystals. It is a transparent to translucent, glassy mineral. When pure, Fluorite is colourless; however, it usually contains impurities that colour it. The most common colours are violet, blue, green, yellow, brown, pink, and bluish black.

This Brazilian Fluorite gives a perfect example of the gem's multi-colour banding

Arguably, the most popular colour for Fluorite is a deep purple that can rival Amethyst in its finest examples. Indeed Fluorite/Amethyst comparisons are often used to show that colour cannot be relied upon as a gemstone test.

An example of an Oval cut being used to show the glassy lustre often found in Fluorite

An eye catching phenomenon of Fluorite is its distinctive bi-colour and multi-colour banding. Chunky Fluorite bead strands optimize this exceptional effect. Interestingly, the "Blue John" variety mined in England that possesses curved bands of blue purple, violet, yellow and white has been used as an ornamental gem since Roman times.

Bi-Colour Fluorite

Colour Change Fluorite is mined in Bihar, India and shows a dramatic change from green to purple. Colour change gems are those that distinctly change their colour when viewed under two different light sources.

Fluorite

FLUORITE:	Bi-colour & multi-colour banding
Locations:	Brazil, India
Colours Found:	Various
Typical Cuts:	Baguette, Oval
Family:	Fluorite
Hardness:	4.00
Refractive Index:	1.43
Relative Density:	3.20

GARNET

Fantastic array of colour change Garnet in this popular design

The very rare and beautiful colour change variety of Garnet

Garnet has a history spanning more than 5,000 years. Deriving its name from the Latin word for seed, "granatus" Garnet was so named because of its similar colour to pomegranate seeds.

From the svelte necklines of Abyssinian princesses to the powdered décolletages of Marie Antoinette, the captivating mystique of Garnets has made them a timeless symbol of feminine beauty. The imaginative lure of this "queen of gems" intoxicates the senses.

Understanding the Garnet family

Garnets are a group of minerals all having essentially the same crystal structure but varying in chemical composition, physical properties and colours. Unlike many other gemstones, colour in Garnet does not come from chemical impurities - when pure, a Garnet still has colour. Garnets very rarely occur in nature with their compositions precisely matching their "pure ideal". A natural Garnet's composition typically falls somewhere in between the pure ideals of other Garnet members.

Group	Species	Pure Types	Mixed Types
Pyralspites	Almandine	Almandine	Rhodolite (Pyrope & Almandine)
	Pyrope	Pyrope	Mozambique (Pyrope & Almandine)
	Spessartite	Spessartite (Mandarin & Tangerine)	Malaia (Intermediate composition range between Spessartite & Pyrope)
			Umbalite (Pyrope & Almandine with small traces of Spessartite)
Ugrandites	Andradite	Demantoid	Mali (Andradite & Grossular)
	Grossular	Grossular, Tsavorite, Merelani Mint & Hessonite	
	Uvarovite		

Legends and lore

Garnet's associated symbolism with pomegranates has been longstanding. Interestingly, several ancient pieces of jewellery have been unearthed that are studded with

Hessonite Garnet - a must for all gem lovers

tiny red Garnets in cluster-like patterns reminiscent of pomegranates. The pomegranate is associated with eternity in Greek mythology and mentioned specifically in the legend of Hades' abduction of Persephone.

Garnet has long been associated with fire, and was thought to possess the ability to illuminate the sky at night. Today, Garnets remain a symbol of faith, truth and light. This story from Grimms fairytales nicely presents this association – "Once upon a time an elderly lady came upon an injured bird. Taking the bird home with her, she nursed it back to health until one day it flew away. Although the lady thought she'd never see it again, it returned to her house with a Garnet that she put by her bedside. To her surprise, she awoke every night to see it shinning as bright as a torch, illuminating the bird's gratitude for her kindness".

According to Jewish legends, during the great flood a radiant Garnet guided the way for Noah, ultimately leading his ark to salvation. For Muslims they are believed to illuminate the fourth heaven.

Garnet jewellery was buried with Norseman to light their passage to Valhalla and was also used to light the palace of Abyssinia's monarch.

The Crusaders set Garnets into their armour, believing their power would lead them to safety. During the middle ages Garnet was also believed to draw out negativity, ward off harm and increase well-being, chivalry, loyalty and honesty.

To receive a Garnet as a gift in the middle ages was considered good luck, however, if ever stolen, bad luck to the thief! It was also believed that a Garnet's loss of lustre was a sign of impending doom.

Although Garnet was the "fashion gem" of the 18th and 19th centuries, the inadequacy of available chemical tests often resulted in it being confused with dark Ruby. Jewellery set with Garnets from Czechoslovakia was particularly admired, and although today the Garnets are mined elsewhere, Bohemian style Garnet jewellery has retained its popularity.

In 1912 Garnets were made the official birthstone for January by the American National Association of jewellers. It is also the gemstone for Aquarians and a traditional gift for 2nd and 6th wedding anniversaries.

Just the facts

Even though there are many types of Garnets (including trade and historic names there are currently 38 known

GARNET

Four pieces of Malaia Garnet set with Diamonds

Malaia Garnet in 9k gold as drop earrings

The beauty of Mali Garnet

Mali Garnet set in a floral style pendant

57

GARNET

Classic Mandarin Garnet and Diamond gold stud earrings

Modern elegance created by Channel set Diamonds and gorgeous Demantoid Garnet

Simple yet chic Demantoid Garnet 9k gold earrings

Garnet names), appearing in as many colours, when you say "Garnet" most people automatically think of small dark red gemstones. In fact, Garnets offer enough variety for every taste and can consequently keep up with the fast pace of changes in fashion!

Over the next six pages there are detailed descriptions of the most popular Garnets.

Champagne Garnet

A distinctive and very attractive colour variety of Malaia Garnet, Champagne Garnet is in fact a mixture of Pyrope and Spessartite Garnet and is mined in Tanzania's Umba Valley.

Colour Change Garnet

Colour Change Garnets are one of the rarest, interesting and phenomenal of all gemstones. An extremely rare variety of Malaia Garnet, Colour Change Garnet is in fact a mixture of Pyrope and Spessartite Garnet.

The colour change can be intense and equal to the colour change of top quality Alexandrite. As a result, Colour Change Garnets can easily be mistaken for Alexandrite.

Colour Change Garnets are mined in Bekily, southern Madagascar and both Songea and Tunduru in Tanzania.

Demantoid Garnet

Demantoid Garnet is one of the most desirable of all coloured gemstones and extremely rare. Discovered in 1855 in the Russian central Ural mountains at two alluvial deposits, it was first assumed to be Emerald, and even took the name "Uralian Emerald" until gemmologists took a closer look.

The name Demantoid originates from the old German word "demant" meaning "Diamond-like", because of a lustre and dispersion that yields a fire even higher than Diamonds!

Commonly known as "horsetail" inclusions, some Demantoid Garnets have golden byssolite strands that form beautiful patterns similar to the tail of a horse. Demantoid Garnets with prominent horsetail inclusions are particularly coveted.

While small scale mining recommenced in Russia in 1991, most Demantoid Garnets are sourced from relatively new deposits beneath the scorched desert sands of Namibia. A favourite of the famous Russian

GARNET

goldsmith Karl Fabergé, due to a fire greater than that of Diamonds, Demantoid Garnet is an absolute "must have" for any serious collector.

Hessonite Garnet

A variety of Grossular Garnet, Hessonite comes in two colours, golden and cinnamon (this variety is commonly known as the "Cinnamon Stone"). A perfectly coloured Hessonite is a bright golden orange that resembles a combination of honey and orange with an internal fire. Some Hessonites have tints of red and brown.

Popular for thousands of years, the ancient Greeks and Romans used it in jewellery, cameos and intaglio (a figure cut into a gem, so as to make the design depressed below the surface, whereas in a cameo the relief rises above the surface). Interestingly, its name comes from the Greek word "esson", meaning "inferior", because it is slightly softer than other Garnet varieties. However, please don't be put off by the origin of its name. Hessonite is still durable and perfectly suited to jewellery.

Widely used in Vedic astrology, Hessonite is known as "Gomedha" in Hindi. The ancient Hindus believed that Hessonite was formed from the fingernails of the great demon Vala, which were scattered in the lakes of the east. Vedic astrologers believe that when set in gold, Hessonite is a powerful talisman that increases your lifespan and happiness.

Hessonite is common in the gem gravels of Sri Lanka and practically all Hessonite is obtained from this locality, although it is also found in Africa.

While the clearest gems are most prized, inclusions in Hessonite are common, with unique treacle-like streaks giving Hessonite an oily or even glasslike appearance.

Malaia Garnet

Discovered in the mid 1960's in Tanzania's Umba Valley, this red-orange to pink-orange variety of Garnet was originally thought to be Spessartite Garnet.

Actually a mixture of Pyrope, Almandine and Spessartite, Malaia Garnets are lively gems that exhibit sparkling red flashes. Once discovered not to be Spessartite, it aptly became known by the Swahili word "Malaia" meaning "outcast".

Malaia Garnets are available in numerous shades of orange, ranging from soft peach to intense reddish orange.

One of our most popular gems - Merelani Mint Garnet

Merelani Mint Garnet accented with Diamonds

The rare Merelani Mint Garnet, elegant and timeless in this magnificent bracelet

GARNET

Superb colours in this pair of Spessartite Garnet earrings by Gems TV

A fine display of Mozambique Garnet in this white gold bracelet

Gems for the gent's in this patriotic design

Mali Garnet

Mali Garnet is one of the latest discoveries in the Garnet family. Mali Garnet is an attractive and very interesting rare mixture of Andradite and Grossular that was only discovered in late 1994 at the Sandaré Mine in Mali's Kayes region (Diakon Arrondissement). Extremely rare, Mali Garnets are a bright, uniform light yellowish green colour.

Mandarin, Tangerine & Spessartite Garnet

Mandarin and Tangerine Garnets are the intensely bright orange red varieties of the rare orange Spessartite Garnet, also known as Spessartine.

Spessartite Garnet is named after its first discovery in Spessart, Bavaria in the mid 1800's. Spessartite Garnet, once an extremely rare gem, is now enjoying a newfound popularity.

In 1991 Mandarin Garnets were discovered embedded in mica in northwest Namibia where the Kunene River borders Namibia and Angola. In 1994 new deposits were unearthed in southwest, Nigeria. Soon after, Tanzania, the powerhouse of African gems, yielded deposits at the fabled gemstone mines of Arusha and Lelatema.

Although initially called "Kunene Spessartine" or "Hollandine", the evocative names Mandarin Garnet and Tangerine Garnet were soon adopted.

Merelani Mint Garnet

Long regarded as a source of the finest coloured gems, it is no surprise that Tanzania is home to some of the world's most coveted Garnets. Displaying stunning mint greens, lustre, sparkly brilliance and excellent durability, Merelani Mint Garnet is a relatively new rare gemstone whose popularity is only limited by its scarcity.

Named for its colour and where it is mined, Merelani Mint Garnet was first discovered around 1998 in the same area as Tanzanite (Merelani Hills, Arusha Region, Tanzania). Merelani Mint Garnet is basically a different hue of its better known relative, Tsavorite Garnet (Grossular Garnet). Extremely scarce, Merelani Mint Garnet is always relatively small in size (under 1 carat) and is usually included with bubbles and/or silk. Not surprisingly, when clean, Merelani Mint Garnet increases in value.

Formed in metasomatic (the process by which the chemical composition of a rock is changed by

GARNET

interaction with fluids) conditions it is typically extracted directly from metamorphic rocks and similar to Tanzanite, it is found in association with graphite.

Stunning green Garnets have historically always been in very high demand and Merelani Mint Garnet is coveted for a very good reason - few Garnets have such a brilliant appeal.

Mozambique Garnet

Originating in the east African nation they are named after, Mozambique Garnets are famed for their high quality and wonderfully warm, red colours.

Mozambique Garnet is a mixture of Pyrope and Almandine Garnet, similar in colour to Rhodolite Garnet, but slightly redder and darker.

Pyrope Garnet

Hear the word "Garnet", and what invariably comes to mind is the image of the deep red Pyrope Garnets belonging to the pyralspites family. Pyrope comes from the Greek word "pyropos", meaning "fiery eyed".

Fine Pyrope Garnets may be visually confused with dark rubies. It was the "fashion gem" of the 18th and 19th centuries and many Rubies of this period were later found to be Pyrope Garnets.

Two Baguette cut Rhodolite Garnets set in 9k yellow gold

A Trilliant cut Rhodolite Garnet set in 9k gold

Rhodolite Garnet

The name "Rhodolite" is taken from the Greek "rho'don" and "lithos", which literally translates to "rose stone". Possessing a colour reminiscent of the rhododendron flower, this name was first used in the late 19th century to describe Garnets discovered in North Carolina, USA.

Unusually striking, Rhodolite is a naturally occurring blend of Almandine and Pyrope Garnet. While raspberry is the most prized colour, Rhodolite is also found in shades of pink through lavender.

Rhodolite is typically found as water worn pebbles in alluvial deposits but it is also occasionally mind directly from host metamorphic rock. The most spectacular Rhodolite is mined in Sri Lanka, Zimbabwe, and from a relatively new deposit in the Kangala area of Tanzania that was discovered in 1987. Since then, gorgeous raspberry hued Rhodolite has been found in other regions of Tanzania including Ruvuma, Mtwara and Lindi.

Tough, durable, never enhanced and easily cleaned,

Raspberry Rhodolite Garnet from Tanzania

GARNET

Tsavorite, a favourite of our designers

Fantastic and rare - Tangerine Garnet

Unusual hues of orange in this Tangerine Garnet and Diamond ring

Rhodolite is ideal for jewellery. Due to its bright transparent clarity, Rhodolite is often cut into fantasy shapes.

Star Garnet

A highly unusual form of Garnet is the rare four-rayed Almandine Star Garnet. While Almandine Garnets (also known as "Almandite") are the most common variety of Garnets, those displaying the star are not at all common. Available in deep reds, Almandine Star Garnets are found in Nigeria and Tanzania.

Asterism or the star effect is a reflection effect that appears as two or more intersecting bands of light cross the surface of a gem.

Tsavorite Garnet

For some the sixties swung, for gemmologists they rocked. The decade which had most people looking to the sky for Lucy's Diamonds had gemmologists transfixed by a myriad of precious gemstones hailing from Africa's arid savannas: Fancy Sapphires, Rubies, Tourmaline, Tanzanite, a plethora of gorgeous coloured Garnets, among them a brilliant green Grossular Garnet, Tsavorite. Tsavorite, east Africa's beautiful green gemstone is rightful heir to the title "the king of Garnets".

Some 37 years after its discovery, Tsavorite has comfortably established itself as one of the world's most beautiful and desirable gemstones. Tsavorite Garnet, comparable in scarcity to Demantoid Garnet, is extremely rare. In fact, it is so rare that it might be unavailable in future years.

First discovered in 1967 by the now legendary Scottish geologist, Campbell R. Bridges, Tsavorite has quickly found favour as a coloured gem of choice. Bridges first discovered Tsavorite in Tanzania, but in those days getting an export license to take the gems out was impossible. Bridges, aided by the local Masai and Kikuu tribesmen persisted in his search, but this time turned his attention to the neighbouring country of Kenya. In 1971 Bridges discovered Tsavorite for a second time in Kenya's Tsavo region.

Life in Africa's bush is dangerous and the Tsavo region is well known as the domain of man eating lions and poachers. In order to protect himself from predators and brigands, Bridges was forced to live in a tree house. And as he didn't want his treasure to be stolen, he cunningly used the local's fear of snakes by placing a python in amongst the Tsavorite rough.

Tsavorite eventually found its way to America where Henry Platt of Tiffany & Co. named the gemstone, basing its name on the famous Tsavo National Park in Kenya. Tsavorite took the world by storm and interest increased dramatically when in 1974 Tiffany's started a special campaign promoting Tsavorite making it well known in the USA. International promotional campaigns followed and soon global demand for Tsavorite reached epic proportions.

While Tsavorite was once being mined in 40 different areas throughout Tanzania and Kenya, only four mining ventures are still producing commercial quantities. While some 50 deposits have been found in Kenya, Tanzania, Madagascar and even Zambia, only a handful of small mines are viable. This is because Tsavorite is notoriously difficult to mine, requiring a good understanding of geology. Seams suddenly disappear, giving no indication where to look next and its crystals are often found inside Quartz or Scapolite "potatoes" that must be cracked open to reveal the Tsavorite.

Tsavorite's intense green colours, similar to the very best Emeralds, are due to the presence of vanadium in the host rock. Like all Garnets, Tsavorite possesses few inclusions and its high index of refraction, results in a superb brilliance.

Umbalite Garnet

Umbalite Garnet is an attractive light pinkish-purple Garnet that was first unearthed in Tanzania's Umba Valley in 1978. A cocktail of Pyrope, Almandine, with small traces of Spessartite Garnet, production of this unusual gem material has been irregular and highly sought after by connoisseurs of fine gemstones the world over.

GARNET:	January's birthstone
Locations:	Kenya, Madagascar, Mali, Mozambique, Namibia, Nigeria, Russia, Sri Lanka, Tanzania
Colours Found:	Various
Typical Cuts:	Various
Family:	Garnet
Hardness:	6.5 - 7.5
Refractive Index:	1.70 - 1.73
Relative Density:	3.51 - 3.65

Merelani Mint Garnet from Tanzania

GREEN AMETHYST (PRASIOLITE)

Green Amethyst can be a confusing gem as it is traded under a variety of names and is even sometimes mistaken for other gemstones such as Peridot and Tourmaline. The green variety of Quartz, Green Amethyst is also known as Vermarine, Green Quartz, and Lime Citrine or by its gemmological name, Prasiolite. Although reasonably affordable, it is unusual and remains a collector's gemstone.

Mostly mined in Brazil, Green Amethyst's gemmological name is derived from the Greek words "prason" meaning leek (due to its colour similarities with the vegetable) and "lithos" meaning stone.

Legends and lore

Green Amethyst is believed by crystal healers to facilitate the gap between the physical and spiritual aspects of life, attracting prosperity through strengthening the mind, emotions and will.

Just the facts

Unusual Green Amethyst set in gold with White Topaz

Simple but effective. Green Amethyst and gold earrings

A stunningly cut Green Amethyst pendant

Although Quartz of sufficient beauty to be set into jewellery is not available in great abundance, Quartz is found in many geological environments and is a component of almost every rock type. It is also the most varied in terms of varieties, colours and forms. Quartz gemstones are often separated into two groups based on the size of their individual crystals. Green Amethyst is a macrocrystalline Quartz (large crystal) and this group includes many popular gemstones such as Amethyst, Citrine and Ametrine. All forms of Quartz are piezoelectric (when heated or rubbed they create an electrical charge becoming a magnet that attracts lightweight objects), making for important applications in electronics. Tourmaline is the only other gemstone that possesses this property.

With beautiful colours ranging from pastel yellow green to deep forest green, Green Amethyst is a tough gemstone making it ideal for everyday wear.

GREEN AMETHYST:	Green variety of Quartz
Locations:	Brazil
Colours Found:	Pastel yellow green to deep forest green
Typical Cuts:	Buff Top, Cabochon, Fancy, Mirror, Octagon, Oval, Round
Family:	Quartz
Hardness:	7.00
Refractive Index:	1.54 - 1.55
Relative Density:	2.65

Green Amethyst

HELIODOR

Heliodor was first discovered in Rossing, Erongo in western Namibia in 1910 and was named from the Greek "helios" and "doron", meaning "gift from the sun".

Appearing in yellow, yellowish green and yellowish orange colours, Heliodor is the yellow variety of Beryl, the "mother of gemstones". Interestingly, pure Beryl is colourless, with traces of different elements being responsible for Beryl's great colour range.

Just the facts

Heliodor's main characteristic is its colour, which is a yellowish green similar to olive oil. However, the shade may vary and it is often difficult to establish a dividing line between Heliodor and Golden Beryl. Originally, Golden Beryl found in Namibia was called Heliodor but today the name is used to describe the yellow varieties of Beryl, with the golden colours being aptly referred to as Golden Beryl. To see a complete list of all the gems in the Beryl family please turn to page 27.

The yellow colour is produced when iron replaces some of the aluminium in the crystal structure. Not surprisingly, Heliodor was discovered in a location that also produced Aquamarine, a Beryl also coloured by iron.

Heliodor is famous for their perfect, six-sided prismatic hexagonal crystals that usually occur individually. These are often enormous and some 8 meter, well crystallized examples are known to have existed. Understandably, only very small amounts of these enormous crystals are of a sufficient quality to be used in jewellery.

Heliodor can be faceted into various gem cuts, and some gems display chatoyancy (cat's eye effect) when cut and polished into cabochons. When perfectly transparent, six-sided crystals are discovered, they are sometimes set uncut in necklaces and pendants.

While the best Heliodor hails from Namibia, beautiful specimens are also found in Minas Gerais, Brazil and the Ural Mountains, Russia.

Extremely durable and displaying invigorating summery colours, Heliodor is well suited to jewellery.

A delicate heart shape gem Bezel set in 9k gold to produce this elegant ring

Brazilian Heliodor and Diamonds make this children's pendant delightful

Heliodor

HELIODOR:	Perfect, prismatic hexagon crystals
Locations:	Brazil, Madagascar, Namibia, Nigeria, Russia
Colours Found:	Brown, orange, yellow & yellow-green
Typical Cuts:	Various
Family:	Beryl
Hardness:	7.50 - 8.00
Refractive Index:	1.57 - 1.60
Relative Density:	2.80

65

HELIODOR

*Brazilian Heliodor
Oval cut and Claw
set in yellow gold*

Typically appearing in vivid and pastel limes, Herderite is an extremely attractive yet very rare gemstone. It was named for Siegmund August Wolfgang Von Herder (1776 - 1838), a mining official in Freiberg, Saxony, Germany where it was first discovered.

HERDERITE

Just the facts

Herderite has a vitreous lustre and a very complicated crystal structure, with its twinned crystals (one crystal growing within another) being its most noteworthy feature.

One of Herderite's other characteristics is that it is thermo luminescent, meaning it may glow with a weak blue light upon extreme heating. It is also sometimes fluorescent, showing a deep blue in long wave ultraviolet (UV) light.

Herderite appears in a range of vivid to pastel colours including white, yellow, green and blue.

Herderite is predominately mined in Minas Gerais, Brazil, Germany and Russia. In the USA there are several locations that mine Herderite including Newery, Maine, New Hampshire and San Diego, California. Regardless of the locale, the percentage of rough crystals unearthed suitable for jewellery is extremely limited.

Don't expect to see a lot of Herderite at Gems TV. In 2005, we were only able to source less than a dozen pieces of this incredibly rare and exotically beautiful gem. Whenever we do discover it, as it is so rare, we always set it in 18k gold.

A fine example of the lapidarys art, stunningly cut Herderite in 18k gold

A very unusual cut in Herderite set with Diamonds in 18k gold

Herderite seen here in 18k gold with Channel set Diamonds

Don Kogen, the Gem Hunter says:

"Our buyers are constantly travelling the globe hunting gems. On our travels, we occasionally come across a small quantity of gems that we weren't expecting to find. When this happens, regardless of the economics involved, we will always try and obtain them in order to offer the widest selection of gems to our customers and collectors. Herderite was such a find. We have included it in this guide in the hope that we will soon discover more of this beautiful gem."

HERDERITE:	Thermoluminescent
Locations:	Brazil, Germany, Madagascar, Russia, USA
Colours Found:	Colourless, green or light blue, white & yellow
Typical Cuts:	Various
Family:	Herderite
Hardness:	5.00 - 5.50
Refractive Index:	1.59 - 1.62
Relative Density:	2.90 - 3.00

HIDDENITE

Hiddenite is an attractive and rare gemstone. It has an unusual green colour that is unlike either Peridot or Emerald. Hiddenite was discovered in 1800 in Hiddenite, a city in Alexander County, North Carolina, USA. Both the city and the gem mineral were named after William Earl Hidden, a mineralogist and mining director from Newark, New Jersey who was mining in the area.

Just the facts

Hiddenite is actually one of the two varieties of Spodumene. The other is Kunzite, typically a pink to lilac variety, but Yellow Kunzite is a trade name used to describe yellow Spodumene. While all varieties of Spodumene are scarce, Hiddenite is the rarer of the two, with Kunzite better known by most gemstone collectors.

The green colour of Hiddenite ranges from a yellowish to a bluish green. Hiddenite is strongly pleochroic meaning that it can change colour when viewed from different angles, thus a gem cutter must take great care to orient the gem in a position that accentuates its deepest colour. The top and bottom of the crystal reveal the deepest colours and knowledgeable gem cutters take advantage of this effect to produce the finest quality Hiddenite.

The brilliance of Hiddenite is maximized by our expert gem cutters

Hiddenite is formed from lithium aluminium silicate. The crystals are vitreous and can be either transparent or translucent. For many years, the occurrence of Hiddenite was limited to North Carolina, however new deposits were recently discovered in Madagascar and Brazil.

With Hiddenite at its centre this pendant is extremely eye catching

Typing Hiddenite into an internet search engine will provide hundreds of results about the city of Hiddenite in North Carolina, USA. As you start to discover the lifestyle of this historic city, you can't help but become attached to this wonderful gem.

Simple and elegant this pendant is timelessly beautiful

While Hiddenite is prized both as a collectors gem and as a jewellery gemstone, because it's so scarce, if you fall in love with Hiddenite, when you see it you better - Snatch It!

HIDDENITE:	Pleochroism
Locations:	Brazil, Madagascar, USA
Colours Found:	Yellowish to bluish green
Typical Cuts:	Baguette, Emerald, Fancy, Pear, Princess
Family:	Spodumene
Hardness:	6.50
Refractive Index:	1.65 - 1.68
Relative Density:	1.66

Idocrase derives its name from Greek words "eidos", meaning likeness and "krasis", meaning composition. Collectively meaning "mixed form", this is an allusion to its crystals showing a mixture of other minerals.

Idocrase is a fascinating gem originally discovered at the volcano, Mount Vesuvius. Not surprisingly, one of its other names is Vesuvianite.

Idocrase is both a rare and beautiful gem and extremely popular among gemstone collectors.

Just the facts

Idocrase's colour is normally green, but can also be brown, yellow, blue or purple. Idocrase forms as a result of contact between metamorphic rock and impure limestone, and is usually found with other exotic minerals. Due to variations in its composition, a range of physical properties occurs. Idocrase's crystals are typically thick and stubby and striated along their length.

A massive green translucent gem variety of Idocrase is called Californite, after the location of its initial discovery. Often confused with Jade, this variety of Idocrase is sometimes incorrectly called Californian Jade or Vesuvian Jade. However, upon closer inspection, its crystal shape reveals its true identity.

Another popular variety of Idocrase is Cyprine. Sky blue in colour, Cyprine is mostly found in Norway.

Transparent Idocrase suitable for jewellery is typically faceted using table or step cuts. However, gem quality crystals of Idocrase are incredibly scarce, making this gemstone highly collectable.

IDOCRASE

The combination of Idocrase and Purple Diamonds in white gold

Three gems used to great effect. Idocrase, Yellow Sapphire and Diamond

Idocrase

IDOCRASE:	Vitreous to resinous lustre
Locations:	Brazil, Mexico, Namibia, Russia, South Africa
Colours Found:	Blue, brown, green, purple & yellow
Typical Cuts:	Cabochon, Emerald, Octagon, Oval, Round, Trilliant
Family:	Idocrase
Hardness:	6.50
Refractive Index:	1.70
Relative Density:	3.30 - 3.50

IOLITE

The name Iolite comes from the Greek word "ios" which means violet. Iolite is a transparent, violet blue, light blue or yellow grey gemstone. A pleochroic gem (different colours are displayed when the gemstone is viewed from different angles), Iolite will show many colours in a single piece.

Legends and lore

According to ancient Scandinavian sagas, Norse navigators used thin pieces of Iolite (their magical "sun stone") as the world's first polarizing filter. Looking through an Iolite lens, they could determine the position of the sun on overcast days and navigate their boats safely. Hence Iolite is also known as the "Viking Compass" or "Viking Stone". The story of the "Viking Compass" triggered the curiosity of a 10 year old boy who just happened to be the son of the Chief Navigator of the Scandinavian Airline System, Jorgen Jensen. The "sun stone" described in Norse lore sounded similar to the twilight compass used by his father at higher latitudes where a magnetic compass is unreliable. His father's twilight compass was equipped with a polarizing filter that enables a navigator to locate the sun, even when it is behind the clouds, by light polarized by the atmosphere. Intrigued by his son's observation, Jensen passed it onto Danish archaeologist Thorkild Ramskau, who immediately recognized its scientific implications. Collecting minerals found in Scandinavia whose molecules are aligned similarly to the crystals in a polarizing filter, Ramskau put Iolite (the gem variety of the mineral Cordierite) to the test. Accompanying navigator Jorgen Jensen on a flight to Greenland, Ramskau kept track of the sun with a piece of Iolite while Jensen used the twilight compass. Incredibly, his observations were accurate to within 2.5 degrees of the sun's true position!

Known as the gemstone of clear vision, when worn as an amulet, Iolite was believed to have the power to guide lost sailors to the brilliance of the sun, allowing them to safely find their way home.

Just the facts

Iolite is a popular and interesting gemstone. It has a pretty violet blue colour that is unlike other gemstones although it has been compared to light blue Sapphires. It is for this reason that it is sometimes known as "Water Sapphire".

While we believe an Iolite necklace or Iolite earrings are

Cushion cut Iolite, White Topaz and gold

The classic cross pendant. Seen here with Iolite

The beauty of Iolite with White Topaz

Iolite gemstones

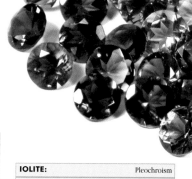

IOLITE

probably the best ways to showcase this gem's unique colour, Iolite rings are also desirable, as it is a durable gem well suited to everyday wear.

Pleochroism (meaning that it can change colour when viewed from different angles) is very pronounced in Iolite and is seen as three different colour shades in the same gem. In viewing an Iolite, the colours violet blue, yellow grey and a light blue can be seen. When correctly faceted, Iolite will show its best violet blue colour through the top or table of the gem, but when viewed from another angle the gem may display other colours.

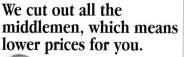
IOLITE:	Pleochroism
Locations:	India, Madagascar, Sri Lanka
Colours Found:	Violet blue, light blue or yellow grey
Typical Cuts:	Various
Family:	Cordierite
Hardness:	7.00 - 7.50
Refractive Index:	1.50
Relative Density:	2.53 - 2.65

Twelve Pear shaped Iolites set into a watch face

JADE (NEPHRITE)

For centuries, Nephrite Jade and the other Jade variety Jadeite were considered one and the same. It was not until 1863 in France that they were identified as different minerals with a similar appearance and properties.

The name Jade was first used around the time of the Spanish conquest of Central and South America and is from the Spanish "piedra de ijada", meaning hip stone, as it was thought to cure kidney stones and other kidney ailments.

While Jade was known as the "stone of heaven" in ancient China, the Chinese word for Jade "Yu" is not generally used. Jade was excavated from the Kunlun Mountains of northwest China, from 5000 BC, and even today China remains an important source for this gemstone.

Legends and lore

In Russia, it has been mined and crafted since 3000 BC. Tsar Alexander III's sarcophagus was carved from Jade. For about 3,000 years Jade has been highly prized by the Native North Americans of British Columbia, Canada who called it "Greenstone" and for centuries the New Zealand Maori have made beautiful Nephrite carvings.

Just the facts

Nephrite is composed of silica and magnesia and its colour is determined by the amount of iron present in the mineral. A lesser iron content produces lighter colours such as white, cream, yellow, grey, green, blue, red, brown and lavender. A greater iron content produces darker coloured Nephrite, such as darker grey and darker green.

Nephrite has the highest tensile strength (toughness as opposed to hardness) of all natural gemstones and in fact has a tensile strength greater than some steel. It is so strong that it cannot be chiselled. It must be ground using sharp abrasives.

Interestingly, less than 0.05% of Nephrite extracted is of gem quality. Nephrite is typically not treated as it is less likely to take up dye or stains than Jadeite. Older pieces benefit from polishing to retain their lustre.

The subtle colour of Lavender Jade

Rare Red Jade set in gold

Jade set with Citrine in this white gold pendant

Jade

JADE:	Highest tensile strength
Locations:	China
Colours Found:	Blue, brown, cream, green, grey, lavender, red, white & yellow
Typical Cuts:	Cabochon, Ornamental
Family:	Jade
Hardness:	6.50
Refractive Index:	1.61 - 1.63
Relative Density:	2.90 - 3.10

JASPER

The name comes from the Latin name for Jasper "iaspis", which probably also referred to the other types of Chalcedony Quartz. Jasper is an opaque and fine grained variety of Chalcedony Quartz. It is typically found in red, yellow, brown or green colours and generally has spots.

Jasper is normally cut as cabochons and has traditionally been used as a gemstone for jewellery such as brooches, earrings, necklaces, pendants, intaglios (a gem carved in negative relief) and cameos (a gem carved in relief).

Legends and lore

Jasper was a favourite amulet gem in ancient times and is referenced in Greek, Hebrew, Assyrian and Latin literature. For example, Jasper is one of "the stones of fire" (Ezekiel 28:13-16) that were given to Moses at the mountain of God and said to possess the power to summon angels. Moses then decreed them mounted into a sacred breastplate for his brother, the high priest Aaron (Exodus 28:15-30). In the New Testament (Revelations 21:19), Jasper is one of the twelve gemstones set in the foundations of the city walls of Jerusalem. As compiled by Andreas, Bishop of Caesurae, one of the earliest writers to tie the Apostles with the symbolism of the twelve gems of Jerusalem, Jasper was denoted for the Apostle St. Peter.

Handcrafted beauty in gold and Jasper

In some native American cultures, Jasper is considered to be the symbolic blood of the earth, and was thus thought to be one of the best gems for connecting with the deep, stabilizing energies of the earth.

According to crystal healers, Jasper is an intensely protective gem, acting to stabilize the aura and rid it of dysfunctional energy thereby facilitating relaxation, contentment and compassion.

Red Jasper and White Topaz in this Gems TV favourite

Just the facts

Quartz gemstones are commonly separated into two groups based on the size of their individual crystals. The macrocrystalline Quartz (large crystal) group includes many popular gemstones such as Amethyst, Ametrine, Citrine and Green Amethyst (Prasiolite). Cryptocrystalline Quartz includes species whose individual crystals are too small to be easily distinguished. Apart from being a variety within the group, Chalcedony is also a catch all term to describe cryptocrystalline Quartz and includes Jasper as well as many other gems that have been coveted since antiquity.

Dalmatian Jasper set in classic gold stud earrings

JASPER:	Mentioned in the Bible
Locations:	India, Madagascar, Mexico
Colours Found:	Brown, green, greyish white, pink, red, shades of blue/purple & yellow
Typical Cuts:	Beads, Cabochon
Family:	Chalcedony
Hardness:	6.50 - 7.00
Refractive Index:	1.54
Relative Density:	2.59 - 2.61

73

JASPER

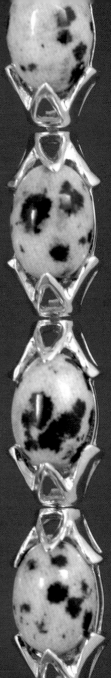

Red Jasper from India and
Dalmatian Jasper from Madagascar

KORNERUPINE

Kornerupine (also known as Prismatine) was discovered in Fiskernaes, Greenland in 1884 and was named after the Danish geologist and explorer Andreas N. Kornerup (1857-1881). It is a rare gemstone well known for its pleochroism (different colours seen from different viewing angles) and its green colour, which can be intense as Emerald.

Legends and lore

Amongst crystal healers, Kornerupine is considered a gemstone for teaching and communication. Kornerupine is also said to help stabilise the emotional swings of manic-depressives and assist in seeing through the false agreements in one's current reality.

Just the facts

A metamorphic mineral, Kornerupine is a complex magnesium aluminium borosilicate whose crystals are often found in alluvial deposits collected behind rocks or in the bends of rivers. Kornerupine is often deposited with other gems including Sapphire, Chrysoberyl, Ruby, Topaz, Garnet, Zircon, Diopside, Andalusite, Spinel and Iolite.

A cluster of Kornerupine

While Kornerupine has a similar but slightly higher index of refraction to Emeralds as well as their characteristic inclusions, the two gems are easily distinguished by Kornerupine's pleochroism. Depending on the angle which Kornerupine is viewed, its colours can range from brown, colourless, green, greenish-yellow, yellow, pink or lavender. However, wherever possible Kornerupine is faceted on the green axis as this colouration is its rarest and most coveted colour.

Elegance in gold - Kornerupine

Kornerupine also occasionally exhibits chatoyancy or the cat's eye effect. When polished as cabochons Kornerupine can display a reflection effect that appears as a single bright band of light across its surface. This effect is caused by inclusions of fine, slender parallel fibres in the gem.

White Topaz used to accent the beauty of Kornerupine

While Kornerupine is a rare gem that used to be limited to collections, it is now becoming increasingly popular in jewellery due to its suitability for everyday wear.

Kornerupine

KORNERUPINE:	Pleochroism
Locations:	Sri Lanka, Madagascar, Tanzania
Colours Found:	Brown, green & orange
Typical Cuts:	Baguette, Cabochon, Fancy, Oval
Family:	Kornerupine
Hardness:	6.50 - 7.00
Refractive Index:	1.66 - 1.68
Relative Density:	3.28 - 3.35

KUNZITE

Kunzite, discovered in California in 1902, was named after Tiffany's chief gemmologist, George Frederick Kunz.

Kunz described this durable pastel pink gemstone as having two distinct properties: "phosphorescence" where Kunzite, in this aspect similar to Diamonds, is observed to glow in a darkened room after it has been exposed to the sun's ultraviolet rays and "pleochroism", showing different colours when viewed from different directions.

These phenomena are best seen in larger sized gems set into jewellery like pendants, drop and chandelier earrings, and rings with open Prong or Bar settings that let light flow freely through them, accentuating Kunzite's fire to full effect.

Kunzite radiates pure Parisian chic, revealing delicate raspberry pinks, frosty lilacs, cool lavenders and hot fuchsias under the warm glow of incandescent light (candlelight). Its subtle colouring perfectly compliments "décolleté" eveningwear, dreamy candlelight and tender blushes, hence its colloquial name the "Evening Gemstone".

Legends and lore

Aside from their obvious physical beauty, pink gemstones possess potent metaphysical properties. Alternative healers use a multitude of pink gems in conjunction with the "heart chakra". The 4th of 7 energy points that run the course of the human body, the heart chakra is believed to carry the emotional sensibilities of love and compassion.

Some believe that when the 4th chakra is blocked we experience emotions such as anxiety, fear, anger and frustration. Crystal healers use the properties of pink gems like Pink Tourmaline and Kunzite to free the heart chakra from this negative energy.

This alternative approach of enhancing the "power of pink" is a viewpoint shared and supported by traditional methods of medicine and psychology:

"The colour Pink causes the brain to send signals that reduce the secretion of adrenalin, reducing the heart rate and consequently dissipating states of extreme excitement such as anger."

Science Digest, 1980

Sophisticated and elegant - 18k yellow gold and Kunzite

A stunning example of the colour of Kunzite

18k gold with Kunzite

A large piece of oval Brazilian Kunzite

KUNZITE

Just the facts

The lithium in Kunzite's chemical composition, lithium aluminium silicate, gives it a wonderful pink violet colour that compliments both autumn and spring wardrobes.

As a member of the Spodumene family, Kunzite is closely related to Hiddenite, the green variety of Spodumene. Hiddenite is an attractive gem, but is extremely rare and for the most part is known only by collectors (see page 68). While Kunzite is usually thought of as a pink to violet gemstone, Yellow Kunzite is a trade name used to describe Yellow Spodumene. Displaying delicate pastel lemon meringues, Yellow Kunzite hails from Madagascar and Afghanistan, and possesses all the attributes of Kunzite, albeit in another colour, providing Kunzite lovers with a delightful alternative.

Kunzite is strongly pleochroic, meaning there is a colour intensity variation when a crystal is viewed from different directions. The top and the bottom of the crystal reveal the deepest colours and our experienced gem cutters always take this into consideration when faceting Kunzite for Gems TV.

A beautifully finished Kunzite set in 9k gold

Kunzite

Yellow Kunzite

KUNZITE:	Pleochroism
Locations:	Afghanistan, Brazil, Madagascar, Pakistan
Colours Found:	Pink & yellow
Typical Cuts:	Various
Family:	Spodumene
Hardness:	6.00 - 7.00
Refractive Index:	1.65 - 1.68
Relative Density:	3.16 - 3.20

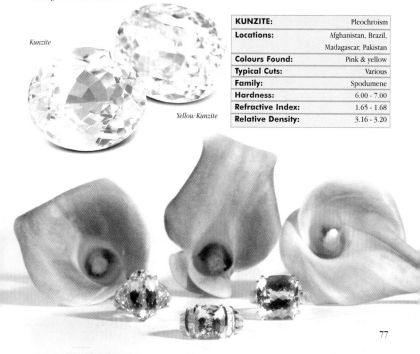

KYANITE

Also called Disthene, the name Kyanite is derived from the Greek "kyanos", meaning blue. The most popular varieties display intensely beautiful colours reminiscent of top Ceylon and Kashmir Sapphires. Although the name Kyanite has been used since 1789, Kyanite was sold in Europe as Sapphire until the turn of the 20th century.

Legends and lore

The powerful blue hues of Kyanite have long been thought to inspire calmness, composure, serenity, loyalty and respect.

Kyanite is used by alternative healers as a tool for mediation and relaxation. These healers use Kyanite to open the 3rd Eye chakra to enhance creativity, broaden perception and to reach a better understanding of others. Kyanite is also said to foster tranquillity, and believed to have a positive effect on dreams, visualization and foresightedness.

Just the facts

Like Diamonds, Kyanite has perfect cleavage in one direction, a unique characteristic amongst gemstones. This combined with its varying hardness (Kyanite is a rare polymorph, displaying two harnesses within one gem), makes Kyanite a challenging gem to facet. Understandably, the cutting of Kyanite is an extremely important quality consideration.

Occurring in a wide variety of locations around the world, the best quality Kyanite hails from a deposit discovered in 1995 in the Kali Gandaki region of west central Nepal and Tibet. Tibetan Kyanite is arguably the best ever found, displaying rich cobalt blues evocative of superb Sapphires.

The ever popular Kyanite seen here in 9k gold

Kyanite and White Topaz - a great gem combination

Kyanite

KYANITE:	Perfect cleavage, varying hardness
Locations:	Nepal, Tibet
Colours Found:	Blue
Typical Cuts:	Emerald, Octagon, Oval
Family:	Kyanite
Hardness:	4.50 - 7.00
Refractive Index:	1.71 - 1.73
Relative Density:	3.56 - 3.68

Gavin "Gemstone Gav" Linsell says:

"Emerging from a deep slumber, you push back the covers and slip out of bed, pondering what jewellery to wear. As you draw back the curtains on a revitalising summer's morning, your question is answered with the clear blue skies embodied in the atmospheric hues of cool blue Kyanite. Suitability is a key word when describing Kyanite, as it suits all skin tones and looks great set into yellow, white or rose gold jewellery."

LABRADORITE

Labradorite is named after the Labrador Peninsula in Canada where it was discovered. Displaying brilliant pastels and deep golden colours, it even includes varieties colloquially known as "Black Rainbow", which feature a spellbinding play of colour. Labradorite is a stunning gemstone perfect for wardrobes of all seasons.

Legends and lore

Calling it "Firestone" because of its captivating play of colour, the Native Indians of Labrador attributed mystical qualities to Labradorite, using the powdered gem as a magical potion to cure their ailments.

Interestingly, some modern mystics believe that Labradorite is a gem that assists the practice of magic, unleashes the power of the imagination and helps to overcome personal limitations.

Just the facts

Labradorite is a sodium rich variety of plagioclase Feldspar. While transparent Labradorite is relatively free from inclusions and appears red, orange, yellow or colourless, the smoke grey varieties that show a play of colour or "schiller" are most frequently used in jewellery.

A 9k gold Labradorite pendant made by Gems TV

Valued for its lustrous metallic reflections that are said to resemble a butterfly's wing, this schiller is aptly called "labradorescence" by gemmologists and appears as stunning rainbow coloured reflections when light strikes the gem in a particular direction. Mainly caused by the interference of light from lattice distortions, this effect often appears in violet, blue, green, yellow, gold and even reddish orange tints. Spectrolite, an extremely rare variety found only in Finland, can even display the complete colour spectrum.

The perfect accessory - Labradorite bracelet in gold

When appreciating the play of colour in Labradorite, observe the strength and intensity of the labradorescence when the gemstone is viewed from different angles. This may result in different colours being visible or even a range of colours all visible at the same time.

White gold set with Labradorite

Labradorite

LABRADORITE:	Labradorescence
Locations:	China, Madagascar, India
Colours Found:	Colourless, orange, red, smoke grey & yellow
Typical Cuts:	Various
Family:	Feldspar
Hardness:	6.00 - 6.50
Refractive Index:	1.55 - 1.57
Relative Density:	2.70 - 2.72

LAPIS LAZULI

The word "lapis" is the Latin word for stone. The names of both "lazuli" and Lazurite are derived from the Persian word "lazhuward" and the Latin word "lazulum", meaning blue or heaven. The Lapis Lazuli name, often shortened to Lapis, is sometimes mistakenly used for the mineral Lazurite.

Legends and lore

Lapis was mentioned in writing in 2650 BC in the Sumerian epic of Gilgamesh and in the Book of Exodus in the Bible. The ancient Egyptians used Lapis extensively in religious ceremonies (it appears in various passages in the Egyptian Book of the Dead), and Lapis items were found in tombs near the ancient city of Ur, including that of Tutankhamen. The ancient city of Ur had a thriving trade in Lapis as early as the fourth millennium BC.

The Greeks and Romans used it as a reward for bravery and the Romans (typically) also believed Lapis to be a powerful aphrodisiac. The Greeks and Romans also employed it for inlaid work and for jewellery, amulets and talismans. They named it "sapphirus" (blue), which is now used for blue variety of Corundum, Sapphire.

Prized by Romans, to this day Lapis remains a striking gem when used in gent's jewellery

When Lapis was first introduced to Europe, it was called Ultramarinum, meaning beyond the sea. Lapis was once powdered and mixed with oil to produce the pigment ultramarine, which is seen in the beautiful blues of Renaissance paintings. Ultramarine has been made synthetically since 1828.

In the Middle Ages, it was thought to keep the limbs healthy and free the soul from error, envy and fear. In the 17th century, it was used in medicine to prevent miscarriages, epilepsy and dementia.

Attributed with great healing, purifying and curative properties, Lapis allegedly points the way to enlightenment, and aids in the opening of the 3rd Eye. Popular with ancient alchemists, it was used in

Lapis Lazuli

medicine, cosmetics and paintings. It was also believed to confer ability, success, divine favour, ancient wisdom and cure sore throats. No wonder it was once as valuable as gold!

The Arab geographer Istakhri record a visit to the Afghanistan Lapis mines in the 10th century and Marco Polo visited and wrote about them in 1271.

Just the facts

Mined in the Kochka river valley of Badakhshan, Afghanistan for over 7,000 years, the "Armenian Stone" is an enduring rock - and yes, it is a rock! Lapis is a contact metamorphosed limestone that contains Lazurite, Pyrite and Calcite. Unlike other gems, it is a composite of several materials with sparkling flecks of Pyrite, or fool's gold, adding to its mystical allure.

Arguably, the finest Lapis Lazuli is a dark royal blue colour and as with all gems, the quality of its cutting is also a consideration.

LAPIS LAZULI

LAPIS LAZULI:	Early jewellery gem
Locations:	Afghanistan, Pakistan
Colours Found:	Ultramarine
Typical Cuts:	Cabochon
Family:	None
Hardness:	5.00 - 5.50
Refractive Index:	1.50
Relative Density:	2.40

Want to learn more about gemstones? Visit our Gemstone Buyer's Guide at www.GemsTV.com

MALACHITE

A modern gent's 3ct Cabochon Malachite ring

This Azurite Malachite from Arizona shows why the Romans called it the Peacock Stone

Demonstrating different shades of green, this Silver Malachite ring proved popular with younger customers

Malachite is named after the Greek word "moloche", meaning mallow, due to its similarity in colour to mallow leaves.

A secondary copper mineral, Malachite is a popular gem that has light and dark vivid green banded areas. Many beautiful specimens of Malachite contain special combinations with other minerals, such as Azurite, Cuprite or Chrysocolla..

Legends and lore

Malachite was admired by ancient Greek followers of the goddess Venus and thought to possess great powers.

In Rome, it was called the "Peacock Stone" and dedicated to the goddess Juno, who protects against lightning and other perils of nature. Continuing these ancient traditions, to this day some Italians wear Malachite as protection from the evil eye

Popular with the ancient Egyptians, according to legend, their hippo goddess Toeris (also associated to Hathor) wore a necklace of many beads including Malachite.

According to legend, it was worn to detect impending danger, and is believed to break into pieces when danger was near. Hence, it was often regarded as the guardian gem of travellers.

According to modern crystal healers its powers include protection, power, peace, hope, love, and success in business.

Just the facts

Malachite's banded, light and dark green designs are unique, and give it a visual appearance unlike any other gem. The light and dark green bands are so distinctive that it is arguably one of the most easily recognisable gemstones.

Its ability to mix with other minerals has lead to Malachite being unearthed in a wide array of attractive colours and patterns. These unique combinations create some intriguing gemstones.

MALACHITE:	Known as the Peacock Stone
Locations:	Namibia, Tanzania, Zambia
Colours Found:	Banded light & dark green
Typical Cuts:	Beads, Cabochon, Ornamental
Family:	Malachite
Hardness:	3.50 - 4.00
Refractive Index:	1.85
Relative Density:	3.90 - 4.00

Popular with the Romans, who thought it was formed out of moonlight, and in India, where it is considered a sacred zodiac gem, Moonstone is one of the most coveted varieties of Feldspar.

MOONSTONE

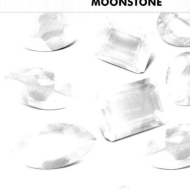

Legends and lore

In antiquity, men used Moonstone to predict the future by placing them in their mouths.

A symbol of the 3rd eye, Moonstone was once believed to balance yin/yang, protect against epilepsy and sun stroke, cure headaches and nose bleeds, and ensure a high yield in crops. Today, crystal healers believe that it can help men open their feminine emotional aspects.

Moonstone is a highly prized gift for lovers as it is believed to arouse tender passion. In some cultures, it is also believed to accentuate the wearer's nature, whether positive or negative.

An unusual Cat's Eye Moonstone pendant

Just the facts

Moonstone is a member of the Feldspar group of minerals and is closely related to Sunstone. The name Feldspar comes from the German "feldt spat", meaning "field stone". This is because when Feldspar weathers, it releases large amounts of plant nutrients, such as potassium, which enrich the soil.

A contemporary setting for this Sri Lankan Rainbow Moonstone

Moonstone's characteristic shimmer or sheen is also known as "schiller" or "aventurescence" and is caused by the intergrowth of two different types of Feldspar with different refractive indexes. Moonstones are often cut as cabochons to maximize this effect.

Traditionally, Moonstone has a silver to blue sheen, near perfect clarity and a colourless body colour. Sri Lankan Rainbow Moonstone possesses all these qualities and as it is quite rare and becoming rarer, it is definitely a "must have" for any jewellery collection. Sri Lankan Rainbow Moonstone is laboriously chipped directly from a host deposit in Meetiyaguda, Sri Lanka. Interestingly, Sri Lankan Rainbow Moonstone typically displays such a stunning transparent clarity (not usually associated with this gemstone), intense bright blue shimmer and dazzling play of colour that it can be cut as a faceted gemstone.

Sri Lankan Rainbow Moonstone in gold

This is truly unique and further accentuates the desirability of this highly collectable exotic gemstone.

MOONSTONE:	June's birthstone
Locations:	Brazil, India, Madagascar, Sri Lanka, Tanzania
Colours Found:	Colourless to brown, green, grey, pink, rainbow & yellow
Typical Cuts:	Cabochon
Family:	Feldspar
Hardness:	6.00 - 6.50
Refractive Index:	1.51 - 1.57
Relative Density:	2.56 - 2.62

MORGANITE

Morganite, or Pink Beryl as it was initially described, was discovered in Madagascar in 1911. It was Tiffany's celebrated gemmologist, George Frederick Kunz who renamed this unique gemstone in homage to the New York banker and his benefactor, John Pierpont Morgan.

Legends and lore

While Morganite has had little time to generate myths and legends, aside from their obvious physical beauty, all pink gemstones are believed by some to possess potent metaphysical properties connected with love and compassion.

Just the facts

Morganite, a member of the Beryl family and sister gem to Aquamarine and Emerald, is coloured by trace amounts of manganese that find their way into the Beryl crystal structure. Morganite is found as flat, tabular crystals that resemble Rose Quartz, but they are easily differentiated by their lustre and brilliance.

Medina Morganite - a favourite of Gems TV

When mother nature created Morganite she made the ideal gemstone to complement all complexions. Coming in pinks from subtle lavenders to hot fuchsias and even pastel pink apricot blends, Morganite exudes feminine charm and tenderness. Putting a unique twist on fashionable pink, Morganite provides the perfect antidote to the stress of modern life.

Subtle colours and stunning design - Morganite

Its durability, lustre, clarity, brilliance and myriad of beautiful pink hues, makes Morganite immensely suitable as a jewellery gemstone, appropriate for everyday wear. The only factor impeding Morganite's popularity is its scarcity.

The summer pinks of Morganite

MORGANITE:	Pink variety of Beryl
Locations:	Brazil, Madagascar
Colours Found:	Pink
Typical Cuts:	Various
Family:	Beryl
Hardness:	7.50 - 8.00
Refractive Index:	1.57 - 1.60
Relative Density:	2.71 - 2.90

Morganite

MOTHER OF PEARL

While Queen Elizabeth I gave Mother of Pearl its name in the 15th century, the beauty of Mother of Pearl was used in the decoration of jewellery and ornaments 3,000 years before the birth of Christ. Also known as nacre (from the Arabic word for shell "naqqarah"), the name reflects the fact that these shells are the "mother" from which Pearls are harvested.

Mother of Pearl is the smooth lining of iridescent lustre found in some mollusc shells such as oysters, abalone, mussels and paua shells.

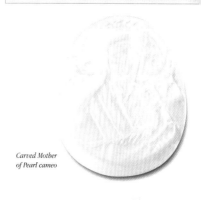

Carved Mother of Pearl cameo

Legends and lore

In the 1920's, a series of tombs were excavated to the east of Babylon in the Middle East. The tombs were of Sumerian royalty from ancient Mesopotamia and yielded a treasure of gold, silver, gemstones and several beautiful wooden ornaments and musical instruments inlaid with Mother of Pearl (a testament to the wealth and sophistication of this ancient culture). The silver lyre of Ur, found in one of the graves in the royal cemetery, dates to between 2600 and 2400 BC. The lyre was entirely covered in sheet silver and inlaid with Mother of Pearl.

Just like a butterfly, this Mother of Pearl pendant displays many colours

In Asia, centuries before the birth of Christ, the Chinese learned that beads or tiny figures of deities slipped between the soft mantle and the shell of a living mollusc soon became coated with Mother of Pearl. These beads and carvings were then taken to temples and offered to the gods in the hope that they would bestow good luck.

A simple, elegant and contemporary design

The Yaqui Indians of Mexico, immortalised in the shamanic tales of Carlos Castaneda, wear a necklace called the "hopo'orosim". The necklace is made of Mother of Pearl and is believed to provide the wearer with protection from evil.

By the 15th century Europe's growing demand for Mother of Pearl for use in gold and silver rings, necklaces and brooches had all but depleted the supplies of Mother of Pearl in the Persian Gulf.

A stunning example of Mother of Pearl from China, flanked by Diamonds and set in sterling silver

In 1568 the Solomon Islands, known as "the pearl of the pacific", were discovered by the Spanish explorer, Alvaro de Mendana. On discovering the island's rich bounty of gold and Mother of Pearl, he gave the archipelago its current name, believing that he had found the mythical source of King Solomon's mines.

In Polynesian lore, the iridescence of Mother of Pearl is attributed to the spirits of coral and sand, Okana and Uaro, who as legend has it adorned Tahitian oysters in

Our craftsmen will often shape Mother of Pearl into various modern shapes

MOTHER OF PEARL

This piece demonstrates how we take our creative inspiration from around the globe

An unusual combination of Mother of Pearl and gold which was chosen for its complementary colours

glistening cloaks covered in all the colours of the fish of the sea.

Just the facts

High quality Mother of Pearl is produced by the members of mollusc family called bivalves (two part shells).

Mother of Pearl's nacre (also see Pearls on page 95) forms when an organic particle becomes trapped within the mollusc or if the mollusc is injured in some way.

Sensing the object or damage, the living organism within the mollusc secretes calcium carbonate, a derivative mineral of aragonite, and the binding protein conchiolin. The layers of calcium carbonate settle and are interspersed by the conchiolin, which acts as a kind of organic glue binding the crystals together.

Mother of Pearl is created by a living organism and thus environmental factors play a crucial role in its formation. As Mother of Pearl producing molluscs cannot regulate their body temperature, they are susceptible to changes in external conditions. Mother of Pearl appears in a wide variety of colours and derives its colour from its genetic make-up and the water in which it grows.

MOTHER OF PEARL:	Ancient gemstone
Locations:	China, Japan
Colours Found:	Various
Typical Cuts:	Beads, Cabochons, Cameo
Family:	Organics
Hardness:	3.00 - 4.50
Refractive Index:	1.52 - 1.65
Relative Density:	2.60 - 2.80

MOTHER OF PEARL

*Pink Bezel set
Mother of Pearl
from Japan*

OBSIDIAN

Fashionable necklace in Rainbow Obsidian

Unusual Mahogony Obsidian as a trilogy

Snowflake Obsidian in 9k yellow gold

This gem is supposedly named after Obsidian, a Roman said to have brought the first gems from Lake Shalla, Ethiopia to Rome.

Legends and lore

Obsidian is regarded as one of the most important "teachers" of the New Age movement. Obsidian is said to sharpen both external and internal vision. For some crystal healers, it is the warrior of truth, and shows the self where the ego is at, and what we must change in order to advance to the next step of evolutionary growth.

Just the facts

Obsidian is formed by the rapid cooling of viscous lava due to volcanic explosions. It is made of the same minerals as granite but cools so quickly that they do not have time to crystallise.

Obsidian has a glassy lustre and is usually black or a very dark green, but it can also be found in an almost colourless form.

Obsidian may be fashioned into a razor sharp cutting edge and ancient civilizations used it for jewellery, mirrors, arrow heads, spear heads, scrapers and cutting tools, such as the sacrificial knives of the Aztecs. Because of this, Obsidian has been found in locations far from its original source. This might have confused a few gemmologists but it has helped us understand more about the travels of our ancestors.

Today, transparent specimens are faceted, usually into steps cut, while less transparent pieces are fashioned into cabochons.

Especially prized in jewellery, Snowflake Obsidian is a striking black, lustrous opaque gem with white bold markings, formed by internal bubbles or crystals of potassium feldspar, much like beautiful patterns of snowflakes on a black background. Snowflake Obsidian was very popular with Gems TV collectors in 2005.

OBSIDIAN:	Natural glass of volcanic origin
Locations:	Mexico, USA
Colours Found:	Almost clear, black & very dark green
Typical Cuts:	Cabochon
Family:	Obsidian
Hardness:	5.50 - 7.00
Refractive Index:	1.48 - 1.53
Relative Density:	2.33 - 2.60

ONYX

Commonly known as "Black Magic", this gem's name comes from the Greek word "Onyx", which means fingernail or claw. Legend says that one day while Venus was sleeping Cupid cut her fingernails and left the clippings scattered on the ground. Because no part of a heavenly body can die, the gods turned them into a gem, which later became known as Onyx.

Onyx is a Chalcedony Quartz with a fine texture and parallel bands of alternate colours.

Legends and lore

In Greek times, almost all colours of Chalcedony Quartz from fingernail white to dark brown and black were called Onyx. Later, the Romans narrowed the term to refer to black and dark brown colours only. Today when we think of Onyx we often preface the word with black to distinguish it from other varieties of Onyx that come in white, reddish brown, green, brown and banded colours. Onyx which is reddish brown and white is known as Sardonyx.

One for the gent's - Onyx in 9k gold

With its consecutive layers of different colours, the ancient Romans believed Onyx to be an excellent cameo (a gem carved in relief) gemstone. Sardonyx was highly valued in Rome, especially for seals, because it was said to never stick to the wax. Roman General Publius Cornelius Scipio was known for wearing lots of Sardonyx.

Related to its mythological origin, Onyx is believed by some to encourage the growth of fingernails, hair and skin.

Two classic gems - Marcasite and Onyx used to stunning effect

Ideally suited to men, Onyx is often associated with instincts and intuition. It is believed to give one the power to deeply analyze a situation before reacting to it, as well as better business acumen and management skills. Crystal healers also believe that it restores confidence in life and love, thereby increasing your happiness.

Just the facts

Quartz gemstones are commonly separated into two groups based on the size of their individual crystals. The macrocrystalline Quartz (large crystal) group includes many popular gemstones such as Amethyst, Ametrine, Citrine and Green Amethyst (Prasiolite). Cryptocrystalline Quartz includes species whose individual crystals are too small to be easily distinguished. Apart from being a variety within the group, Chalcedony is also a catch all term to describe cryptocrystalline Quartz and includes many gems that have been coveted since antiquity.

Onyx

ONYX:	Also known as Black Magic
Locations:	Brazil, India, Madagascar, Uruguay
Colours Found:	Black & white
Typical Cuts:	Beads, Cabochon, Cameo
Family:	Chalcedony
Hardness:	6.50
Refractive Index:	1.54
Relative Density:	2.59 - 2.61

89

OPAL

Black Opal with Blue Diamond

Black Opal with Blue and White Diamond

Jelly Opal with Diamond in this magnificent pendant

One of the world's most coveted gemstones, Opal's name evolved from the Roman word "opalus" from the Greek word "opallios" meaning "to see a change of colour". The Greek word was a modification of the ancient Indian Sanskrit name for Opal, "upala", which meant "precious stone". If one spoke in mixed tongues, then Opal would be opallios upala, "to see a change of colour precious stone".

While their body colour covers a broad spectrum of colours, Opal's are most prized for their unique fiery play of colour or "opalescence", which gives them the ability to reflect and refract light into flashes of multiple colours.

Legends and lore

Historically, Opal was considered a lucky charm that brought beauty, success and happiness to its wearer. The early Greeks believed Opals embodied the powers of foresight and prophecy.

The Romans also cherished Opals, considering them to be a symbol of hope and purity - an appropriate attribute for a gem with a rainbow locked within it!

The Arabs thought that Opals must have fallen from heaven in flashes of lightning. According to Arab tradition, it is believed that Opals prevent lightening strikes, shield its wearer from any undesirable elements in their day-to-day lives and give a cloak of invisibility to its wearer when desired.

Opal featured in literature with Shakespeare referring to it in the Twelfth Night as "the queen of gems".

The history books would have us believe that the European supplies of Opal came from India and the Middle East, but it is far more likely that they came from Hungarian mines.

Opal made the headlines in the 1890's with the first samples of Australian Opal. The Hungarians declared that the all new Australian variety was not the real thing, as Opals with such a fusion of fire and colour had never been seen before.

Queen Victoria intervened in the near destruction of the 19th century Opal market when the writer Sir Walter Scott started a superstition that Opals were bad luck for people not born in October. In one of his novels, the heroine owned an Opal that burned fiery red when she was angry and turned ashen grey upon her death. Queen Victoria finally dispelled the curse by giving Opal jewellery as gifts at a royal wedding.

Scandinavian women still wear Opal hair bands to ward off the onset of grey hair and maintain their lustrous blonde locks while some people believe that this gemstone has therapeutic properties that rejuvenate the inner spirit, invigorating the mind.

Just the facts

Opals possess a special quality generically called "iridescence" but specifically "opalescence" when used in reference to this gemstone. The effect is similar to the rainbow colours displayed on a soap bubble, only much more dramatic.

The physical structure of Opal is unique. Tiny spheres of silicon dioxide form a pyramid shaped grid interspersed with water. Tiny natural faults in this grid cause the characteristic play of colour.

Depending on the colour of their "potch", the host rock on which the Opal formed, Opals will either be classified as black, grey, white, fire, crystal or jelly. Opal actually exhibits many different colours including cherry coloured specimens that rival Ruby, fiery-orange Opals that sparkle like Spessartite Garnet, tropical blue gems as intense as Chalcedony, and even deep gorgeous pinks.

A fine example of Pink Opal

Today 95% of the world's Opal is sourced from a handful of prominent mining areas in Australia, namely Lightening Ridge, Coober Pedy, Andamooka and Mintabe.

Black Opal

Black Opal is principally found at Lightning Ridge in New South Wales, Australia. This magnificent gemstone is the most coveted form of Opal. Its dark background colour, usually black, blue, brown or grey, sets the spectral colours ablaze much like a storm cloud behind a rainbow. So prized is Black Opal that even wafer thin slices are made into doublets or triplets to give them enough strength and depth to set into gold rings and other jewellery items.

Blue Opal with gold in this ring by Gems TV

Boulder Opal

Boulder Opal is found sparsely distributed over a wide area of Australian Ironstone or boulder country where the Opal fills cracks and crevices in Ironstone boulders. Opal bearing boulder is always cut to include the host brown Ironstone. Boulder Opal is in very high demand and extremely popular. Boulder Opal is usually cut to

The rare and opulent beauty of Yellow Opal

African Fire Opal

OPAL

*Peruvian Pink Opal
set into an 18k gold
ring*

OPAL

the contours of the Opal vein creating a baroque wavy surface and is often freeform and irregular in shape, making each Boulder Opal unique.

Crystal Opal

Crystal Opal is transparent and is pure Opal (hydrated silica). It typically has a sharp clarity of diffracted colour visible from within and on the surfaces of the Opal. When held out of the direct light, Crystal Opal displays some of the most intense Opal colours. This is the type of Opal used in Opal inlay jewellery which has the base of the setting blackened before a precisely cut crystal Opal is set within.

White Opal

White Opal is translucent with a creamy appearance that dominates the diffracted colours. While all the Australian Opal fields produce White Opal, the majority is mined in Coober Pedy.

White Topaz accenting Fire Opal in this stunning cluster

Fire Opals

Fire Opals are appropriately named for their fiery cherries, sunburst yellows and deep tangerines. Unique and mysterious, Fire Opal is remarkable in that unlike many other Opals its "opalescence" is minimal. Also known as Mexican Opal, Mexican Fire Opal or Sun Opal, its legendary popularity instead comes from its breathtaking brilliance, extraordinary fiery hues and stunning clarity. Fire Opals have been treasured in the Americas since the time of Aztecs, where they were named "Quetzalitzlipyollitli" or "gemstone of the bird of paradise". Coveted by the Aztecs as symbols of intense love, such radiant gemstones were believed to have emerged from the primordial waters of creation. While Fire Opal is mainly mined in Mexico, it is also found in small quantities in other Opal producing locales. A new deposit in Tanzania, aptly called African Fire Opal, displays breathtakingly intense honey hues.

Cherry Fire Opal

Rough Opal

Jelly Opal

Jelly Opal (also known as Water Opal) is predominately mined in Mexico. Jelly Opal offers an attractive blend of indistinct, blended colours. It is transparent with a gelatinous appearance and an occasional bluish sheen. The "opalescence" is a subtle sheen of colour dancing through the gem, rather than colour patches. Very occasionally it is also found in Lightning Ridge,

Black Opal

OPAL

Fine White Opal set into a floral pendant

Pear shaped Opal in 9k gold

White Opal

OPAL:	October's birthstone
Locations:	Australia, Brazil, Mexico, Peru, South Africa, Tanzania, Zimbabwe
Colours Found:	Various
Typical Cuts:	Various
Family:	Opal
Hardness:	5.50 - 6.50
Refractive Index:	1.73 - 1.46
Relative Density:	1.80 - 2.30

Australia, where it is essentially Black Opal without the black potch background.

Peruvian Opal

Hailing from the Andes and coveted by the ancient Incas, Peruvian Opal is extremely rare and exhibits an exquisite translucent colouring. While it typically comes in blue or pink colours, greens are also occasionally found.

Opals from Lightning Ridge, Australia

Opals are one of Australia's national treasures and one of the world's most prized gemstones.

Lightning Ridge is 965 km north of Sydney and the only place on Earth where the "King of Opals", the Black Opal, is found.

The Black Opal mining fields of Lightning Ridge and the majority of Australia's Opal fields are located in a geological phenomenon called "The Great Australian Basin". The basin was formed from sediments of a large inland sea that existed over 140 million years ago. Approximately 120 million years later, sandstones were deposited by waterways over the top of these sedimentary rocks. Eventually these younger rocks weathered, and their silica filtered down to cavities in the older host rock in the form of a gel. The silica gel hardened forming around a nucleus, creating the Opals characteristic regular spheres and voids. It's the diffraction of light through these transparent spaces that produce Opal's brilliant play of colours.

Opal mining involves hard digging with picks and shovels 6-18 meters underground. Buckets are then loaded and hauled to the surface using simple mechanical winches. The rough Opal (called "nobbies") is initially separated by hand, prior to sieving. The remaining Opal nobbies are then taken to small converted cement mixers to wash off the excess dirt.

Commenting that "the fire of the Carbuncle, the brilliant purple of the Amethyst, the sea green colours of Emerald all shining together in incredible union", Opal clearly impressed Pliny the Elder (23-79 AD), Roman historian and author of the world's first encyclopaedia. With only a mere quarter of a percent of Opal mined making it into jewellery, if you're looking to be impressed with Opals, there is no better place to start building your Opal collection than on Gems TV!

PEARL

Pearls are one of the oldest known gems and for centuries were considered the most valuable. So valuable if fact, that the Roman General Vitellius allegedly financed an entire military campaign with just one of his mother's Pearl earrings!

Thankfully, the days of island inhabitants free diving into azure oceans to harvest Pearls are more or less over. The lust for uncultured Pearls once decimated entire species of molluscs, relegating this gem of the sea to the elite few. Today, thanks to the son of a Japanese noodle maker, these fragile ecosystems are now safe, with natural uncultured Pearls usually appearing only as antiques.

Legends and lore

Classic Pearl studs, a must have for any jewellery collection

The Romans were particularly enamoured of this gem of the sea. Rome's Pearl craze reached its zenith during the 1st century BC when upper class Roman women (the lower ranks were forbidden from wearing them) wore their Pearls to bed so they could be reminded of their wealth immediately upon awakening. They also sewed so many into their gowns that they actually walked on their Pearl-encrusted hems. The famously excessive Emperor Caligula, having made his beloved horse a Consul, decorated it with a Pearl necklace.

Cleopatra in describing her enormous wealth and power, demonstrated to Marc Anthony how she could "drink the wealth of nations" by crushing Pearls into a glass of wine.

A simple solitaire Pearl ring with Diamonds

The first known source of Pearls was the Persian Gulf and the ancients of the area believed that Pearls were a symbol of the moon and had magical powers. Indeed, the oldest known Pearl jewellery is a necklace found in the sarcophagus of a Persian princess who died in 520 BC.

A classic princess length Pearl necklace

The earliest written record of their value is in the Shu King, a 23 BC Chinese book in which the scribe sniffs that a lesser king sent tribute of "strings of Pearls not quite round". The Chinese also used Pearls in medicinal ways to cure eye ailments, heart trouble, indigestion, fever and bleeding. To this day Pearl powder is still popular in China as a skin whitener and cosmetic.

In India, Pearls were believed to give peace of mind and strengthen the body and soul.

Chinese pearls with the traditional gem of China, Jade

Europeans thought that swallowing whole or powdered Pearls cured matters of the mind and heart, and strengthened nerves.

PEARL

The Koran states that a good Muslim, upon entering the kingdom of heaven, "is crowned with Pearls of incomparable lustre, and is attended by beautiful maidens resembling hidden Pearls".

While Queen Isabella had to hock her impressive collection of jewellery to fund Christopher Columbus' expedition to discover the new world, the investment paid off as the discovery of Pearls in Central American waters added to the wealth of Spain. The flood of American Pearls on to the European market earned the newly discovered continent the nickname "land of Pearls". Unfortunately, greed and lust for these gems of the sea resulted in the depletion of virtually all the American Pearl oyster populations by the 17th century.

During the Dark Ages, while fair maidens of nobility cherished delicate Pearl necklaces, gallant knights often wore Pearls onto the battlefield. They believed that the magic possessed by the lustrous gems would protect them from harm.

Pearls have long been considered ideal wedding gifts because they symbolize purity and innocence. In the Hindu religion, the presentation of an un-drilled Pearl and its piercing has formed part of the marriage ceremony. While in the western hemisphere Pearls are the recommended gift for couples celebrating their 3rd and 30th wedding anniversaries.

A freshwater Pearl from China nestled in a twist of silver

Just the facts

The Pearl begins life as a foreign body, a grain of sand or coral, which makes its way into the shell of a marine or freshwater mollusc – usually oysters or clams. The mollusc's defence mechanism starts to coat the intruder with layers of a slightly iridescent substance "nacre" (from the Arabic word for shell "naqqarah"), which is the attractive outside of the Pearl. In its natural environment this will, after many years, form a Pearl that is of a significant size and quality.

A multicoloured array of Chinese Pearls

Unlike natural Pearls, cultivated Pearls do not begin as accidental intruders. First cultivated by the Chinese as early as the 12th Century, the process starts with "nucleation". A cultivated Pearl usually begins its life when a spherical bead is placed inside the mollusc. After this seeding process, the Pearl farmers place the molluscs in wire-mesh baskets and suspend them in water. The aqua-culturists carefully tend to the molluscs, overseeing their development for 18 months to 5 years. The depth of the nacre coating, an important factor in determining the colour of Pearls, depends on how long the seeded Pearls are left in place before being harvested.

Mozambique Garnet and Chinese Pearls

PEARL

While Pearls are classified as coloured gems, there is a unique appeal about them. Unlike other gemstones that are born of earth and fire, Pearls are water born organic gems that originate from living animals. They are also unique in the sense that the principals of the 4 C's (colour, cut, clarity and carat weight) cannot be applied to them. The evaluation of Pearls requires a different set of criteria. A Pearl is appraised according to the display of colour, lustre, surface clarity, shape and size.

The two colours of pearls

The body colours themselves can be white, cream, pink, rose, golden, silver, grey and black. As colour preference is subjective, there is no such thing as a bad body colour - it is purely a matter of choice. Apart from the obvious body colour, there is actually a second colour to consider when evaluating Pearls. This second colour is actually a result of subtle iridescence. While not instantly obvious, especially when similar to the body colour, this effect lends Pearls much of their allure. Typically, this iridescence is seen most

PEARL

A perfect round Tahitian Pearl is set in a sweeping white gold band

The deep Orient of Tahitian Pearls is complemented by white gold and Diamonds

A touch of glamour with Tahitian Pearl earrings accented with Diamonds

strongly on the crest of a Pearl's horizon. This beautiful, shimmering effect is known as the "orient" or overtone and denotes the depth of the nacre. Pearls with rich colourful orients are generally more coveted than those that have little or no orient.

Lustre of Pearls

Pearls are bright, reflective gemstones. While Pearls with clean and even surfaces reflect more light than Pearls with blemished surfaces, please remember that as a natural creation, like inclusions in mineral gems, most Pearls do have blemishes. Intelligent jewellers solve this problem by concealing blemishes near the drill holes.

Weight, size & shape

As with other gemstones, value and size are intrinsically linked. The bigger the Pearl the more desirable it becomes. However, there is one important difference: Pearls are measured and expressed by their size not weight (e.g. 8.5 millimetres).

Pearl locations

As with all things natural, Pearls can only grow in the right conditions. Different Pearl varieties from different locations command different prices. The best quality Pearls are found in the waters of French Polynesia, Japan and China. However, due to the different environments, mollusc species and farming techniques, all cultivated Pearls have their own distinctive qualities. The three main Pearl varieties on Gems TV are Freshwater Pearls, Tahitian Pearls and South Sea Pearls.

Freshwater Pearls

Although historically originating in Japan, China is a now a major producer of Freshwater Pearls. Our Chinese Freshwater Pearls are farmed in the Fuchum, Wu and Ling Rivers of the Zhejiang Province in southern China. China has successfully concentrated on Freshwater Pearls using not oysters but freshwater clams. The humble clam, while not as widely celebrated as its cousin the oyster, is equally capable of producing high quality Pearls.

Tahitian Pearls

Tahitian Pearls are from French Polynesia and are named after the tropical island of Tahiti. Grown in the large black-lipped saltwater oyster (Pinctada

Margaritifera), Tahitian Pearls are celebrated for their exceptional beauty. Tahiti's pure and tranquil waters are the ideal cultivation grounds for the dramatic Tahitian Pearl.

Tahitian legend says that Te Ufi (Pinctada Margaritifera) was given to man by Oro, the god of peace and fertility, who came to earth on a rainbow and offered the Pearl to the beautiful princess Bora Bora as a sign of eternal love.

First appearing in Europe in 1845, Napoleon III's wife, Empress Eugenie was responsible for bringing Tahitian Pearls into fashion. After the fall of Napoleon, Empress Eugenie's necklace was auctioned at Christies for US$20,000. "Azra" was the most famous natural Tahitian Pearl, the centrepiece of a necklace that was part of the Russian crown jewels.

Tahitian Black Pearls are prized and admired throughout the world. The first Pearl farms were established on the atoll of Hikueru and the island of Bora Bora in the early 1960's. Exports began in 1972 and production was subsequently expanded on the islands of Marutea Sud and Mangareva. Today, Tahitian Black Pearls are cultivated in Pearl farms in a sprawling group of atolls and islands in French Polynesia, primarily the lagoons of the Tuamotu-Gambier Archipelago.

Tahitian Pearls generally range in size from 8 mm to 16 mm and consist of many thousands of layers of Aragonite (a variety of calcium carbonate). In contrast to many other Pearl varieties, Tahitian Pearls are cultured for 4-5 years and have a nacre thickness of 3-10 mm.

Tahitian Pearls display a shimmering orient that is green, blue, pink or violet in colour. These orient colours are in striking contrast to their silver to black body colour. Their orient or overtone colours are sometimes given specific names (deep green is called "fly wing", "peacock" is termed for the combination of green & pink, and "eggplant" is a dark toned body colour combined with pink).

South Sea Pearls

Highly coveted, South Sea Pearls come from Australia, Indonesia and the Philippines. Cultured in varieties of Pinctada Maxima, this large, warm water loving, gold and silver-lipped oyster produces Pearls of fabulous colours.

PEARL

A beautiful colour range of drop Pearls set in silver

Single Pearls

PEARL:	June's birthstone
Locations:	Australia, China, Indonesia, Japan, Philippines, Tahiti
Colours Found:	Black, cream, gold, golden yellow, grey, orange, pink, silver & white
Typical Cuts:	N/A
Family:	Organics
Hardness:	3.00 - 4.00
Refractive Index:	1.53 - 1.68
Relative Density:	2.60 - 2.78

PEARL

*Chinese Pearl strand
necklace*

PERIDOT

Shining with a bright green glow even at night, Peridot was called the "gem of the sun" by the ancient Egyptians and the "evening emerald" by Romans. Peridot was a favourite gemstone of Cleopatra and was historically mistaken for Emerald. The pronunciation of this popular gem is often confused and should be pronounced "Pair-ee-doh" as opposed to "Pair-ee-dot".

Legends and lore

Popular in early Greek and Roman jewellery, Peridot has been coveted since 1500 BC when the Egyptians started mining it on Zeberget, later known as St. John's Island, about 80 kilometres off the Egyptian coast in the Red Sea.

Peridot mining was traditionally done at night when the gem's natural glow made it easier to spot. The ancient Egyptians even believed that Peridot became invisible under the sun's rays. Interestingly, they also believed that Perdiot was coloured by the golden glow of their sun god Ra, and was thus a powerful protector from harm.

Over 2ct of Kenyan Peridot, perfectly Prong set

Hawaiian natives believe Peridot is the goddess Pele's tears, while it is mentioned in the Bible (using its old name Chrysolite) as being one of the "stones of fire" (Ezekiel 28:13-16) that were given to Moses and set in the breastplate of Aaron (Exodus 28:15-30). Peridot is also one of the twelve gemstones set in the foundations of the city walls of Jerusalem (Revelations 21:19) and associated with the Apostle Bartholomew.

All 23 of these gems have been Antique cut to perfection

While Cleopatra reportedly had a fine collection of Emerald jewellery, it was in reality predominantly Peridot.

The Ottoman Sultans gathered the largest collection of Peridot during their 600 year reign from 1300-1918, with an impressive array of both loose gemstones as well as earrings, rings and other jewellery.

The clarity of this Chinese Peridot is so good that flashes of fire can be seen

Powdered Peridot has been used to cure asthma and a Peridot placed under the tongue of someone in the grip of a fever was believed to lessen their thirst. Legend has it that drinking from a Peridot goblet can increase the potency of medicines.

Pirate's believed Peridot had the power to drive away evil spirits (and the night's terrors), especially if set in gold. But as protection from evil spirits they believed it must be pierced, strung on donkey hair and worn on the left arm.

Pear cut Chinese Peridot, set in a regal 9k gold necklace

Possibly the most unusual Peridot is that which comes

PERIDOT

The V-Claw setting gives these earrings a designer look

One hundred and ninety five carats of Peridot band strung to create a twist of vibrant green gems

Peridot

from meteorites called pallasites. Some have even been facetted and set in jewellery, one of the few extraterrestrial gemstones known to man.

Just the facts

Peridot is the gem variety of Olivine and exhibits colours ranging from golden lime greens to rich grass greens. Traditionally, the most coveted colour hues have been the rich grass greens. However, many Peridots with slight yellowish hues still exhibit attractive colours that are extremely popular. This once again demonstrates that your individual preference should always be the primary factor when collecting coloured gemstones.

The elements that give gemstones their colour are termed "idiochromatic" or "self coloured" if they are an intrinsic ingredient of the gem (meaning the colour results from a colouring element that is always incorporated into the crystal structure of the mineral) and "allochromatic" or "other coloured" if they are trace elements (small amounts of an element that is not part of the normal crystal causes the colour). In many gems, the major element in the chemical composition is colourless in a pure state such as Topaz or Sapphire. If these "allochromatic" gems occur in a variety of colours such as Ruby or Sapphire, then it is usually the result of trace elements. In the case of an "idiochromatic" gem like Perdiot, the colouring element iron is actually part of the crystal, meaning the gem is always the same colour (Peridot is always green).

Because of the way Peridot splits and bends light, it has an attractive velvety, "sleepy" appearance with a shining rich glow.

In 1994, an exciting new deposit was discovered in Pakistan, producing some of the finest Peridot ever seen. The new mine is located 4,500 metres above sea level in the Nanga Parbat region in the far west of the Himalayan Mountains in the Pakistani part of Kashmir.

PERIDOT:	August's birthstone
Locations:	China, Kenya, Pakistan, South Africa, Tanzania, USA
Colours Found:	Green & yellowish green
Typical Cuts:	Various
Family:	Olivine
Hardness:	6.50
Refractive Index:	1.64 - 1.69
Relative Density:	3.34

Gavin "Gemstone Gav" Linsell says:

"Imagine sitting on a royal lawn, basking in the mid summer heat. The beautiful, vivid, slightly golden shimmering green of Peridot is the perfect gem to go with any summer outfit. Even after sunset when one enters indoors, the brilliant green sparkle of Peridot still magically dances and sings under artificial light. Is it really a coincidence that it is the official Birthstone of August?"

Displaying gorgeous deep raspberry pinks, Pezzottaite is a relatively new gemstone that has been subject to much confusion due to its similarities with the Red variety of Beryl, Bixbite.

PEZZOTTAITE

Just the facts

Pezzottaite was discovered in November 2002 at the Sakavalana mine located about 140 kilometres southwest of Antsirabe in southern Madagascar. The initial deposit yielded some extremely rare large crystals and it is now practically depleted although small amounts are now mined elsewhere in Madagascar. The Sakavalana pegmatite where Pezzottaite was discovered was mined by the French for Tourmaline during the 1940's. The initial Pezzottaite deposit was discovered in a large crystal bearing cavity that also contained Tourmaline and Spodumene. Not surprisingly, Pezzottaite was initially mistakenly sold as Tourmaline in Madagascar.

Pezzottaite is mined from granitic pegmatite's using hand tools, making its extraction slow and difficult.

Having a slightly different chemical composition to Bixbite ($Be_3Al_2Si_6O_{18}$) it was named Pezzottaite ($Cs[Be_2Li]Al_2Si_6O_{18}$) in September 2003 after Dr. Federico Pezzotta of the Museo Civico di Storia Naturale, Milan, Italy, in recognition of his contributions to the mineralogy of Madagascar.

Pezzottaite has a variety of trade names including Madagascan Raspberyl, Raspberyl and Raspberry Beryl. While Pezzottaite is closely related to the Beryl family and is visually similar, it is in fact a unique species, making its trade names somewhat of a misnomer.

Like Emeralds, inclusions in Pezzottaite are common, especially in the larger carat weights. However, their rarity and novelty for gemstone collectors has always been the primary factor. Pezzottaite has all the attributes a gem needs - beauty, durability and rarity. Scarcer than Ruby, these rare gems truly are a unique fashion statement.

Stunning Madagascan Pezzottaite in an organic asymmetric design

A classic design accented with Diamonds

Pezzottaite

PEZZOTTAITE:	Initially confused with Bixbite
Locations:	Madagascar
Colours Found:	Pink to raspberry
Typical Cuts:	Cabochon, Octagon, Oval
Family:	Pezzottaite
Hardness:	7.50 - 8.00
Refractive Index:	1.60 - 1.62
Relative Density:	3.04 - 3.14

PYRITE (MARCASITE)

Pyrite has a shiny golden yellow colour and a metallic lustre. The name comes from the Greek word "pyr" word meaning "a gemstone that strikes fire". This is due to the sparks produced when Pyrite strikes iron. While Pyrite is often mistaken for gold, they are quite different. Pyrite grains are lighter and tougher than gold, and have broken faces, properties that are not normally found in gold. Thus only a fool would mistake it for gold, which is why Pyrite is also known as "fool's gold".

Gorgeous semi-hoop earrings Pave set with Marcasite

Marcasite is often used as a jewellery trade name for Pyrite. Although they are called Marcasite, they are actually Pyrite, as true Marcasite is unsuitable for jewellery. The confusion between the two dates back several hundreds years due to their similar appearance. Marcasite's name was derived from "marqashith", the Arabic word, for Pyrite, after an old province in northeastern Persia. Marcasite jewellery (Pyrite) is a popular style that became fashionable during Queen Victoria's reign. Marcasite jewellery normally uses Pyrite cut and polished in a circular outline (square cut gems are occasionally used) and pavé set between sterling silver beads to enhance their brilliance. They were originally used because they catch the light and glow like small diamonds. Today, Marcasite jewellery is often fashioned into 925 sterling silver rings, earrings, pendants, broaches, necklaces and bracelets.

Fashionable in the UK since the reign of Queen Victoria, this gem's classic appeal is celebrated in this Marcasite and Pearl brooch

Legends and lore

Used by the ancient Greeks in pins, earrings and amulets, Pyrite was once polished by Native Americans and used as mirrors. Pyrite is also known as "Healer's Gold" and is highly regarded by crystal healers as a gemstone of intellect and protection.

The lustre of Marcasite is beautifully contrasted by Onyx and Mother of Pearl in these timeless earrings

Just the facts

Pyrite is composed of iron sulphide. When found in its raw state, Pyrite crystals can be shaped as cubes, octahedrons and pyritohedrons (12 faces). Twinning causes "iron crosses" that look like interpenetrating cubes. Collectors particularly favour a flattened nodular variety called "Pyrite Suns" or "Pyrite Dollars".

Pyrite is present in igneous rocks as an accessory mineral, in sedimentary rocks, especially black shale, and in metamorphic rocks, most notably in slates. Pyrite is sometimes found as a replacement mineral in fossils.

PYRITE:	Called Marcasite in the jewellery trade
Locations:	Austria, China, Mexico, Romania, Russia, South Africa
Colours Found:	Golden yellow
Typical Cuts:	Round, Square
Family:	Pyrite
Hardness:	6.00 - 6.50
Refractive Index:	None
Relative Density:	4.90 - 5.20

QUARTZ

The Greeks originally named Quartz "krystallos" meaning "ice", but this term was soon applied to any crystal. In fact, the modern name of Quartz is derived from the Saxon word "querklufterz" meaning "cross-vein-ore".

Although Quartz of sufficient beauty to be set into jewellery is not available in great abundance, Quartz is found in many geological environments and is a component of almost every rock type. It is also the most varied in terms of varieties, colours and forms. The gem varieties of Quartz have been used as gemstones for thousands of years.

Legends and lore

The ancients of India considered Quartz to have special properties as transformers as well as keepers of energy. To this day Quartz crystals are used universally in meditation, as they are believed to possess healing properties and other diverse metaphysical powers.

Champagne Quartz mixes the warm yellows of Citrine with the smoky tones of Smoky Quartz

Folklorists classify Quartz as a receptive gemstone credited with the ability to attract positive energies, such as peace and love. The subtle energy of Quartz is said to balance the emotions, giving inner peace, harmony and enhancing the bonds of relationships. It is also said to calm aggression and increase self-esteem.

A modern design shows off the misty pinks of Rose Quartz

Just the facts

Quartz gemstones are commonly separated into two groups based on the size of their individual crystals.

The macrocrystalline Quartz (large crystal) group includes many popular gemstones such as Amethyst, Ametrine, Citrine, Green Amethyst (Prasiolite), Rose Quartz, Rutilated Quartz, Smoky Quartz and Tiger's Eye.

Cryptocrystalline Quartz includes species whose individual crystals are too small to be easily distinguished. Apart from being a variety within the group, Chalcedony is also a catch all term to describe cryptocrystalline Quartz and includes many gems that have been coveted since antiquity such as Agate, Cornelian, Sard, Chrysoprase, Bloodstone and Jasper.

Quartz gemstones

Phenomena sometimes observed in Quartz include asterism (star effect) and chatoyancy (cat's eye effect).

Amethyst is the queen of the Quartz varieties and in better qualities it is amongst the most coveted Quartzes (please see page 15 for more).

QUARTZ

Smoky Quartz has been Fancy cut to complete this design by Mike Matthews

Rainbow Quartz displays an explosion of colours

Rough Rose Quartz

QUARTZ:	Ancient gemstone
Locations:	Brazil, Madagascar, Mozambique
Colours Found:	Various
Typical Cuts:	Various
Family:	Quartz
Hardness:	7.00
Refractive Index:	1.50
Relative Density:	2.60 - 2.65

Ametrine is a bi-colour variety that is part Amethyst coloured and part Citrine coloured (please see page 18 for more).

Citrine is a yellow variety of Quartz that takes its name from "citron", the French word for lemon (please see page 34 for more).

Phantom Quartz (also known as Ghost Crystals, Specter Crystals and Shadow Crystals) is an unusual gemstone that exhibits a phenomenon called a "phantom". Phantoms can sometimes be seen in the interior of Quartz crystals as a permanent record of earlier stages in the crystal's formation, much like growth rings in a tree.

Green Amethyst (Prasiolite) is a confusing gem as it is traded under a variety of names and can easily be mistaken for other gem types (please see page 64 for more).

Rainbow Quartz (including Lavender Quartz, Neptune Quartz, Fuchsia Quartz and Coral Quartz) is visually similar to Mystic Topaz and is produced using the same physical vapour deposition (PVD) coating process. Applied to top quality natural Rock Crystal, the treatment is permanent with normal wear (please see page 190 for more of the PVD process).

Smoky Quartz is an earth toned transparent Quartz of all shades, including cognac. Also known as "Champagne on Ice", Smoky Quartz gets it rich warm colour from aluminium. A variety of Smoky Quartz is Cairngorm, which owes its name to the legendary source in the Scottish Highlands. Smoky Quartz is the national gem of Scotland, whose national sceptre includes a large Smoky Quartz on its top.

Rock Crystal is colourless Quartz.

Rose Quartz is the pink variety of Quartz. Rarely transparent, facet grade gems will usually display a beautiful misty appearance.

Rutile Quartz (also known as Rutilite, Rutilated Quartz, Venus' Hair or Cupid's Darts) is a beautiful gemstone produced by large inclusions of golden rutile needles in clear colourless Quartz.

Tiger's Eye is simply chatoyant Quartz (please see page 139 for more).

Star Quartz is a fascinating gem that clearly displays asterism (star effect) and is colourless, blue, pink or silver. The stars are six-rayed and roll around the gem as it is moved.

Rhodochrosite (whose name means rose-coloured from the Greek words "rhodon", rose and "chroma", colour) is a very attractive gem with an absolutely beautiful colour.

Rhodochrosite's jewellery qualities make it extremely popular. The colour of a single gem can astound the observer with its vivid pink-rose hues that seems to radiate from the crystal as if lit from within.

Legends and lore

Rhodochrosite is believed by crystal healers to be a gemstone of love, balance for emotions, male and female energies, assisting in expanding consciousness and for healing mother earth.

Rhodochrosite was a popular gem during the 1930's and was often carved into decorative figurines.

Just the facts

Rhodochrosite is a manganese carbonate with colours ranging from very pale pink, pale to deep orange red, mahogany red, burnt orange, pale to dark chocolate and black. The vivid pink-rose and red colours are due to a higher manganese content. Some fine transparent crystals of Rhodochrosite are faceted into gems but this is difficult because of its perfect cleavage. As a result, Rhodochrosite is often cut and polished as cabochons, displaying bands of pink and red as well as pink and white.

Rhodochrosite occurs in hydrothermal mineral veins containing ores of silver, lead and copper. Individual crystals are found in rhombohedrons and sometimes scalehedrons but large crystals are extremely rare.

Rhodochrosite is found in a number of locations worldwide. For several years now the Sweet Home Mine in Alma and Sunnyside Mine in Silverton, Colorado USA have been mined exclusively for Rhodochrosite specimens. The Hotazel Mine in South Africa is famous for producing deep red clusters of Rhodochrosite crystals. However, the most famous mines are in the provinces of Catamarca and LaRioja, Argentina. The mines there produce an attractive pink and red banded Rhodochrosite that is colloquially called "Inca Rose".

RHODOCHROSITE

The rose red tones of this gem require the simplest of gold work to maximise it's beauty

A 32ct Cabochon cut Rhodochrosite Claw set in yellow gold

Rhodochrosite

RHODOCHROSITE:	Perfect cleavage
Locations:	Australia, Brazil, Namibia, South Africa
Colours Found:	Brown, red, pink & white
Typical Cuts:	Cabochon
Family:	Calcite
Hardness:	3.50 - 4.50
Refractive Index:	1.60 - 1.80
Relative Density:	3.40 - 3.70

RUBY

This 242ct Ruby has been hand carved by our skilled Thai artisans

A classic cluster draws the eye to these beautiful earrings

White gold is used to contrast with the Rubies in these stud earrings

Majestic Ruby

Ruby derives its name from the Latin word for red, "rufus". The beauty, rarity and historical mystique of Rubies are undeniable. Ruby is July's birthstone, the gemstone for Capricorns and the traditional 15th and 40th anniversary gift.

Legends and lore

With the earliest record for the mining of Rubies dating to more than 2,500 years ago, the historical mystique and beauty of Rubies is as colourful as the legends and lore that surround this most precious of gems.

Prized throughout history, many believed that mystical powers lay hidden within this intensely coloured red gemstone. The fiery crimson colour of Rubies caused many civilizations to associate them with passion, love and romance. Rubies were also thought to bestow wisdom, health and luck in gambling.

Mentioned in Sanskrit texts, the ancient Hindus were so enchanted by the colour of Rubies that they called them Ratnaraj "the king of gems". The ancient Hindus thought that the colours of Rubies were due to an inextinguishable fire that burned inside the gem which would endow its' wearer with long life and even cause water to boil!

As in Sanskrit texts, biblical references to Ruby (all red gemstones were collectively called Carbuncle at this time) refer to it as a most precious gem. In the King James version of the Bible, Ruby (Carbuncle) is mentioned four times:

Exodus 28:17

And thou shalt set in it settings of stones, even four rows of stones: the first row shall be a Sardius, a Topaz, and a Carbuncle: this shall be the first row.

Exodus 39:10

And they set in it four rows of stones: the first row was a Sardius, a Topaz, and a Carbuncle: this was the first row.

Ezekiel 28:13

Thou hast been in Eden the garden of God; every precious stone was thy covering, the Sardius, Topaz, and the Diamond, the Beryl, the Onyx, and the Jasper, the Sapphire, the Emerald, and the Carbuncle, and Gold: the workmanship of thy tabrets and of thy pipes was prepared in thee in the day that thou wast created.

Isaiah 54:12

And I will make thy windows of agates, and thy gates of

Carbuncles, and all thy borders of pleasant stones.

RUBY

Interestingly, the gems called "Rubies" in the Old Testament may have actually been Spinel or Garnet. Up until the 18th century, when chemical testing was improved, most red gems were called Rubies. In fact, many of the famous Rubies in the crown jewels of Europe have since been identified as Spinel or Garnet. For example, the Black Prince Ruby that rests proudly at the centre of the British Imperial State Crown is actually a red Spinel!

Ancient Ceylonese legends (modern day Sri Lanka) relate the story of the destruction of their demonic King Ravana. They believed that after his demise, his blood set into Rubies resulting in their intense red colour.

Native Americans believed that offerings of a fine Ruby resulted in rebirth as a powerful Chief.

Encrusted with 41 Square cut Rubies, this heart pendant is the ultimate in romance

Some cultures believed Ruby's blood-like colour would protect the wearer from injury. In fact, ancient Burmese warriors believed that when a Ruby was inserted beneath the skin it generated a mystical force, making them unconquerable in battle.

In the 13th century, the renowned explorer Marco Polo wrote that Kublai Kahn, the Mongol Emperor of China, once offered an entire city for a Ruby the size of a man's finger.

A stunning solitaire ring featuring a Cabochon cut Indian Ruby

Because of its fluorescent properties, a giant Ruby once lit an entire chamber in a palace of a Chinese emperor!

In the Middle Ages, Rubies were thought to contain prophetic powers. It was believed that a Ruby could warn its owner of misfortunes by deepening in colour.

Just the facts

Like many "allochromatic" (other coloured) gems whose colours are due to trace elements, apart from their colour, Rubies are identical to Sapphires. Rubies and Sapphires are comprised of the mineral known as Corundum. The crystalline form of aluminium oxide, the name Corundum is believed to be derived from three ancient Tamil, Hindi and Sanskrit words for Rubies and Sapphires, "kurundam", "kurund" or "kuruvinda" respectively.

Diamond accents give this Ruby pendant an antique feel

Did you know that Rubies are rarer than Diamonds? In the last 60 years hardly a month has passed without a new Diamond deposit being discovered. In contrast, Rubies are only found in a handful of mines worldwide.

Ruby

Did you know that Rubies are more expensive than Diamonds? A 16 carat Ruby that sold at Sotheby's in

RUBY

18 Channel set Rubies from Tanzania create a clean and contemporary look

A designer look with a central Royal Ruby accented with Diamonds at each corner

A massive 67ct Royal Ruby bracelet

Rough Ruby

RUBY:	July's birthstone
Locations:	China, India, Kenya, Madagascar, Tanzania, Thailand, Vietnam
Colours Found:	Red
Typical Cuts:	Various
Family:	Corundum
Hardness:	9.00
Refractive Index:	1.76 - 1.77
Relative Density:	3.90 - 4.10

New York in October 1988 fetched a staggering $3,630,000!

Second only to Diamonds in hardness, Rubies are one of the toughest gemstones and with no cleavage, breakage rarely occurs. This combined with the fact that Rubies come in many different shapes and sizes, makes them perfect for all types of jewellery.

While colour preferences are subjective, the best Rubies possess an intense, almost electric red effect due to fluorescence. Colour is the most important factor when evaluating Rubies. While cutting and size (fine Rubies over 3 carats are very scarce) is also important, transparency is secondary. Why is this? Coloured by chromium and other trace elements, Rubies formed millions of years ago deep within the earth. As very few Rubies crystallized undisturbed, a whole host of tiny irregularities (inclusions) are a characteristic of their formation. Far from being flaws, inclusions are also a fascinating hallmark of authenticity that records a gem's natural relationship with the Earth.

Microscopic rutile inclusions, commonly known as "silk", are a normal characteristic of Rubies. When evenly distributed, small quantities of "silk" enhance a Ruby's beauty by creating a soft uniform distribution of light or sparkle.

Asterism or the "star effect" is a reflection effect that appears as two or more intersecting bands of light across the surface of a gem. This rare phenomenon is found in both Rubies and Sapphires.

As Rubies come in many different colours and sizes, ultimately, your personal preference should be your primary concern. But what is the difference between a Royal and Majestic Ruby? At Gems TV, "Royal" relates to size (2 carats or more) and "Majestic" relates to quality (colour and clarity). However, by calling a gem "Majestic" we are not suggesting that it is the best quality available anywhere, simply some of the best available at Gems TV.

Our Madagascan Rubies are mined at high altitude, deep within an impenetrable jungle. The only way to reach the Ruby mines near the mining village of Moramanga is by helicopter or a gruelling long day's trek (11 hours) on a muddy trail through dense mountainous rainforest from the Madagascan town of Andilamena. A relatively new deposit found in July 2004 yields our Majestic Ruby.

Apart from Madagascar, we also source Rubies from Vietnam, Tanzania, Kenya, Sri Lanka, China, and of course Thailand. However, strict environmental regulations combined with depletion have resulted in the reduction of Thai gem mining.

With approximately 80% of the world's Rubies passing though Chanthaburi, Thailand (the home town of the Gems TV workshops) our craftspeople are the first to choose the finest examples. We use Rubies when handcrafting all manner of gorgeous jewellery and being the gem of love and passion, heart shaped Rubies are hard to resist. Next time you need a bit of passion in your life, tune into Gems TV.

Sixteen inches and over 1400ct of Indian Ruby

SAPPHIRE

Sapphires derive their name from the Latin word "sapphirus", meaning blue, and are often referred to as the "gem of the heavens" or the "celestial gem" as their colours mirror the sky at different times of the day.

The word Sapphire, stated without a prefix, implies Blue Sapphires only. Sapphires of all other colours are assigned a colour prefix or are collectively termed "Fancy Sapphires".

Legends and lore

Blue is one of the favourite colours of both men and women and is a colour psychologically linked to the emotions of sympathy, calmness and loyalty.

Vibrant Hot Pink Sapphire from Sri Lanka in 18k white gold

Legend has it that the first person to wear Sapphire was Prometheus, the rival of Zeus, who took the gemstone from Cacaus, where he also stole fire from heaven for man.

The ancient Persians believed Sapphires were a chip from the pedestal that supported the earth, and that its reflections gave the sky its colours.

Ceylon Sapphire, thought to be some of the finest blue Sapphire in the world

Sapphire is mentioned in the Bible as being one of the twelve "stones of fire" (Ezekiel 28:13-16) that were given to Moses and set in the breastplate of Aaron (Exodus 28:15-30). Sapphire is also one of the twelve gemstones set in the foundations of the city walls of Jerusalem (Revelations 21:19) and associated with the Apostle St. Paul.

The guardians of innocence, Sapphires symbolize truth, sincerity and faithfulness, and are thought to bring peace, joy and wisdom to their owners. In ancient times it was believed that when the wearer of a Sapphire faced challenging obstacles, the gem's power enabled them to find the correct solution.

In India it was believed that a Sapphire immersed in water formed an elixir that could cure the bite of scorpions and snakes. Alternatively, if it were worn as a talisman pendant, it would protect the wearer against evil spirits.

Precision Cut Sapphires

The following legend is Burmese in origin and highlights Sapphires' connection with faithfulness: "Eons ago Tsun-Kyan-Kse, a golden haired goddess with Sapphire blue eyes, presided lovingly over the temple of Lao-Tsun. Everyday, the temple's chief monk Mun-Ha, meditated before the golden goddess accompanied by his devoted companion, a green-eyed cat named Sinh. One day the temple was besieged by a group of terrible outlaws. When they threw Mun-Ha to the floor, Sinh

leapt fiercely at the bandits, jumping up on his master's chest to protect him. The wrong doers fled screaming in fear, never to return and in gratitude for his courage, the golden goddess awarded Sinh with her Sapphire blue eyes. To this day, Sinh's ancestors guard over the temple." The temple still stands and is populated by Siamese cat's with striking blue eyes (typically this breed has green eyes).

For hundreds of years Blue Sapphires were the popular choice for engagement and wedding rings.

Just the facts

The modern popularity of Padparadscha and Pink Sapphires aside, Blue Sapphires are traditionally the most coveted members of the Sapphire family. Coming in a wide variety of hues, Sapphires range in colour from pastel blues all the way through to the depths of midnight blue. Sapphires are identical to Ruby (the red variety of Corundum), except for one key component, their colour. Sapphires are "allochromatic" (other coloured) gems and obtain their colours due to the presence of trace elements including iron and titanium. The crystalline form of aluminium oxide, the name Corundum is believed to be derived from three ancient Tamil, Hindi and Sanskrit words for Rubies and Sapphires, "kurundam", "kurund" or "kuruvinda" respectively.

While personal preference should always be your primary concern when purchasing coloured gemstones, Sapphires that sit in the middle of the blue colour range are historically the most coveted.

Sapphires are one of the toughest gemstones, second in hardness only to Diamonds. Corundum is primarily mined from alluvial deposits and only occasionally from host rock deposits just beneath the earth's surface.

Asterism or the "star effect" is a reflection effect that appears as two or more intersecting bands of light across the surface of a gem. This rare phenomenon is found in both Sapphires and Rubies.

Sapphire Locations and Varieties

As Sapphires from different locations can vary slightly in appearance, we have detailed some of our main sources and varieties below.

SAPPHIRE

Vivid canary Yellow Sapphire hailing from Madagascar

Split band detail leads the eye to this stunning Green Sapphire

A gorgeous Colour Change Sapphire in a fashionable gold twist

The crystal clear tones of Sky Blue Sapphire are complemented by Diamonds

113

SAPPHIRE

Ceylon Sapphire

A big look - over 9ct of Royal Sapphire from China

Madagascan Green Sapphire with phenomenal clarity

Sunset Sapphire, rich reds in 9k yellow gold

Ceylon Sapphire

The island of Ceylon (known as Sri Lanka since 1972) holds the earliest records for the mining of Sapphires. Noted for their cornflower blues, Ceylon Sapphires are synonymous with top quality Sapphires and are highly coveted. A classic source of quality Sapphires throughout history, mining occurs in the gem rich alluvial gravels found beneath the tea-covered slopes of Elahera and Rathnapura.

Ceylonese Sapphires received a boost in their popularity in 1981 when Prince Charles gave Lady Diana an engagement ring set with a stunning 18 carat Ceylonese Sapphire.

At Gems TV, we use the prefix "Ceylon" to denote a quality as well as an origin (not all Sri Lankan Sapphires can be called "Ceylon").

Madagascan Sapphire

Today, Madagascar also provides some of the highest quality Sapphires. Sapphires were first unearthed on this island in the early 1990's. The Madagascan gem fields now account for approximately 20% of the world's Sapphires. The majority of Madagascar's Sapphires come from the prolific gem fields of Ilakaka and Antiermene.

Pailin Sapphire (Cambodia)

The Cambodian city of Pailin (the ancient Khmer word for "Blue Sapphire") is steeped in local folklore regarding its precious treasures: "Long ago when the men folk sharpened their spears to go out hunting, the gods feared for the local wildlife. The gods told the townsfolk to lay down their arms, explaining that if they promised not to hunt the beasts of the forests they would find something of far greater value in the streams and rivers. Sure enough, they found Sapphires in abundance".

Kanchanaburi Sapphire (Thailand)

The sleepy province of Kanchanaburi, renowned for the bridge over the River Kwai, rests amongst the jungle clad valleys of western Thailand. Kanchanaburi's Bo Ploi Sapphire mines were discovered in 1919 and today remain one of world's premier sources of Blue Sapphires. The Sapphires of Bo Ploi are mined from alluvial deposits spread over 3.2 square kilometres. The miners of Bo Ploi must unearth over 50 tons of alluvial soil to extract just 1 carat of Sapphire crystal. Sapphires have been heavily mined from the Bo Ploi mines in the last ten years and are approaching depletion. This increasing rarity makes these Sapphires a must for any jewellery collection.

SAPPHIRE

Australian Sapphire (Australia)

Some of the finest Sapphires in the world herald from this sun-burnt country. Top quality Australian Sapphires exhibit brilliant cornflower blues usually associated with those from Ceylon (Sri Lanka). Sapphires have been mined in Australia for over 100 years. The majority of Australian Sapphires come from three fields; the Anakie fields in central Queensland, the Lava Plains in northern Queensland and the New England fields around Inverell in the northeast of New South Wales.

During the 1980's Australia produced about 70% of the world's Sapphires and although production has decreased, the demand from the international market for Australian Sapphires remains very high. Sapphires found in Australia originate from similar geological conditions to those of Thailand and Cambodia, and thus possess similar characteristics.

Hours of workmanship are dedicated to creating our handcrafted jewellery

Nigerian Sapphire (Nigeria)

Nigeria plays a key role in supplying the world with some of the most popular gemstones. Nigerian Sapphire is mined at Nisama Jama'a in Nigeria's Kaduna State.

An icy lilac shade of Sri Lankan Sapphire

Umba River Sapphire (Tanzania)

On the Great North Road in Tanzania, between the plains of the Serengeti and the foothills of Mount Kilimanjaro lies Arusha, the gateway to the beating heart of Africa and home to the fabled gemstone mines of the Umba Valley. Collecting in rich alluvial deposits that run the course of the valley, Umba River Sapphire is sourced using age-old mining techniques by Waarusha and Wameru miners whose knowledge of gemstones has been handed down for generations.

A Ceylon Padparadscha displaying its characteristic lotus blossom hues

Midnight Blue Sapphire

Midnight Blue Sapphire combines deep rich colours and a spellbinding lustre all in one gemstone. Blue and black intermingle in Midnight Blue Sapphire as if to reveal the secret of the sky at night. This accentuates their lustre and is one reason for its enduring popularity. Mined in a wide variety of countries

SAPPHIRE

including Madagascar, Australia, Nigeria, Thailand, Vietnam and China, Midnight Blue Sapphire is a gemstone whose colours are beyond vivid. But there is nothing black about Midnight Blue Sapphire. To visualize this, think of the colour of a desert sky shortly after the sun has set, with stars rising in the distance. This is the colour of Midnight Blue Sapphire, an intense azure hue unmatched in the gem kingdom.

Royal Sapphire

As larger Sapphires increase in scarcity exceptionally, regardless of locale, we clearly identify these for you in our product descriptions. At Gems TV, "Royal" denotes Sapphires 2 carats and over.

FANCY SAPPHIRE

Since the dawn of time, Sapphires have captivated and mesmerized jewellery connoisseurs the world over. From hot pink to forest green, Sapphire's spectrum of colours is truly kaleidoscopic.

Royal Ceylon Sapphire

Fancy Sapphires get their unique colours from the iron, chromium, titanium and other trace metals present within the Corundum.

Chanthaburi Sapphire (Thailand)

Black Star Sapphires have only ever been found at one place on Earth - Ban Kha Ja, Chanthaburi (located approximately 245 kilometres east of Bangkok close to the border of Cambodia). From these mines, no more than 7 kilometres from the Gems TV workshops, stunning bluish green, green and yellow Sapphires are also unearthed. Displaying, gorgeous golden tangerine hues, a stunning Sapphire variety we aptly called "Chanthaburi Sapphire" from a new alluvial pocket at Ban Kha Ja proved hugely popular in 2005. Today, mining in Chanthaburi is very limited making top quality Sapphires from this town exceedingly rare.

Rare Tanzanian Colour Change Sapphire Bezel set in yellow gold

A red-carpet look crafted with Fancy Sapphires

What our Craftsmen say:

Miss Bang-on Lakbiri - Gem Matcher

"There is nothing more satisfying in gem sorting than to work on a multi-coloured Sapphire bracelet. Even though the task of matching colours is simplified by the fact that they are all different, the skill in balancing all of the different colours and hues is a true art in itself."

SAPPHIRE

A town steeped in gem lore, Chanthaburi has been a centre of gem mining and cutting in Thailand for generations. Chanthaburi first gained its gemstone reputation as early as 1407 when the intrepid Chinese traveller Ma Huan wrote of a special place near Chanthaburi where hundreds of families sold bright clear Rubies. Thanks to its skilled artisans, Chanthaburi continues to garner international recognition as a global headquarters for coloured gemstone faceting and trading. Known specifically for its expertise in processing Rubies and Sapphires, Chanthaburi is responsible for processing more than 80% of the world's supply of these gemstones. If you own Ruby or Sapphire jewellery, there is a very good chance your gems once visited Chanthaburi! With Gems TV being the biggest jeweller in the province, it is easy to understand why we are one of the world's largest handcrafters of high quality gemstone jewellery.

Colour Change Sapphire

Colour Change Sapphire

While Colour Change Sapphires come from a variety of locations, the gem gravels of Tanzania is the main source. Colour Change Sapphires present gem lovers with an opportunity to own the rare and stunning colour change effect in a gem other than Alexandrite or Garnet.

Ten Oval cut Ceylon Padparadscha Sapphires create the sparkle in this beautiful bangle

Green Sapphire

Green Sapphires display a range of green hues, from tropical limes to wine bottle greens.

Ceylon Padparadscha, sourced from modern day Sri Lanka

Padparadscha Sapphire

While Sapphires have mesmerized jewellery connoisseurs since the dawn of time, there is one Sapphire variety that mesmerizes above all others, the mysterious and coveted Padparadscha Sapphire.

Marquise cut Ceylon Padparadscha Sapphire in 18k gold stud earrings

Padparadscha Sapphire derives its name from its resemblance to the beautiful and famed pinkish orange red lotus flower known to the Sri Lankan people as "Padparadscha" or in botanical terms *Nelumbo Nucifera Speciosa*.

Padparadscha Sapphires must combine elements of yellow, pink, red and orange in one gem to rightly claim their Padparadscha title. One way to picture the colour of Padparadscha Sapphires is to imagine sitting in front of a lazy fire on an isolated beach painted by the soothing hues of a tropical sunset. You then hold a fragrant lotus bloom to your nose and at that instant,

Ceylon Padparadscha Sapphire

117

SAPPHIRE

Drop earrings add a touch of Hollywood chic to the simplest outfits

Bright citrus shades of Orange Sapphire in 18k yellow gold

Eleven and a half carats of Ceylon Padparadscha Sapphire in a classic tennis bracelet

Sunset Sapphire

the colours meld creating an aurora of orange, red and pink. This is Padparadscha Sapphire!

Wonderfully romantic and delightfully seductive, Padparadscha Sapphires are so rare and beautiful that they are highly prized by collectors. But what are the origins of the word Padparadscha?

Often misunderstood, with no universal agreement as to its meaning, the modern word "Padparadscha" was in fact adopted from a German gemmological text early in the 20th century. The word Padparadscha is actually a corruption of two Sanskrit and Singhalese words "padma raga". While "padma" means lotus, the word "raga" is a more complex meaning colour, attraction, desire and musical rhythm all in rolled into one! Interestingly, the original term had much broader applications and was even used in ancient times to describe a variety of Ruby. A medieval Prakit text on gemmology called the Thakkura Pheru's Rayanaparikkha describes Padparadscha Sapphires as "that which spreads its rays like the sun, is glossy, soft to the touch, resembling the fire, like molten gold and not worn off is Padma Raga".

Although the exact description is often debated, the beauty of these rare gemstones is not. While some continue to narrowly define Padparadscha as a Sri Lankan Sapphire, today Padparadscha Sapphires are recognized as also hailing from Madagascar, Vietnam and Tanzania. Regardless of the locale, Padparadscha Sapphires, especially in larger sizes, are incredibly scarce.

Don't forget that like many of the rarer gemstones we offer, there is never a guarantee of continuous supply. Padparadscha Sapphire certainly fits into this category and it can take months of hard work to accumulate enough even for a few jewellery lines.

Don Kogen, the Gem Hunter says:

"A true Sapphire connoisseur's delight! When I manage to source Padparadscha Sapphire, don't hesitate to acquire it or you will be too late. With my global contacts when Mother Nature passes over her prized possession, I ensure my team of buyers are always first on hand".

SAPPHIRE

Purple Sapphire

Prized by collectors, purple Sapphires can display rich purple-pink colours reminiscent of orchids. One word of warning: when we manage to source Purple Sapphires, they don't stay in our vaults for a very long and are quickly snapped up by collectors and jewellery connoisseurs alike.

Yellow Sapphire

Ranging from pleasing pastel daisies to intensely beautiful canary yellows, Yellow Sapphires are renowned for their amazing lustre and brilliance. Yellow Sapphires are not just beautiful, but are also one of the most coveted of all yellow gemstones.

Star Sapphire

With their very bright and lustrous star formations, Star Sapphires have traditionally been the most popular of all star gemstones. Glance at a Star Sapphire and you will see six or even twelve rayed stars silently gliding across the gemstone's surface. This wonderful gem has long been coveted for their beautiful and mysterious optical effects know as "asterism". "Asterism" or the "asteric effect" is caused by sets of parallel needle-like inclusions within the gemstone. While the gem gravels of Rathnapura in Sri Lanka is one of the world's main sources of Star Sapphires, Black Star Sapphires are only found in the Ban Kha Ja district in the Chanthaburi province of Thailand.

Star Sapphire

Sunset Sapphire

While it might not have the chromium to be Ruby or the pinks to be Padparadscha, there is nothing about the beauty of Sunset Sapphires that is lacking. Displaying a bright blend of crimsons tangerines reminiscent of an African sunset, Sunset Sapphire (also called Songea Sapphire) was only discovered in 1992. The world's only Sunset Sapphire deposit is located 60 kilometres West of Songea, with the Masuguru district being the main mining area. Discoveries like Sunset Sapphire have helped Songea become the second most important Tanzanian mining area after Merelani (the home of Tanzanite).

White Sapphire

White Sapphire

The ancient Egyptians associated White Sapphire with the all-seeing eye of Horus, while the Greeks linked it to their god Apollo, using it in the prophesizing of the

SAPPHIRE:	September's birthstone
Locations:	Australia, Cambodia, China, Kenya, Madagascar, Nigeria, Sri Lanka, Tanzania, Thailand, Vietnam
Colours Found:	Various
Typical Cuts:	Various
Family:	Corundum
Hardness:	9.00
Refractive Index:	1.76 - 1.77
Relative Density:	3.90 - 4.10

SAPPHIRE

oracles at Delphi. The ancient Greeks unearthed White Sapphires from the island of Naxos in the Aegean Sea. With none of the iron, chromium, titanium and other trace metals that give Fancy Sapphires their unique colours, White Sapphire is arguably Sapphire in its purest form. Displaying an exceptional lustre and brilliance, it has become a popular alternative to Diamonds.

Pink Sapphire

Immensely popular, Pink Sapphires range from pastel to vivacious pinks and share a colour border with Ruby. Many Pink Sapphires are so close to this boundary they are termed as "Hot Pink". Sharing exactly the same position on the colour wheel, red and pink are technically the same colour. It is the saturation or strength of this red hue that differentiates red from pink. The problem is that the border region where pink stops and red starts is open to interpretation. To put the issue to rest, the International Coloured Gemstone Association (ICA) stated the following: "Pink is really just light red. The International Coloured Gemstone Association has passed a resolution that the light shades of the red hue should be included in the Ruby category since it was too difficult to legislate where red ended and pink began. In practice, pink shades are now known either as Pink Ruby or Pink Sapphire."

SCAPOLITE

Coming in colourless, pink, purple, blue, yellow and silver hues, Scapolite was discovered in 1913 in the Mogok Stone Tract of upper Myanmar (Burma). Scapolite comes from the Greek words "scapos", meaning rod and "lithos", meaning stone. It gets its name from the stick or rod-like appearance of its crystals. Scapolite is also known as Wernerite for the German explorer and mineralogist Abraham Gottlob Werner (1750–1817).

Legends and lore

While Scapolite has no specific legends and lore, its Cat's Eye variety has been attributed with some metaphysical attributes. Wearing a Cat's Eye is believed by some to make one wealthy, healthy, strongly determined, knowledgeable as well as providing protection from enemies. It is also believed to help one gain insight and psychic powers.

Just the facts

As Scapolite is a mixture of minerals, with varying specific gravity and refractive indexes, it can easily be confused with Amethyst, Citrine, Chrysoberyl and Golden Beryl. However, Scapolite can be differentiated from these other gems by the use of a long-wave ultraviolet (UV) light. Scapolite fluoresces with a yellowish to orange colour, while Quartz and Beryl do not display such fluorescence.

Scapolite minerals are silicates of aluminium with calcium and sodium. Scapolite is usually found as prismatic crystals in metamorphic rocks and only very occasionally in igneous rocks.

While facet grade Scapolite can be transparent with a fine colour, less transparent crystals are often polished as cabochons to exhibit exquisite Cat's Eyes.

Although very attractive, Scapolite is not a well known gemstone, mainly due to its extreme scarcity. Definitely one for collectors, this gem only makes a few rare appearances on Gems TV.

A rare Cat's Eye Scapolite weighing over 15ct

Two unusual gems - Scapolite and Kornerupine together in this striking ring

The canary Scapolite yellows and rich Amethyst purples perfectly compliment one another

Scapolite

SCAPOLITE:	Mixture of minerals
Locations:	Brazil, China, India, Kenya, Madagascar, Mozambique, Sri Lanka, Tanzania,
Colours Found:	Yellowish to orange
Typical Cuts:	Various
Family:	Scapolite
Hardness:	5.50 - 6.00
Refractive Index:	1.54 - 6.00
Relative Density:	2.56 - 2.77

SILLIMANITE

Beautiful and rare, Sillimanite is named for the famous American geologist Benjamin Silliman (1779-1864). Sillimanite is sometime referred to as Fibrolite. Sillimanite is not only scarce, but also difficult for miners to identify and problematic for cutters. These three attributes combine to ensure that Sillimanite remains a true exotic gemstone.

Just the facts

Sillimanite is formed from aluminium silicate and is usually found as silky, fibrous crystals suitable for cabochons. Transparent crystals suitable for faceting display a glassy lustre and are exceedingly scarce. Sillimanite is colourless, white, brown, yellow, blue and green in colour.

Sillimanite is typically found scattered within layers of metamorphic rocks that have been put under great pressure and high temperature. This is why Sillimanite is commonly found in volcanic or hot spring areas. Because of the way it is scattered within the host rocks, miners often have difficulty in detecting Sillimanite.

Sillimanite is a polymorph with two other minerals, Kyanite and Andalusite. A polymorph is a mineral that shares the same chemistry but a different crystal structure with another, or other, minerals. This is unusual, and due to its brittleness, Sillimanite is very difficult to facet. Some 50% of gem quality crystals can be damaged during the faceting and fashioning process alone!

Some Sillimanite crystals demonstrate chatoyancy (also known as the "Cats Eye Effect", caused by minerals reflecting a single band of light back to the eye), and make stunning cabochon rings and earrings.

High quality Sillimanite with stunning clarity and brilliance

A yellow example of Sillimanite

A striking Brazilian Sillimanite solitaire ring

Sillimanite

SILLIMANITE:	Polymorph
Locations:	Brazil, India, Sri Lanka
Colours Found:	Blue, brown, colourless, green, white & yellow
Typical Cuts:	Various
Family:	Sillimantine
Hardness:	6.00 - 7.00
Refractive Index:	1.65 - 1.68
Relative Density:	3.24

Sodalite is a rare, rich royal blue gemstone and a component of Lapis Lazuli. Discovered in the early 1800's in Greenland, Sodalite was named because of its high sodium content.

SODALITE

Sodalite did not become important as a gemstone until 1891 when it was unearthed at a deposit near Bancroft, Ontario by Frank D. Adams while he was investigating the geology of the Haliburton-Hastings area for the Geological Survey of Canada.

Legends and lore

Sodalite has been named, "Princess Blue", after Princess Patricia who visited Ontario shortly after Sodalite's discovery in Canada. She subsequently selected Sodalite for the interior decoration of Marlborough House in England.

Sodalite is believed by some to foster knowledge, learning proficiency, consciousness, communication and wisdom, and is sometimes called the "Wisdom Gemstone".

Lemon yellows give these gems their unique look

Just the facts

Well known for its blue colour Sodalite may also be grey, yellow, green or pink and is often mottled with white veins or patches. Sodalite is the main mineral of the Sodalite group which is composed of minerals with a similar isometric structure and related chemistry. Its members are also part of a larger group called the Feldspathoids (similar to Feldspars but with less silica content).

A Marquise cut solitaire set in stunning 18k yellow gold

Although Sodalite appears similar to Lapis Lazuli, Sodalite is a royal blue rather than ultramarine and rarely contains Pyrite, a common inclusion in Lapis. Clear crystals are very rare and are hardly ever large enough to be faceted. Most Sodalite is polished into beads and cabochons.

The feathered appearance of Sodalite makes this gem very unique

There are two main varieties of Sodalite. One called Hackmanite, which contains a higher concentration of sodium than the basic form and Molybdosodalite, which contains less chlorine than the basic form. A relatively new variety of green Sodalite found in Greenland is colloquially called the "Chameleon Sodalite".

Rough Sodalite

SODALITE:	Transparent to translucent crystals
Locations:	Brazil, Namibia, South Africa,
Colours Found:	Blue, green, grey, pink or yellow with white veins or patches
Typical Cuts:	Beads, Cabochon
Family:	Feldspathoids
Hardness:	5.00 - 6.00
Refractive Index:	1.48
Relative Density:	2.10 - 2.30

SPHENE

Sphene is named after the Greek word for wedge, because its crystals are typically wedge shaped. As it contains titanium, Sphene is also sometimes referred to by its mineral name Titanite.

One of the world's newest and rarest gems, Sphene possesses the rather unusual ability to take a beam of light and break it into all of the spectral colours. A feature gemmologically referred to as fire or dispersion. In this regard, Sphene is superior to Diamond. This combined with its strong pleochroism (different colours are displayed when the gemstone is viewed from different angles) has the effect of making the gem appear to change colour. Occasionally pink, black or chocolate, most Sphene is predominantly green or yellowish-green, with just about every other colour of the rainbow displayed by its intense fiery brilliance.

A Sphene solitaire, flawlessly faceted to enhance it's great fire

Just the facts

Sphene makes gorgeously brilliant, fiery gems that have a higher dispersion (fire) than Diamonds.

A minimalist design draws the eye to this fiery gemstone

Sphene's magnificent fire, unique colour shades, strong pleochroism, adamantine (Diamond like) lustre and double refraction (birefringence) make it ideal for earrings and pendants that catch the light, displaying its sparkling qualities to full effect. A unique characteristic of Sphene is birefringence (doubly refractive), meaning that light splits into two rays as it passes through the gem. As a result, the back facets appear as double images giving it a beautiful soft hazy appearance similar to the doubling seen in Zircon.

If well polished the lustre can approach or equal that of Diamond, but Sphene is notoriously difficult to polish well. A well polished Sphene is testament to an experienced jeweller. The cutters at Gems TV always take great care to ensure that our Sphene is finished in a manner that maximizes its intense natural beauty.

Sphene and Chrysoberyl combined to great effect

Clean Sphene larger than a few carats is extremely scarce.

SPHENE:	High dispersion
Locations:	Brazil, Madagascar, Pakistan
Colours Found:	Yellowish-green
Typical Cuts:	Various
Family:	Sphene
Hardness:	5.50
Refractive Index:	1.885 - 2.05
Relative Density:	3.40 - 3.56

Don Kogen, the Gem Hunter says:

"Ignore the name, its got more fire than Diamonds! Sphene is one of my favourite gems. It's got beauty, it's got rarity and because of the way I can source it, we make it affordable too!"

SPINEL

Spinel was once mistaken for Ruby, but it's no impostor, rather a "master of disguise". One of the gem kingdom's best kept secrets, Spinel is treasured for its eternal brilliance and spectacular colours. Whether your fascination with gems is for their beauty, rarity or history, Spinel is a superb addition to your jewellery collection.

Spinel's name is derived either from the Latin word for thorn "spina", as a result of its characteristic octahedral crystals having pointed ends, or from the Greek word for spark "spintharis", in reference to the gem's bright red hues.

Legends and lore

Due to its mistaken identity, Spinel has few historical references. However, Spinels have a bizarre association with sorcerers and alchemists. Spinels were used by practitioners of the "dark arts" to summon demons and also used as amulets to protect them from fire. One tale describes how Spinels could be used to work against their masters. Those thought to possess supernatural powers were found guilty, if they began to shake when approached with a Spinel wrapped in paper!

Rich Red Spinel has been mistaken for Ruby

Spinels occupy a unique place in gemstone history. Despite being recognized as a separate gem species in 1587, up until the 19th century the intense colouration displayed by Noble Red Spinel lead some to mistakenly identify this gem as Ruby. The source of confusion stemmed not only from colour similarities but also the close proximity of their deposits.

Reminiscent of Fancy Sapphire, the master of disguise lives up to it's name

Noble Red Spinel's near identical resemblance to Ruby lead to it being a prodigious, albeit accidental feature in many of the world's most famous gem collections, including the Vatican's and the Crown Jewels of Russia, Iran and England. Interestingly, both the legendary 352 Carat "Timur Ruby" and the 170 Carat "Black Prince's Ruby", which feature in the British Imperial State Crowns proved to be Noble Red Spinel!

Deep Purple Spinel in a classic religious design

In 1415 at the "Battle of Agincourt" the English King, Henry V wore a helmet garnished with jewels including the "Black Prince's Ruby". During the battle, the French commander, the Duke of Alenon, struck Henry's head a mighty blow with his battle-axe, nearly killing the King. Surprisingly, the force of the blow glanced off the Spinel saving his life, allowing Henry to lead his troops to what many thought would be an impossible victory.

Noble Red Spinel

SPINEL

*Bezel set Fancy Spinel
from Madagascar*

Just the facts

Spinel occurs in many colours including red, blue, pink, orange and a plethora of other fancy colours. Apart from colour prefixes, some of Spinel's other names include:

Almandine Spinel:	The violet variety of Spinel
Balas Ruby:	This is an historical name for Spinel, which referred to their country of origin; either Badakshan in Tajikistan or the Balaksh region of Sri Lanka
Cobalt Spinel:	Resembling fine Sapphires, these exceptional Blue Spinels from Sri Lanka and Tanzania are coloured by Cobalt
Flame Spinel:	The orange-red variety of Spinel
Gahnite or Gahnospinel:	Named after Swedish chemist L. G. Gahn, it is the rare greenish or bluish, zinc rich variety of Spinel
Noble Red Spinel:	The Ruby red variety of Spinel was historically mistaken for Ruby
Rubicelle:	The yellow to orange variety of Spinel

Pink Spinel, mimicking the colours of Hot Pink Sapphire

The reality behind Noble Red Spinel's Ruby like appearance is due to it being found in proximity to corundum, the base mineral of Rubies and Sapphires, and chromium, the midas element responsible for giving both Noble Red Spinels and Rubies their deep red colour.

Fancy Spinel exhibits a beautiful range of strong colours

Today, Spinels can be easily identified by their refractivity. Since Noble Red Spinels are singly refractive and Rubies doubly refractive, the primary colour in Noble Red Spinels appears purer and more intense than the reds seen in many Rubies.

Spinels are mined from alluvial deposits or directly from large granular granite or other igneous host rocks. Spinels come from a handful of sources including Madagascar, the Mahenge region of south central Tanzania, Tundura in Tanzania's remote south east and central Vietnam's Luc Yen region. Perfect octahedral crystals are sometimes set into jewellery in their original uncut octahedral shapes. The Burmese refer to these gems as "nat thwe", meaning spirit polished. Sometimes "nat thwe" Spinels will receive a very light polishing.

Black Spinel with Marcasite in these gothic inspired earrings

Pure Spinel is white, but impurities give it a wide range of colours. Almost all colours are used in jewellery, but the most valuable and popular colour is Noble Red Spinel. Occasionally, colour change varieties are found,

The Black Spinel in this pendant is accented by Marcasite set silver

SPINEL

turning colour from a light grey blue in daylight to a light purple under candlelight.

Even though they are more affordable, did you know that Spinels are rarer than Rubies? In the gem kingdom, "rare" can be both a blessing and a curse, as this affects market prices and availability. This is unfortunate for the Spinel miner, but great news for everyone else as they are one of nature's most beautiful treasures.

Spinels are intensely coloured durable gemstones perfect for all jewellery. Spinel's high refractive index makes cutting very important, as the quality of the cut will affect its brilliance. Naturally, all Spinels sold at Gems TV are faceted by experienced cutters who always take each gemstone's physical properties and individual attributes into consideration.

SPINEL:	Once confused with Ruby
Locations:	Madagascar, Tanzania, Vietnam
Colours Found:	Various
Typical Cuts:	Various
Family:	Spinel
Hardness:	8.00
Refractive Index:	1.715 - 1.720
Relative Density:	3.60

Cobalt Blue Spinel

Rough Red Spinel

SUNSTONE

Tibetan Sunstone

Radiating with the power of eternal light, Sunstone has been coveted since antiquity for its ability to guide its wearer through the journey of life. Sunstone is also known as Aventurine Feldspar or Heliolite, from the Greek "helios" for sun and "lithos" for stone.

SUNSTONE

Legends and lore

An ancient gem, Sunstone has allegedly been discovered in Viking burial mounds. Among the Vikings, Sunstone was thought to aid navigation both in reality and during ones journey to Valhalla and the afterlife. Interestingly, the Sunstone referenced in Norse literature probably refers to Iolite (see page 70) rather than the modern gem we call Sunstone.

Pope Clement VII (1478 - 1534) was reputed to have in his possession a Sunstone with a golden spot that moved across the surface in accordance with the apparent motion of the sun from sunrise to sunset.

Native Americans in Oregon, USA used Sunstone for trade and barter. Oregon Sunstone was declared the official Gemstone of the State of Oregon in 1987.

Crystal healers believe Sunstone to be useful for adding personal insight and alleviating depression. Historically, Sunstone has been linked with benevolent gods, luck and good fortune.

Just the facts

Sunstone is a member of the plagioclase Feldspar group of minerals and is closely related to Moonstone and Labradorite. The name Feldspar comes from the German "feldt spat", meaning "field stone". So named, this is because when Feldspar weathers, it releases large amounts of plant nutrients, such as potassium, which enrich soil.

Sunstone has a beautiful glittering sunlight effect as a result of its tiny metallic inclusions. The copper or pyrite inclusions cause sparkling flashes of light as millions of particles playfully interact with light. While known to gemmologists as "schiller" or "aventurescence", African miners call this feature "flowers". Sunstones are nearly always cut as cabochons to reflect this phenomenon but the deeper colours may also be faceted to exhibit their superior lustre.

Sunstone is formed and crystallized in lava flows. Sunstones range in colour from water clear through pale yellow, soft pink and red to deep blue and green. Some of the deeper coloured gems have bands of varying colour while others exhibit pleochroism,

Incredible Tibetan Sunstone Trilliant cut and set in yellow gold

Octagon cut Tibetan Sunstone

Tibetan Sunstone

Beautiful Sunstone from Madagascar displays golden flecks and rich reds

SUNSTONE

A striking pair of Sunstone earrings

A Pear cut Sunstone, creates a striking solitaire ring

An imposing gent's Sunstone ring

showing different colours when viewed from different directions.

Sunstones are mined from the surface from partially decomposed rock (with a pick and shovel) or from shallow pits and shafts dug to retrieve the rough.

Sunstone is mined in the USA (Warner Valley, Oregon – the high copper content of Oregon Sunstones gives them their unique bright red orange colours), India, Canada, Tanzania, Tibet, Madagascar, Norway and Russia. Interestingly, some Sunstones from Madagascar display asterism (also known as the "star effect", this is caused by minerals reflecting a star of light back to the eye), which further accentuates Sunstone's natural sparkle.

One of the newest and most beautiful rare gems to be discovered, Tibetan Sunstone (also known as Andesine, for the location of this minerals discovery in the lava flows of the Andes Mountains, Bolivia in 1841) was first unearthed in 2002 in central Tibet. Initially bumping into some rough Tibetan Sunstone during a buying trip in east Africa, our gem hunters were perplexed by its origin. While many incorrectly claim that the Democratic Republic of Congo is the source of this gemstone, we know better. Using our network of mining and gemstone contacts around the globe, we were able to get to the bottom of this modern gem mystery. Tibetan Sunstone is characterized by a swirling mix of coppery oranges, honeys, ambers, lemons and limes with a beautiful glittering sunlight effect caused by tiny copper inclusions. While the copper inclusions are predominantly orange, they often disperse a fiery multitude of electric colours. With such an attractive blend of shimmering colours, Tibetan Sunstone has a unique appearance unlike any other gemstone. Nevertheless, supply is erratic and very limited, making this beautiful rare gemstone even more collectable.

Tibetan Sunstone is somewhat similar to Maasai Sunstone from Tanzania. First found by a young Maasai man on tribal grazing lands near Arusha in 2000, Maasai Sunstone's basic red orange colour mimics the bright hues of the Maasai people's dress. Since the Maasai have found several of east Africa's gem deposits (Tsavorite and Tanzanite), it is fitting that at least one of their gem discoveries carries their tribal name.

Sunstone

SUNSTONE:	Aventurescence
Locations:	Madagascar, India, Tibet, USA
Colours Found:	Orange, red & yellow
Typical Cuts:	Various
Family:	Feldspar
Hardness:	6.00 - 6.50
Refractive Index:	1.53 - 1.55
Relative Density:	2.62 - 2.65

As far back as AD 77, Pliny the Elder in his Historis Naturalis cited India as a major source of the world's most coveted gemstones. Today, India continues this tradition with our discovery of Tanolite™, a stunning new variety of Iolite trademarked by Gems TV.

TANOLITE™

Just the facts

Nestled in the Bay of Bengal, two thirds of the Indian state of Orissa is covered with pre-cambrian rocks that have long been known to include many gemstones. Orissa yields a plethora of coloured gemstones including Ruby, Sapphire, Aquamarine, Garnet, Topaz, Zircon, Tourmaline and of course, Iolite. By virtue of their colour, transparency, size, brilliance and flawlessness, Orissa's gemstones are known the world over.

It is in Orissa, with its tradition of gemstone excellence, that we recently unearthed new deposits of Iolite (please see page 70). And herein lay the problem; this Iolite was nothing like anything we had ever seen before. Sporting beautiful violet hues, on a cursory glance more than one of our buyers would muffle, "Is this Tanzanite?" Knowing better, Don "The Gem Hunter" would crack a smile before revealing its Indian lineage. But this also gave him an idea. He had discovered this gem, so why not trademark a special name? In homage to its visual similarities with Tanzanite, a new gem was born.

A combination of Tanolite™ and Iolite, the purple-blues are beautiful against white gold

Tanolite™ is mined in the metamorphic rocks of Orissa's Kalahandi and Nawapada districts. It occurs as large, transparent violet crystals with excellent lustre and brilliance. While Iolite is know as "Water Sapphire" due to its similar appearance to light Blue Sapphire, Tanolite™ is a wonderfully affordable alternative to one of the world's most popular gems, Tanzanite. Jokingly referred to as "Water Tanzanite" by our gem sorters, its similarity to Tanzanite is not just skin deep. Both Tanzanite and Tanolite™ are strongly pleochroic, meaning they show many colours in a single gem depending on the viewing angle.

A Pear cut gem beautifully set in white gold

The only place you will ever obtain Tanolite™ is on Gems TV.

A simple Round cut Tanolite™ perfectly faceted and Prong set

Tanolite™

TANOLITE™:	Pleochroism
Locations:	India
Colours Found:	Violet
Typical Cuts:	Various
Family:	Cordierite
Hardness:	7.00 - 7.50
Refractive Index:	1.50
Relative Density:	2.53 - 2.65

131

TANZANITE

Displaying an aurora of stunning royal blues, violets, indigos, lilacs, periwinkles, and ultramarines, Tanzanite's popularity is well deserved. Demand for Tanzanite has rocketed in recent years, outstripping sales of all other coloured gemstones, with the exception of Sapphire. A thousand times rarer than Diamonds and with a little over a decade of mine life remaining, Tanzanite is the fashion gem of the millennium.

Legends and lore

The romance of Tanzanite begins in the arid Merelani foothills of Mount Kilimanjaro. Born of fire, Tanzanite's beauty remained secret to Tanzania's nomadic Massai until 1967. Legend has it that a short lived grass fire caused by a lightening strike was the first catalyst that turned burgundy violet surface pebbles of Zoisite (Tanzanite's gemmological name) into the vibrant blues spotted by Massai herdsmen. While wonderfully romantic, it is now generally regarded as unlikely that enough heat could be generated by a grass fire to affect such a dramatic transformation.

Sourced only in D block, AAAA Tanzanite is characterised by deep blues with flashes of red

AAAA Tanzanite represents some of the finest quality Tanzanite sold at Gems TV

In reality, the story of Tanzanite's discovery is as fascinating as the gem. While it is not known exactly who first found Tanzanite, the most popular story is that a local tribesman, Ali Juuyawatu discovered a translucent Tanzanite crystal at the base of Mount Kilimanjaro. Sharing his find with a local prospector called Manuel D'Souza, D'Souza was actually searching for Rubies in the region and initially thought he'd discovered a new source of Sapphires. However, their multitude of blues and complex composition soon revealed Tanzanite's true identity to gemmologists. Interestingly, the legendary Scottish geologist, Campbell R. Bridges, first discovered Tsavorite in Tanzania in 1967 during some Tanzanite consulting work for Tiffany & Co. and was the first person to bring Tanzanite to the USA for identification by the GIA (Gemmological Institute of America) Gem Trade Laboratory.

A 4ct high quality AAAA Tanzanite ring

AAAA Tanzanite

Tanzanite soon found its way to America, arriving at the New York based jewellers Tiffany & Co. Henry B. Platt, great grandson of Louis Comfort Tiffany and later President and Chairman of Tiffany & Co., was immediately enraptured by their beauty, but disturbed by its gemmological name "Blue Zoisite". To him the name echoed "Blue Suicide". As with anything in fashion, it's all in the name, so this rare and exotic African gemstone was christened Tanzanite. At Tanzanite's official launch in October 1968, Platt

TANZANITE

*AAAA Tanzanite set in
18k gold accented
with Diamonds*

TANZANITE

remarked that it "was the most beautiful blue gemstone discovered in over 2,000 years".

Tanzanite's blue-purple fire soon took the fashion world by storm and was heralded "the gemstone of the 20th century". Demand for Tanzanite jewellery grew dramatically as its global appreciation increased, and in 1998 and 1999 Tanzanite was proclaimed the world's best selling coloured gemstone.

While Tanzanite was adopted as one of December's official birthstones in 2002 (the first time the list changed since 1912), it is increasingly regarded as the ideal gem to celebrate new life and new beginnings. This belief has its roots in Massai tradition, where blue is believed to be a sacred spiritual colour and bestowed in the form of blue beads and robes to women who have borne children. Today, this tradition has evolved, with Massai chiefs giving Tanzanite to wives on the birth of a baby. This gift is believed to bless their child with a healthy, positive and successful life.

Tanzanite continues to be all the rage in contemporary jewellery. Tom Ford, "enfant terrible" of the Paris and Milan fashion house Gucci, once dominated the catwalks with a collection modelling exotic blue gems, including Tanzanite.

At the 2004 Oscar's, Eileen Penn, mother of Oscar winner Sean Penn, stole the limelight from her son with a stunning Tanzanite and Diamond cross pendant.

Just the facts

A key ingredient in Tanzanite's success is that it exhibits more shades of blue than a clear midnight sky due to a phenomenon call pleochroism, whereby different colours are seen in different directions of the gemstone. Frequently, Tanzanite exhibits a colour change from the more bluish hues under daylight, to pinkish violets under incandescent light (candlelight). Most of the time, you can actually see both colours simultaneously; this is especially true in larger carat sizes where Tanzanite's colourful brilliance intensifies.

Tanzanite is also coveted because of its rarity. Tanzanite's production is slowly but surely decreasing and many experts are of the opinion that Tanzanite will disappear in years to come. This has led to Tanzanite gaining considerable kudos; after all, the desire to own something beautiful and unique has always been a decisive factor in fashion. Tanzanite is exclusively mined in East Africa in an area of Tanzania known as Merelani. The conditions involved in Tanzanite's formation 585

A romantic trilogy design with a beautiful variety of Tanzanite hues

A striking Trilliant cut Green Tanzanite

This piece demonstrates the fantastic colour range of Tanzanite

The textbook lilacs of Tanzanite

TANZANITE

million years ago saw the random incorporation of vanadium during an event so unique it is often described as a geological phenomenon. Some experts even go as far as to maintain that the chance of Tanzanite occurring elsewhere is one in a million.

The Tanzanite deposits are hosted in metamorphic rocks, marbles and schists that belong to the Mozambique Belt (Rift Valley). The deposits run through the low hills of Merelani that rise from the hot Sanya plains, close to Mount Kilimanjaro. Running at an angle of 41 degrees to the surface, the deposit line or horizon periodically folds over itself, creating pockets of Tanzanite.

Barely covering 20 square kilometres, the Tanzanite mining area has been divided into four different sections known as "blocks" (lettered A, B, C & D) that have been allotted to different mining groups. While the largest scale and most sophisticated techniques used in Tanzanite mining take place in C block, the per tonne yields for rough Tanzanite in C Block average only 22 carats (4.4 grams) per processed tonne!

A piece from the designer gent's range at Gems TV

Representing less than 1% of all Tanzanite mined, although AAA colours come from all blocks, the "D block" section has earned the reputation for supplying some of the highest quality AAA Tanzanite. Characterised by intensely deep purples with glistening flashes of red, the finest D block Tanzanite can be likened to an old French wine of an impossibly hard to obtain vintage. Many jewellers will not have been fortunate enough to see D block AAA Tanzanite, as the vast majority of higher quality Tanzanite on the market comes from the neighbouring C block. While AAAA Tanzanite is sometimes called AAA "D block" Tanzanite (a very unromantic way to describe the most romantic of gemstones), at Gems TV we use the term AAAA to clearly differentiate fabulous colour D block Tanzanite from AAA Tanzanite coming from other blocks. AAAA Tanzanite is the very best quality Tanzanite sold at Gems TV.

A pretty floral design highlighted with Diamonds

A designer piece for the gentlemen

Tanzanite typically starts its life as bluish burgundy crystals that are heated to reveal their vibrant lilac, violet and blue colours. Occasionally, this process produces highly coveted and extremely rare fancy colours (Pink Tanzanite, Green Tanzanite, Ultramarine Tanzanite, Bi-Colour Tanzanite etc.). Possessing all the kudos of regular Tanzanite, these coloured varieties are far less common and are highly coveted by collectors. In gemmology, the technically correct name for these gems is "(Colour Prefix) Zoisite". However, Coloured

An elongated flower cluster - one of the most popular designs by Gems TV

TANZANITE

The perfect symbol of love, encrusted with pastel purple Tanzanite

The colour of Tanzanite speaks for itself in these simple stud earrings

Exquisitely set Tanzanite form these elegant earrings

Tanzanite is generally accepted in the marketplace due to the gem's popularity and because this name specifies an origin.

Tanzanite exudes sophistication. It is the quintessence of class while at the same time communicating individuality and self confidence. Lavish Tanzanite jewellery is suited to all ages, emphasizing the non conformity of the young and the sophistication of the mature. However, Tanzanite is rare and growing rarer by the moment. Apart from the sheer pleasure of owning one of this century's most spectacular gemstone discoveries, those fortunate to already own a Tanzanite or to purchase one before the only known deposit is depleted, truly are custodians of this spectacular gem whose legacy will be to pass it on as an heirloom to coming generations.

Tanzanite's wonderful colours, clarity and range of imaginative cuts lend itself to prominent display. Fashionable drop-earrings and pendants accentuate Tanzanite to the fullest, but Tanzanite is most popularly featured as large carat sized solitaires mounted into prominent ring settings, showing off its scintillating colours to full effect.

Gavin "Gemstone Gav" Linsell says:

"On a recent visit to Merelani in Tanzania, just outside the gem trading town of Arusha, I was fortunate to experience Tanzanite mining first hand. Apart from the hustle and bustle of a gem mine, one of the reasons I love visiting gem locales around the globe is to gleam local knowledge.

I find gem folklore especially fascinating and one legend surrounding Tanzanite that intrigues me is how grass fires caused by lightning strikes were attributed to its first discovery. While grass fires would be unlikely to generate the heat necessary to reveal Tanzanite's beauty, I was surprised to learn from miners that this story may have originated from the practice of placing Tanzanite rough in grass huts that were then burnt. To this day, Massai artisanal miners use slow burning camp fires to effect Tanzanite's miraculous transformation. Regardless, Tanzanite is a mesmerising gem and much like Kashmiri Sapphire, in my generation it will most likely become a gem of the past."

TANZANITE:	December's birthstone
Locations:	Tanzania
Colours Found:	Blue, indigo, lilac, periwinkle, ultramarine & violet
Typical Cuts:	Cushion, Octagon, Oval
Family:	Zoisite
Hardness:	6.50 - 7.00
Refractive Index:	1.68 - 1.72
Relative Density:	3.35

TEKTITE

We are not alone! Since the beginning of time the curiosity of humankind has been aroused by the descent of "shooting stars" or meteorites into our world. So catch a falling star as we discover the mystery behind this extraterrestrial gemstone.

Tektite comes from the Greek word "tektos" meaning molten and was the name given by Edward Suess who was born in London in 1831. He was a highly regarded professor at the University of Vienna, a geologist and a politician in the Austrian government.

A meteor is a small particle from space that appears as a bright light that completely burns up before it hits the ground. However, a meteorite is a meteor that is large enough to reach the ground, without burning up completely. Frequently exploding on impact, throwing pieces of rare, and highly sought after meteorite debris over a large area, these incredibly scarce and collectable gems are the perfect gift for anyone fascinated by outer space.

Perfectly matched Moldavite set in 18k gold

Just the facts

Collectively known as Tektites, they are assigned specific names based on their location. For example, Moldavites, named after the river Moldu in the Czech Republic are found in this country as well as Austria and Germany, Australites are from Australia, Philippinites are from the Philippines and Southern China, Malaysianites are from Malaysia and Indochinites are from Thailand, Myanmar (Burma), China, Laos and Vietnam.

Considered to be gemstones from space, Tektites are fragments of glass that are formed from meteorite impacts with our planet.

Eye-catchingly stylish Moldavite discovered in the Czech Republic

Scientists believe that Tektite's origin is the result of meteorite impact on either terrestrial or lunar rocks. The Tektites are formed when molten rock, created by the meteorite's hyper-velocity impact, fly through the air hardening into natural glass with aerodynamic forms and surface features.

Some Tektites are smooth but others have rough, strongly eroded surfaces. Most Tektites are jet black but the Moldavites are dark to bottle green and are most suitable for faceting.

The green tones in this Moldavite is brilliantly balanced with Green Tanzanite

Tektites look similar to Obsidian, which is a result of volcanic lava coming in contact with water, but can be differentiated by their colour and chemical composition.

Tektites and associated impact melted rock are found in only a few regions on earth (called Tektite strewn fields)

TEKTITE

TEKTITE:	Extraterrestrial gem
Locations:	Australia, Austria, China, Czech Republic, Germany, Laos, Malaysia, Myanmar, Philippines, Thailand, Vietnam
Colours Found:	Black & green
Typical Cuts:	Various
Family:	Tektite
Hardness:	5.50 - 6.50
Refractive Index:	1.48 - 1.50
Relative Density:	5.50 - 6.50

and are, in most cases, associated with young impact craters on or near land.

Tektites come in two forms. The more common "splash form" Tektites have rounded aerodynamic shapes such as spheres, tear-drops, dumbbells and disks when they are well-preserved.

The second variety call "layered" Tektites are primarily found in Southeast Asia. They have blocky, fragmental shapes and commonly display compositional layering and variations in bubble content. Some larger pieces have a surface reminiscent of lava or "bread crust" lava bombs.

There are far fewer Tektite localities on earth than there are impact craters. This is because Tektites, being made entirely of glass, erode slowly over time when exposed to the elements. Therefore, Tektites are only preserved in abundance from large young impact events.

TIGER'S EYE

Bezel set Indian Golden Tiger's Eye

TIGER'S EYE

Tiger's Eye is the best know variety of chatoyant Quartz (or Cat's Eye Quartz). Tiger's Eye, with its bands resembling the eye of a tiger, received its name due to this similarity. Tiger's Eye is also called Crocidolite Cat's Eye or African Cat's Eye. Tiger's Eye has rich yellow and golden brown stripes, with a fine golden lustre when polished.

Legends and lore

Coveted since antiquity, Roman soldiers wore Tiger's Eye for protection in battle. Due to its appearance, in the ancient world Tiger's Eye was thought to be all seeing, offering protection during travel, strengthening of convictions and confidence.

Many legends say that wearing Tiger's Eye is beneficial for health and spiritual well being. Legend also says it is a psychic protector, great for business and aids in achieving clarity of mind.

Today, crystal healers use Tiger's Eye for focusing the mind.

A fine example of the chatoyant effect found in Golden Tigers Eye

Just the facts

Quartz gemstones are commonly separated into two groups based on the size of their individual crystals. The macrocrystalline Quartz (large crystal) group includes many popular gemstones such as Tiger's Eye, Amethyst, Ametrine and Citrine. Cryptocrystalline Quartz includes species whose individual crystals are too small to be easily distinguished. Apart from being a variety within the group, Chalcedony is also a catch all term to describe cryptocrystalline Quartz and includes many gems that have been coveted since antiquity.

Tiger's Eye is an ideal gem for gent's jewellery

Tiger's Eye is a pseudomorph (the result of one mineral replacing another) that contains oriented fibres of Crocidolite that have been replaced by silica.

Tiger's Eye displays chatoyancy (a vertical luminescent band like that of a Cat's Eye). Tiger's Eye typically has lustrous alternating yellow or brown bands. Cutting is crucial with Tiger's Eye because the rough crystals reveal little or nothing of the exciting chatoyancy of the finished gem.

An eye catching piece, Half Bezel set in 9k yellow gold

TIGER'S EYE:	Chatoyancy
Locations:	Australia, Brazil, India, Namibia, South Africa
Colours Found:	Blue-green, golden brown, green-grey & reddish brown
Typical Cuts:	Cabochon
Family:	Quartz
Hardness:	7.00
Refractive Index:	1.55
Relative Density:	2.65

TOPAZ

The cool hues of Sky Blue Topaz in a contemporary design

This most vibrant shade of Blue Topaz mimics the colour of the sky above the Swiss Alps

This London Blue Topaz was sourced in Brazil

London Blue Topaz

The origin of the name Topaz generates confusion, as some references point to the Sanskrit word "tapaz", meaning fire, while others believe it is named after Zebirget, an island in the Red Sea that the ancient Greeks called Topazius, the ancient source of Peridot. In the past, the name was not consistently or specifically applied (it was once used to describe most yellow gems) and sometimes Topaz and Peridot are mentioned as being the same and sometimes different. Interestingly, in the famous book "The Curious Lore of Precious Stones", the esteemed gemmologist George Frederick Kunz (1856 – 1932) states that these two gems are the same species.

Topaz is an inherently romantic gem and features regularly in the titles of romance novels and honeymoon destinations. Its name indicates beauty, rarity and wealth, and imparts a sense of timelessness.

While the golden yellow and blues of Topaz are the most widely known, Topaz actually comes in a diverse array of striking colours. This combined with its beauty and durability, makes Topaz jewellery ideal for all occasions.

Legends and lore

Many ancient traditions and beliefs have created a brilliant history for Topaz. Similarly to Peridot, the Egyptians called Topaz the "gem of the sun", believing it was coloured by the golden glow of their sun god Ra and thus a powerful protector from harm.

Greeks and Romans also associated the golden crystals with their Sun God, Jupiter. They believed the gem increased their strength and could neutralize enchantments.

Topaz is mentioned in the Bible as being one of the "stones of fire" (Ezekiel 28:13-16) that were given to Moses and set in the breastplate of Aaron (Exodus 28:15-30). Topaz is also one of the twelve gemstones set in the foundations of the city walls of Jerusalem (Revelations 21:19) and associated with the Apostle Matthew.

Bushmen in Africa used Topaz in healing ceremonies and rituals to connect with ancestral spirits.

In medieval courts, Kings, judges and other noble persons were often presented with an engraved Topaz to win favour and cultivate positive relationships.

If you are on a journey of spiritual change, Topaz is believed by crystal healers to make an excellent

TOPAZ

companion. It apparently teaches you to trust in the Universe, aiding you to fully recognize the magical laws of attraction, increasing your ability to manipulate them.

Once believed to make you invincible during danger, Topaz is also believed by some crystal healers to strengthen confidence and to help you make correct decisions by giving you the courage to follow through on choices, thereby changing dreams into reality.

Meditations with Topaz are believed by some to help awaken sleeping talents and illuminate co-creative energies.

Just the facts

Mined from both host rock and alluvial deposits, its unique crystal structure makes Topaz a hard and dense gemstone. Because of this, pure colourless Topaz has often been mistaken for Diamond. Weighing 1,680 carats, the huge Braganza gemstone mounted into the Portuguese crown jewels was originally thought to be a Diamond - in fact it is a beautiful clear Topaz.

A very fashionable look featuring 4.4ct of Pink Topaz

A hydrous aluminium fluorosilicate, Topaz is usually formed in granitic pegmatites and in Quartz veins.

Blue Topaz

As well as the renowned Sky Blue Topaz, the more intense colouring of Swiss Blue and London Blue Topaz are also becoming increasingly popular.

Glacier Topaz™

A unification of fire and ice, Glacier Topaz™ mixes the pure clear whites of glacier ice with a fiery brilliance and lustre reminiscent of Diamonds. Sourced from Russia's frozen wildness, Glacier Topaz™ is a stunning new gemstone exclusive to Gems TV.

Mined from the same region as Russian Alexandrite and Siberian Emerald, Glacier Topaz™ is yet another testament to the quality of Russian gemstones recently unearthed by our tireless gem hunters. Glacier Topaz™, arguably Topaz at its most pure, requires only cutting and faceting to reveal its hidden beauty.

Glacier Topaz

Glacier Topaz™ is mined at one location on the planet, the famous Murzinka mines (named after the Ostyak's Prince Murzin) in the Ural Mountains, Russia. Active for well over a century, the Murzinka mines produce some of the world's finest Topaz, a gemstone for which Russia was once famous. While Brazil is today the recognized powerhouse for Topaz, Russian Topaz is relatively

Glacier Topaz has all the look of a huge flawless Diamond without the huge price tag

141

TOPAZ

*Brazilian Imperial
Topaz with 10 Bezel set
Round Zambian
Citrines*

difficult to source, particularly with respect to the pure natural perfection embodied by Glacier Topaz™.

The miners work the deposits of the Murzinka granite pegmatite fields by tunnelling up to 30 metres below the earth's surface in an effort to carefully extract Topaz crystals directly from the host rocks of the lucrative Mokrusha vein. Painstaking work, only a very small percentage of all the Murzinka Topaz mined has the necessary purity to warrant the distinction of being called Glacier Topaz™.

TOPAZ

Imperial Topaz

At the height of Imperial Russia's power, orange pink Topaz was brought from Brazil to decorate the jewellery of the Czarina's. Since then, these colours have been known as Imperial Topaz and even today remain one of the most coveted varieties. Interestingly, some sources dispute this legend and state that Imperial Topaz was named in honour of Emperor Don Pedro of Brazil.

Mystic Topaz

Displaying a flaming kaleidoscope of colours, Mystic Topaz (also known as Mystic Fire Topaz, Rainbow Topaz, Titanium Topaz, Alaskan Topaz and Caribbean Topaz) is one of this centuries most beautiful new gemstones.

Mystic Topaz is produced using the physical vapour deposition (PVD) coating process. Applied to top quality natural White Topaz, the treatment is permanent with normal wear (please see page 190 for more information on the PVD process).

While Mystic Topaz displays a wide variety of scintillating celestial, earthly and oceanic hues all in one gemstone, the PVD process also produces a range of popular new Topaz colours including Red Topaz, Magenta Topaz, Flamingo Topaz, Twilight Topaz, Cornish Blue Topaz, Moonlight Topaz, Canary Topaz, Kiwi Topaz and Neptune Topaz.

Mystic Topaz emits many stunning colours, especially when Trilliant cut

Mystic Topaz

TOPAZ:	November's birthstone
Locations:	Brazil, Mozambique, Nigeria, Russia
Colours Found:	Various
Typical Cuts:	Various
Family:	Topaz
Hardness:	8.00
Refractive Index:	1.60 - 1.63
Relative Density:	3.50 - 3.60

TOURMALINE

Nigerian Fancy Tourmaline

Fancy Tourmaline from Brazil

Boasting a colourful and romantic history, Tourmaline rivals all but the most unique gems as it is found in an incredible array of gorgeous colours. Coming in a palette of over 100 different hues, Tourmaline is one of the world's most diverse gemstones. This has resulted in the nickname "the chameleon gem", which is doubly appropriate when you consider that one major source of Tourmaline is Madagascar, home to more than half of the world's chameleon species!

The name Tourmaline comes from the Sinhalese word "turmali", meaning mixed, due to a historical tendency for it to be confused and then mixed with other gem varieties.

Legends and lore

Sri Lanka (formerly Ceylon) was also partly responsible for Tourmaline's first appearance in Europe when Tourmaline gems were sold to Dutch traders who imported them to the West in the 15th century.

The Dutch, aside from admiring Tourmaline for its beauty, first discovered that this gem like Quartz possessed a unique property. Tourmaline when heated or rubbed creates an electrical charge, becoming a magnet that attracts lightweight materials.

A monarch particularly enchanted by Tourmaline was the Empress Dowager Tz'u Hsi, the last Empress of China. She loved Tourmaline so much, and was so wealthy, that she bought almost a ton of it!

Just the facts

While Tourmalines occur in large crystal sizes, Tourmaline of sufficient beauty to be set into jewellery is not available in great abundance. Because of their size, crystals are usually cut into long rectangular shapes following the axis of the crystal.

Tourmaline crystals occur in granitic pegmatite veins occurring in the great gem mining districts of Minas Gerias in Brazil, and the east African countries of Kenya, Tanzania, Mozambique, Malawi and Madagascar.

In the summer of 1998 a new Tourmaline deposit was unearthed near the city of Ibadan in Nigeria, West Africa, proving to be one of the most significant Tourmaline discoveries in modern times.

Tourmaline is a group of mineral species. However, it's the mineral Elbaite (named after the island of Elba near Italy's west coast where it was discovered) that is responsible for almost all of Tourmaline's most famous gem varieties. When used, the name "Elbaite" typically references Green Tourmaline, while the other colour forms of Elbaite have their own specific colour related names.

Tourmaline very occasionally displays the cat's eye effect. Chatoyancy or the cat's eye effect is a reflection effect that appears as a single bright band of light across the surface of a gemstone.

All Tourmalines can display pleochroism, meaning that its colour changes when viewed at different angles. However, this can vary from specimen to specimen. In some, this effect is hardly noticeable, while in others it is strongly apparent. To bring out the best colour, gemstone cutters must take this into account when faceting Tourmaline.

TOURMALINE

Bi-Colour Tourmaline

Mentioned in early 20th century gemmological texts, it was not until 1970's that Tourmaline lent its charm to jewellery. Treasured for the magnificent harmony of its two colours, Bi -Colour Tourmaline possesses a distinctive beauty created by chance.

Due to their complex chemical composition, Tourmaline occurs in infinitesimal colour variations. Bi Coloured Tourmaline occurs because of differences caused by environmental changes. At different times, various colour-causing elements (iron, manganese, titanium, chromium and vanadium) were incorporated into the crystal, causing different colour layers. Purposefully cut to showcase this feature, Bi-Coloured Tourmaline displays a gorgeous contrast between its colours, typically pink and green, in one gem.

Given the environmental changes endured by Bi-Colour Tourmaline, like many Tourmalines (Paraiba or Rubellite), inclusions are common. Far from being flaws, inclusions are also a fascinating hallmark of authenticity that records a gem's natural relationship with the Earth.

Bi-Colour Tourmaline should not be confused with Watermelon Tourmaline. Watermelon Tourmaline is a crystal with the inner part showing pink surrounded by green. They are typically thinly sliced in section, like a loaf of bread and polished to show the "watermelon" effect.

This Bi-Colour Tourmaline displays greens through to pinks

A one-off design by Mike Matthews - a stunning Nigerian 51ct Bi-Colour Tourmaline

Bi-Colour Tourmaline

Deep pink gems are a favourite for many

TOURMALINE

Deep greens contrast with the rich tones of yellow gold

A Forest Green Tourmaline surrounded by White Topaz

Electric blues characterise Paraiba, a virtually unattainable gem

A stunning example of the vibrant blue-green hues which are found in these rare gems

Paraiba Tourmaline

Green Tourmaline

Typically inclusion free, Green Tourmaline offers gem consumers everything they want in an Emerald, but with more clarity.

Green Tourmaline has become very popular with collectors over recent years as they realise the true potential of this beautiful gem. Chrome Tourmaline is scarcer variety of Green Tourmaline that bears chromium, the midas element responsible for producing particularly striking colours in a variety of gemstones.

Indicolite Tourmaline (Neon Blue)

Ranging in colour from bright to deep blue, Indicolite Tourmaline is very rare and high quality specimens are highly collectable.

Paraiba Tourmaline

Paraiba Tourmaline is typically a small gem that displays electric swimming pool blues, neon peacocks and sizzling turquoises. Initially discovered at Mina da Bathalha, Paraiba, Brazil, it possesses a unique brilliance that allows the gem to glow and shine even when there is little light.

Named after the location of its first discovery, Paraiba, Brazil, the most interesting thing about this gem is that its name is more than just a location. Most Tourmalines get their gorgeous colours from traces of iron, manganese, chromium and vanadium, but Paraiba Tourmaline owes its spectacular colours to small amounts of copper, an element not typically found in Tourmaline. Paraiba Tourmaline also often contains manganese. When combined, the interaction between copper and manganese adds to the beautiful and fascinating colours displayed.

Prior to 1989, Mina da Bathalha produced Tourmaline for almost 10 years but the crystals were too fractured or broken to be faceted. Heitor Dimas Barbos, the father of Paraiba Tourmaline, was convinced that better quality Tourmaline could be found. He started digging in abandoned mines near the village of Sao Jose da Batalha in early 1981. In autumn 1989 his persistence finally paid off when he discovered a tiny new vein of gem-quality crystals. By 1994 the relatively small mountain range had almost been levelled and exhausted in the hunt for Paraiba Tourmaline. Mining Brazilian Paraiba Tourmaline is laborious, unpredictable and erratic. Chipped by hand directly from host

TOURMALINE

*Sri Lankan
Fancy
Tourmaline
necklace*

TOURMALINE

Pink Tourmaline

Rubellite is the red variety of Tourmaline

A 1.4ct Rubellite ring accented with Diamonds

metamorphic rock (granitic pegmatite), the elusive narrow veins appear and disappear haphazardly, resulting in mines that resemble Swiss cheese, with a multitude of narrow shafts and interconnected tunnels up to 60 meters deep.

With the Brazilian deposit all but depleted, the race has been on to find these geological rarities elsewhere. Thankfully, Africa came to the rescue. The first new find was discovered in 2001 at the Edoukou Mine in Oyo, Nigeria, close to the border of Benin and more recently in Zambezia, Mozambique. African Paraiba is believed to exist due to the theory of continental drift. Roughly 200 million years ago the earth's continents were joined together to form one gigantic super-continent called Pangaea. Comparing the silhouettes of Africa and South America both fit like pieces in a jigsaw puzzle. This suggests they once belonged to a single landmass where similar geological conditions resulted in their formation. In contrast to the Brazilian deposit, African Paraiba Tourmaline is mined from alluvial deposits. Interestingly, the GAAJ (Gemmological Association of All Japan) research laboratory (Japan's leading authority on gemstones), recently determined that as African Paraiba cannot be distinguished from their Brazilian counterpart by standard gemmological tests, it gets down only to colour, copper and manganese.

While mostly small sizes are extracted (less than 10 points) Paraiba Tourmaline from Mozambique has an average size of 2 carats, which is absolutely amazing considering the norm. Like Emeralds, inclusions are common in Paraiba Tourmaline, making its colour the main beauty determinant. However, when Paraiba Tourmaline displays clean clarities, its' rarity and value increase exceptionally.

Its beautiful vivid colours have made Paraiba Tourmaline hugely popular within a short time. An uncommon colour for the gem kingdom, Paraiba Tourmaline even enchants those accustomed to seeing a wide variety of gems. One of the world's most desired gemstones, gem collectors the world over compete for new Paraiba Tourmaline. Paraiba Tourmaline is a gem whose impossible rarity is only surpassed by its unrivalled beauty - there is simply never enough to go around.

Rubellite Tourmaline

Rubellite's sensuous mélange is the personification of seduction; no other colours display its comparable feminine flair. Whispering in passionate pinks and suggestive purples, Rubellite affords the perfect romance in an opulence of red. Once aware of the extravagance and beauty of this gemstone, a woman can not be parted from her Rubellite, a gem of seduction.

Rubellite, deriving its name from the Latin word "rubellus", meaning "coming from red" is a lustrous, reddish pink and purple toned variety of Tourmaline.

In the 17th century, the Tsar of Russia commissioned many items of gemstone jewellery to be made for the Imperial Crown Court. However, recently what were originally thought to be Rubies, in reality have been discovered to be Rubellite.

Extremely rare, Rubellite has taken the jewellery world by storm in recent years following the discovery of deposits in Madagascar and Nigeria. Madagascan Rubellite heralds from mines located 42 km from the town of Betafo, in the Antananarivo province in Madagascar's central highlands. Interestingly, this deposit produces some truly unique Rubellites whose colour is close to that of famous Rubies.

With the exception of Ruby and Noble Red Spinel, Rubellite is the only other gemstone that occurs in such a rich, dark red colour. Similarly to Emeralds, inclusions in Rubellite are common. The chemical element that colours Rubellite (manganese) actually causes a growing crystal to become internally flawed. The more manganese present, the darker the red colour, and the more imperfect the final crystal. It is therefore extremely rare to find richly coloured Rubellite that is internally clean. Rubellites also tend to have more natural inclusions because they are formed near the centre of the crystal pocket, and thus receive more stress and pressure during their formation. Regardless, Rubellite is a durable gemstone, well suited to everyday jewellery.

TOURMALINE

Rubellite
Tourmaline

What our Craftsmen say:
Miss Amphorn Santamyae - Polishing

"With a hardness of 7-7.5, this multitudinous gem is ideal for all types of jewellery setting. Tourmaline earrings, Tourmaline necklaces, Tourmaline rings and other types of Tourmaline jewellery are all well-suited to every day wear."

TOURMALINE:	October's birthstone
Locations:	Brazil, Kenya, Madagascar, Malawi, Mozambique, Nigeria, Sri Lanka, Tanzania
Colours Found:	Various
Typical Cuts:	Various
Family:	Tourmaline
Hardness:	7.00 - 7.50
Refractive Index:	1.62 - 1.64
Relative Density:	3.06

TURQUOISE

Tropical blues make
Turquoise the ideal
choice for the
summer time

A grand design with
a large Cabochon
cut Turquoise

A large solitaire
Turquoise creates a
modern look in white
gold

Turquoise is
commonly feathered
with inclusions which
give the gem it's
uniquely beautiful
appearance

The name Turquoise is derived from the French "pierre turquois" meaning "turkish stone". This is because western Europeans mistakenly thought the gem came from Turkey. In actual fact it came from the Sinai Peninsula or Alimersai Mountain in Persia (now Iran), which has been mining Turquoise since 5000 BC. In Persian, Turquoise is known as "ferozah", meaning victorious and it is the national gemstone of Iran to this day.

Legends and lore

Turquoise was one of the first gemstones ever mined, dating back to 6000 BC in Egypt's Sinai Peninsula.

In ancient times the Egyptians, Persians, Mongols and Tibetans all valued Turquoise highly. The first millennium AD saw a big increase in the popularity of Turquoise with both the Chinese and Native Americans becoming captivated by the blue stone.

Turquoise has been used for thousands of years as jewellery by the ancient Egyptians, who buried fine pieces with mummies. When the tomb of Queen Zer was unearthed in 1900, a Turquoise and Gold bracelet was found on her wrist, making this one of the oldest pieces of jewellery on Earth!

The Persians preferred sky blue Turquoise and the term "Persian Turquoise" is now used as a colour grade, not as a geographical indicator.

In Mexico, the Aztecs began mining Turquoise between 900-1000 AD, often fashioning it into elaborate masks.

The Anasazi people of America mined Turquoise in what are now Arizona, New Mexico and Colorado. The city of Chaco Canyon became very wealthy based on the Turquoise trade, which was often exchanged for the feathers of tropical birds. Turquoise from this area found its way around the trade routes of the American continent and has been unearthed as far away as the great Mayan city of Chichén Itzá in the Yucatán. By the 16th century, the cultures of the American southwest were using Turquoise as currency.

In North America, the Zuni people of New Mexico have created striking Turquoise jewellery set in silver, once believing these protected them from demons. The Navajo believed that Turquoise had fallen from the sky and thus protected them from demons, while Apache warriors believed that wearing Turquoise improved their hunting prowess. These tribes also believed that Turquoise brought happiness and good fortune to all.

European interest in Turquoise can be dated to around 500 BC when the people of Siberia began using the gem, but it did not make an impact on Western European fashion until the late Middle Ages when trading with the near and Middle East increased.

While the Chinese had some mines in their empire, they imported most of their Turquoise from Persians, Turks, Tibetans and Mongols.

In Asia it was considered protection against the evil eye. Tibetans carved Turquoise into ritual objects as well as wearing it in traditional jewellery. Ancient manuscripts from Persia, India, Afghanistan, and Arabia report that the health of a person wearing Turquoise can be assessed by variations in the colour of the gem. Turquoise was also thought to promote prosperity.

It is also believed that Turquoise helps one to start new projects and protects the wearer from falling, especially from horses! In Europe even today, Turquoise rings are given as forget-me-not gifts.

Legend has it that some Native Americans believed that if Turquoise was affixed to a bow, the arrows shot from it would always hit their mark.

Montezuma's treasure, now displayed in the British Museum, includes a fantastic carved serpent covered by a mosaic of Turquoise. In ancient Mexico, Turquoise was reserved for the gods; it could not be worn by mere mortals.

Just the facts

Turquoise, a hydrated phosphate of copper and aluminium, is prized as a gemstone whose intense blue colour is often mottled with veins of brown limonite or black manganese oxide (commonly known as Spider Web Turquoise).

Turquoise jewellery in the USA has long been produced by Native Americans (Zuni and Navajo peoples). Today, Turquoise is prominently associated with Native American culture particularly Zuni bracelets, Navajo concha belts, squash blossom necklaces and thunderbird motifs. The Native American jewellery or "Indian style" jewellery with Turquoise mounted in or with silver is actually relatively new. Some believe this style of jewellery was unknown prior to about 1880, when a white trader persuaded a Navajo craftsman to make Turquoise and silver jewellery using coin silver. Prior to this time, the Native Americans had made solid Turquoise beads, carvings and inlaid mosaics.

Turquoise is almost always opaque and polished as cabochons but rare, translucent gems are known to exist.

TURQUOISE

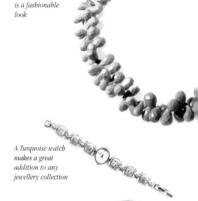

Tumbled Turquoise is a fashionable look

A Turquoise watch makes a great addition to any jewellery collection

Turquoise

TURQUOISE:	December's birthstone
Locations:	Afghanistan, China, India, Iran, USA
Colours Found:	Bluish green & sky blue
Typical Cuts:	Beads, Cabochon, Ornamental
Family:	Turquoise
Hardness:	5.00 - 6.00
Refractive Index:	1.61 - 1.65
Relative Density:	2.60 - 2.80

UNAKITE

Five strands and 773ct of Brazilian Unakite

Unakite is a blend of two minerals; one pistachio green (Epidote) and the other salmon pink (Feldspar). While Unakite is a relatively new gemstone, it has rapidly gained popularity due to its beautiful colour combinations and durability.

Unakite was named in 1874 after the location of its discovery in the Unaka range of the Great Smoky region of the Blue Ridge province of eastern Tennessee and western North Carolina, USA.

Legends and lore

Although a fairly new gemstone, Unakite is well regarded by crystal healers. Looked upon by some as a balancing gem due to its blend of two colours, Unakite is said to help unify our emotional, spiritual and mental aspects. Crystal healers also believe that it can help us to live in the present instead of dwelling in the past.

Because it combines the feminine (pink) with the masculine (green), it is thought by some crystals healers to help foster emotional balance and alignment. They also believe Unakite is an excellent gem for people seeking a more well-rounded existence and helpful in getting to the root of emotional issues.

Associating Unakite's green colours with healing and its pink colours with the heart, some crystal healers consider Unakite important in treating heart problems.

Unakite is also said to be a good gem for those born during "the moon of falling leaves" (22nd September – 22nd October). Crystal healers believe people born during this time can benefit from Unakite's unifying qualities.

Just the facts

Also know as Epidotized Granite, Unakite is a mixture of pink Feldspar, green Epidote and Quartz. The olive green of Epidote combined with the pink hues of Feldspar makes for a striking opaque gemstone. Displaying a good lustre and possessing durability well suited to everyday wear, its varied mottled appearance makes every Unakite unique.

UNAKITE:	Also know as Epidotized Granite
Locations:	Brazil, China, South Africa
Colours Found:	Mixture of pistachio green & salmon gink
Typical Cuts:	Cabochon
Family:	Granite
Hardness:	6.00 - 7.00
Refractive Index:	1.52 - 1.55
Relative Density:	2.85 - 3.20

Unakite

ZIRCON

Zircon's name is either derived from the Arabic word "zarkun", meaning red, or a combination of the ancient Persian words "zar", meaning gold and "gun", meaning colour. Despite this name, Zircon actually occurs in a myriad of colours.

Zircon's brilliant lustre, fire and bright hues make it an enjoyable addition to any jewellery collection.

Legends and lore

Zircon has been found in some of the most ancient archaeological sites.

Zircon has appeared in literature and the gem trade under a variety of names including Jargon (Yellow Zircon), Jacinth (Red Zircon), Matara Diamond (White Zircon), Starlite (Blue Zircon), Hyacinth (Blue Zircon) and Ligure.

Zircon is first mentioned in the ancient Indian tale of the Kalpa Tree. Described by Hindu poets as the ultimate gift to the gods, it was a bright glowing tree with bejewelled leaves of Zircon.

The light dispersion within Zircon gives it a fire similar to Diamonds

The gemstone of fiery starlight, Jewish legends say that Zircon was the name of the guardian angel sent to watch over Adam and Eve in the Garden of Eden.

Zircon is mentioned in the Bible (using the name Jacinth for its red variety) as being one of the "stones of fire" (Ezekiel 28:13-16) that were given to Moses and set in the breastplate of Aaron (Exodus 28:15-30). Zircon is also one of the twelve gemstones set in the foundations of the city walls of Jerusalem (Revelations 21:19) and associated with the Apostle Simon.

Cambodia is one of the world's premiere sources of fine Zircon

The Roman historian, Pliny the Elder, compared Blue Zircon's colour to Hyacinth flowers.

Traditionally, Zircon is a gem of purity and innocence. Zircon is believed to promote inner peace while providing the wearer with wisdom, honour and riches. Legend also has it that a Zircon's loss of lustre is a warning of imminent danger.

Zircon's popularity grew dramatically in the 16th century when Italian artisans featured the gem in jewellery designs. In the 1880's Blue Zircon was widely used in Victorian jewellery.

Just the facts

Although Zircon's existence predates Cubic Zirconia by centuries, Zircon is often unfairly confused with Cubic Zirconia. Cubic Zirconia is a cheap, synthetic Diamond

Blue Zircon

Golden Brown Zircon

ZIRCON

Vibrant blues are set off with crisp white gold

ZIRCON:	December's birthstone
Locations:	Cambodia, Nigeria, Sri Lanka, Tanzania
Colours Found:	Blue, green, honey, red, white & yellow
Typical Cuts:	Various
Family:	Zircon
Hardness:	7.50
Refractive Index:	1.93 - 1.98
Relative Density:	4.60 - 4.70

substitute that resembles colourless Zircon and has a similar sounding name. While Zircon may also be used as a Diamond substitute, it is valuable in its own right.

The fire in Zircon, called dispersion, is caused by light entering the gemstone and separating into a prism of rainbow colours. Possessing dispersion approaching that of Diamond, the brilliance of Zircon is second to none. The Zircon Cut, a variation of the Brilliant Cut that adds eight extra facets to the pavilion, was designed to take advantage of these properties.

A very unique characteristic of Zircon is birefringence (doubly refractive), meaning that light splits into two rays as it passes through the gem. As a result, the back facets appear as double images.

Cambodia is one of the world's premiere sources for gorgeous Zircon. Sixty three miles north of Angkor Wat, close to the Cambodian Thai border, lay the mines of Preah Vihear, the source of some of the world's finest Blue Zircon. Remote, primitive and stunningly beautiful, Ratanakiri is another major centre for Cambodian Zircon. Ratanakiri literally means "gemstone mountain". South of the city, a mining camp has been carved from the forest, where workers toil to extract Blue Zircon from narrow mine shafts that tap into an alluvial layer about 4.5 metres below the surface. Matt McNamara, one of Gems TV's presenters, visited several Cambodian Zircon mines in 2004, "I was amazed at how primitive some mines still are today. Because of the low prices that we see gem set jewellery for at Gems TV, it's easy to forget how much work goes into unearthing these wonderful gems".

Cambodian Blue Zircon Prong set into a gent's design

In addition to this guide, we are constantly updating our website with details on new deposits and new gem discoveries. While we don't have enough space to detail every gemstone, simply click on our "Gemstone Buyer's Guide" at www.GemsTV.com for full details on the following gems:

Amazonite	Gibeon Meteorite	
Anglesite	Hauyne	
Apophyllite	Hematite	
Aquamarine	Hemimorphite	
Aragonite	Howlite	
Aventurine	Larimar	
Axinite	Leifite	
Azurite	Magnesite	
Barite	Malachite	
Bastnaesite	Mammoth Ivory	Rhodonite
Bloodstone	Manganotantalite	Rutile
Boracite	Mawsitsit	Sard
Burbankite	Mellite	Sardonyx
Bustamite	Meteorites	Senarmontite
Calcite	Milarite	Scheelite
Celestite	Monazite	Serandite
Charoite	Mookite	Shortite
Cinnabar	Montebrasite	Siderite
Cobalt Calcite	Morganite	Sinhalite
Creedite	Natrolite	Smithsonite
Danburite	Nuummit	Spectrolite
Datolite	Oligoclase	Sphalerite
Dolomite	Parisite	Spodumene
Dumortierite	Pectolite	Staurolite
Ekanite	Petalite	Sugilite
Enstatite	Phenakite	Thaumasite
Epidote	Pollucite	Tremolite
Euclase	Prehnite	Tugtupite
Eudialyte	Pyroxmangite	Villiaumite
Fossils	Quartzite	Willemite
Genthelvite	Remondite	Wulfenite

155

WHAT IS A GEM?

Although Diamonds are nowhere near as rare as most people believe, they score very highly in beauty and durability.

Amethyst

Tanzanite

Alexandrite, Tanzanite and Padparadscha Sapphire are amongst some of the rarest gems in the world.

For decades, the Gemmological Institute of America (GIA) has taught their students that "gems are specimens of minerals or organic materials used for personal adornment that possess the attributes of beauty, rarity, and durability."

The GIA teaches that all three of these attributes must be present - a gem lacking in one or more of these attributes risks losing its status as a gem.

Beauty

In loose gems, strength of colour is probably the most important factor. Strong colours are expected in the majority of gems, including Ruby, Emerald and Sapphire. However, Kunzite and Aquamarine aren't typically known for strength of colour, yet are greatly appreciated when they display rich, deep colours.

This making of a gem's colour saturation such an important issue limits the potential of less-saturated gem material. For example, lightly-coloured Amethyst, while attractive as light Tanzanite, was traditionally considered among the least valuable of all gems.

In transparent gems, the degree of transparency and light return (brilliance) is considered crucial. However, through market experience, we learn to expect certain degrees of clarity from certain gems. For example, Aquamarine is generally expected to be clean and Emerald is expected to be hazy. Flawless, clean Emeralds are very rare. Generally, jewellery retailers tend to sell the more transparent Emeralds at a huge premium.

Rarity

"What is rare and beautiful is desired..."

Consider the success of copper rich Tourmaline originally from Paraíba, Brazil. Small, often highly included and now so rare that it is practically unavailable on the market, Paraíba Tourmaline broke all pricing rules and now commands higher per-carat prices than fine Sapphire and Diamond. Its remarkable and memorable electric-blue colour and publicity added to its cachet as a rare gem. However, rarity does not always add value. Sometimes the rarity of a gem type jeopardises commercial viability. Tsavorite Garnet is rarer than Emerald, is entirely free of treatments and is frequently more beautiful, but because there aren't enough around, cannot compete with Emerald in terms of the consumer's perception of its value.

Then consider Amethyst. Often beautiful, clean, durable and colourful, it is not as rare as many other popular gemstones. In Medieval Europe, Amethyst was extremely rare and the colour purple was coveted, but today Amethyst is typically only highly regarded by industry professionals when it appears in its top colours.

Given the enormous Diamond stockpiles and new sources springing up around the world, when compared to many coloured gemstones in this guide, Diamonds are not especially rare. Strict control of polished Diamonds on the market, combined with sophisticated consumer advertising, has elevated Diamonds to the extent that they are perceived as a rare and coveted product.

Durability

"The love of precious gemstones is deeply implanted in the human heart," George Kunz wrote in his book The Curious Lore of Precious Stones, "The cause of this must be sought not only in their colouring and brilliancy but also their durability."

Kunz further wrote, "The sheen and colouration of precious stones are the same today as they were thousands of years ago and will be for thousands of years to come. In a world of change, this permanence has a charm of its own that was early appreciated."

A gemstone must be durable enough not to break or fade over years of wear. Its brilliance and beauty are expected to last for a very long time, even to the point where a gemstone will outlast its owners and be passed on to sons and daughters, which, in turn, will help maintain its status as a gem and awaken appreciation in the succeeding generations.

WHAT IS A GEM?

Today, Tsavorite Garnet is far rarer than Emerald yet still demands a slightly lower price.

Given proper care all gemstone jewellery should be suitable to be passed down to many generations

GEMSTONE FORMATION

For millions of years gemstones have formed beneath the surface of the earth in a variety of different environments.

Traditionally, gemstones fall into three rock classifications: Igneous (Magmatic), Metamorphic and Sedimentary. Igneous or Magmatic rocks crystallize from molten magma, lava or gases. Sedimentary rocks crystallize from hydrous solutions on or near the earth's surface, while Metamorphic rocks re-crystallize from existing minerals that have been subjected to great pressure and high temperatures.

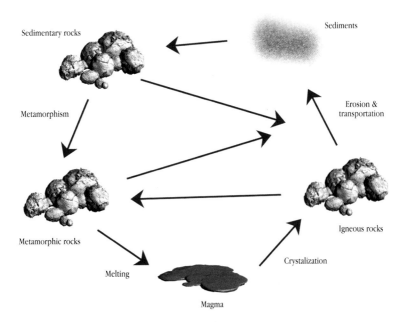

Sedimentary rocks

Sediments

Metamorphism

Erosion & transportation

Metamorphic rocks

Igneous rocks

Melting

Crystalization

Magma

Gemstone formation is generally classified into four processes:

1) **Molten rock & associated fluids**

2) **Environmental changes**

3) **Surface water and**

4) **Formation in the earth's mantle.**

Two famous organic gemstones that are not minerals are Pearl and Amber

GEMSTONE FORMATION

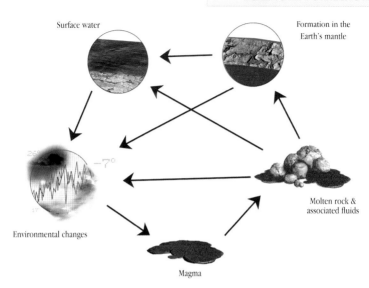

Surface water

Formation in the Earth's mantle

Environmental changes

Molten rock & associated fluids

Magma

While potentially confusing, it should be noted that some gemstone varieties are formed by more than one process.

Molten rock & associated fluids

Molten rock & associated fluids are minerals that are formed in the magma or its escaping fluids. They are created by heat, deep within the earth. Molten rock & associated fluids are further classified into magma crystallization, gas crystallization, hydrothermal and pegmatites.

Magma crystallization

As magma cools its various elements combine to form minerals. When one mineral forms, the available ingredients, temperature and pressure gradually change to create different minerals. While one mineral will occasionally crystallize nicely, if the conditions are not suitable, no crystals will form and the magma will simply cool into aggregate rocks (solid masses of small, interlocking crystals).

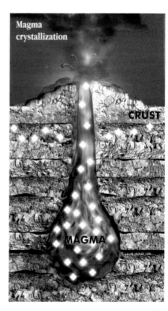

Magma crystallization

CRUST

MAGMA

159

GEMSTONE FORMATION

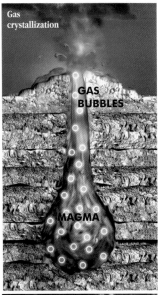

Before all the magma can crystallize it will break into the crust and rush towards the earth's surface. When the pressure and temperature are too low for crystallization, the rest of the magma cools into fine-grained rocks with the original crystals distributed in "phenocrysts" throughout the rocks interior. Gems formed in these conditions include Sapphire, Ruby, Moonstone, Garnet and Zircon.

Gas crystallization

While some gems grow on a solid base, others form inside gas bubbles. Gas bubbles are formed during a volcanic eruption when rising magma undergoes a rapid reduction in pressure. These bubbles often contain high concentrations of certain elements and with the right combination of temperature and pressure, gems including Garnet, Topaz and Spinel are formed.

Zircon, Rubies and Topaz are often created by gas crystallisation

Hydrothermal

Hyrdothermal liquids are created when water and heat interact with magma deep inside the earth. These liquids contain water, carbon dioxide, special elements (such as fluorine and beryllium) and volatiles (substances that are readily vapourised) that have escaped from the magma through fractures and fissures. Hydrothermal liquids may dissolve minerals or combine with ground water as they solidify and form mineral veins. If combined with the right temperature, pressure, time and physical space, gems including Amethyst, Topaz and Emerald are formed.

GEMSTONE FORMATION

Gems such as Emerald and Tourmaline can be formed by hydrothermal liquids

Pegmatites

When magma in the upper part of the mantle becomes concentrated with volatiles it cools into a cavity called a pegmatite. As the molten rock begins to solidify, the elements begin to crystallize into gems including Topaz, Tourmaline, Kunzite, Aquamarine and Morganite.

Environmental changes

Environmental changes, such as changes in temperature or pressure, can alter existing minerals into something new. This process is called metamorphism and it is divided into two types, contact metamorphism and regional metamorphism.

Contact metamorphism

Contact metamorphism occurs when magma forces its way into an existing rock. The intense heat melts these rocks and re-crystallizes new minerals that are stable at higher temperatures. Gemstones formed by contact metamorphism include Garnet, Diopside, Spinel and Lapis Lazuli.

Regional metamorphism

The earth is composed of continental plates that float on the mantle. As some of them compete for the same space, their interaction is responsible for the formation of geographic features such as mountains. The intense heat and pressure generated by these geological events can cause minerals to become unstable, changing them into new varieties over time. Polymorphs are gemstones that re-crystallize into a new crystal system during regional metamorphism. Examples include Andalusite, Kyanite, Sillimanite, Tanzanite and some varieties of Garnet. In contrast,

Pegmatites
CRUST
GEMS
MAGMA

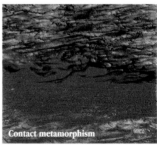

Contact metamorphism

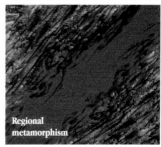

Regional metamorphism

161

GEMSTONE FORMATION

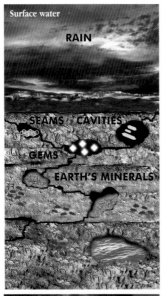

Surface water

RAIN

SEAMS CAVITIES

GEMS

EARTH'S MINERALS

Gems formed in the earth's mantle

MANTLE

MAGMA

pseudomorphs like Tigers Eye change their chemistry through atom-by-atom replacement during regional metamorphism.

Surface water

Rain plays an important role in recycling minerals and creating new gems. As water passes through the earth, it picks up various chemicals that can react with each other in a variety of ways. When a dry season occurs after a period of heavy rainfall, water tables fall, leaving behind deposits of different minerals in seams and cavities. Depending on what chemicals the water has reacted with, gemstones including Opal, Turquoise, Malachite, Amethyst, Agate and Azurite are created.

Opals, Amethysts and Agate are sometimes the bi-product of past rain falls

Gems formed in the earth's mantle

The earth's mantle is composed of molten rock and gases called magma. It is 83% of the earth's volume and 3,000 kilometers thick. Near the centre, the mantle is extremely hot and kept in constant motion due to currents of heat. Where the mantle and crust meet, a tumultuous zone of high pressure and temperature is created.

Peridot and Diamond are examples of gemstones that crystallize at extremely high temperatures. Peridot deposits in Arizona were created on rocks floating in the mantle, approximately 32 to 88 kilometers below the earth's surface. Diamonds crystallize in the magma 176 to 240 kilometers below the earth's surface where the temperatures are higher and the magma is very fluid.

GEMSTONE FORMATION

Diamonds, as well as Moonstones and Sapphires, can be created by magma crystallisation

GEM CRYSTAL PROPERTIES

Mammoth tusks over 10,000 years old are examples of organic gemstones

Tourmaline has a macrocrystalline structure

Jade has a cryptocrystalline structure

Gem crystal structures

All gemstones are broadly split into two categories that depend on their origin:

Type 1: Organic gemstones

These are gemstones that are natural materials which are formed by, or with the help of, organic life processes, such as animals or trees. Examples of organic gemstones are Pearls (from molluscs) and Amber (fossilised tree resin).

Type 2: Inorganic gemstones

This is by far the larger of the two categories. With virtually all other gem types belonging to this category; inorganic means no living organisms were involved in making the material. These gemstones come from an inorganic mineral origin. In simple terms, minerals are generally solid, inorganic, crystalline materials which are formed by geological processes.

Atoms and crystal structure

The earth consists of elements made up of countless atoms. Most of these atoms are in orderly, solid arrangements. Materials with such orderly atomic arrangements are said to be crystalline and each different atomic arrangement is called a crystal structure.

Most natural gem materials are crystalline – they possess crystal structure. Atoms bond together most efficiently as orderly crystal structures and they automatically try to pack into the most orderly structure possible. In simple terms a crystal structure is a regular, repeating, three-dimensional arrangement of bonded atoms.

Crystalline materials can be either:

1. Made from one single piece of crystal. Single-piece crystals are termed macrocrystalline. Most gemstones fall into this category, such as Ruby, Sapphire, Amethyst and Tourmaline.

2. Made up from a crystalline structure so fine that no distinct particles are recognizable under the microscope. Termed cryptocrystalline, examples include Jade, Agate and Chrysoprase.

Some of the resulting properties and phenomena from the possession of crystal structure include:

- Asterism (star effect)
- Chatoyancy (cat's eye effect)
- Colour Change
- Double Refraction
- Pleochroism

It is this possession of different crystal structures offered by many gemstones that gives them their unique properties. Without these unique properties, our ancestors would have never valued them as unusual, rare, desirable or beautiful and, in turn, today, without them, our gemstone choices would be very limited.

Asterism

Gemstones that show asterism include Corundum (Sapphires and Rubies), Almandine Garnet, Spinel, Quartz and Beryl.

Asterism or the star effect is caused by reflections from two or more sets of parallel fibrous or channel inclusions, orientated within a gemstone, which produces a "star" effect on the surface of the gem, when cut into cabochon in a certain orientation.

It is the crystal structure of the gem that arranges the symmetrical placement of the impurities, causing "asterism".

Some gemstones will produce this effect when:

(a) the inclusions are long ("needle-shaped");

(b) the inclusions are in parallel arrangements in at least two different directions;

(c) the inclusions are sufficiently abundant;

(d) the gemstone is cut in such a way that the top is curved and the base is parallel to the direction in which the inclusions lie.

The reflection takes the form of two or more intersecting lines of light, depending on the number of sets of parallel inclusions. The needles crystallise along the atomic planes at 120 degrees to each other, reflecting light back to the eye in a symmetrical and star like manner.

GEM CRYSTAL PROPERTIES

Cat's Eye Alexandrite uniquely demonstrates both colour change and chatoyancy

Asteric gem inclusions

Centre alignment   *Off centre alignment*

Star Diopside and Star Sunstone showing perfect asterism

Star Sapphire and Star Ruby proudly displaying their characteristics and highly coveted stars

GEM CRYSTAL PROPERTIES

Gems TV presenter Caroline Lyndsay (top) and Debby Cavill at the mine in Chanthaburi (only 7km from Gems TV's design centre). This is the only mine in the world where Black Star Sapphire is found.

The pride of Chanthaburi, a Black Star Sapphire

The quality and value of an asteriated gem is judged by:

1. The distinctiveness of its star
2. The length and degree of straightness of each ray
3. The strength & uniformity of the gem's colour
4. The position of the star
5. The gem's size and carat weight. However, in the cases this is done deliberately for artistic affect, particularly in non round cabochons

Asterism is most visible with direct light, such as a fibre-optic light, penlight or other single beam of light, including direct sunlight. With diffused illumination, the stars are not as distinct (often a problem under TV studio lights).

Chatoyancy

Chatoyancy, or the cat's eye effect, is a reflection which appears as a single bright band of light across the surface of certain gemstones, when they are cut as cabochons in a certain orientation. Again, chatoyancy is caused by reflection from oriented, long inclusions, when the inclusions are all parallel to one direction.

Gemstones will show a chatoyant reflection when:

(a) The inclusions are long ("needle-shaped");

(b) The inclusions are in parallel arrangement;

(c) The inclusions are sufficiently abundant;

(d) The gemstone is cut in such a way that the top is curved and the base is parallel to the direction in which the inclusions lie.

These inclusions may be either needles or fibres of other mineral substances, or they may be tube-like cavities. To reveal chatoyancy, the gemstone must be cabochon cut.

Gemstones with chatoyant varieties include Quartz (including Tiger's Eye), Alexandrite, Tourmaline and Beryl. These should not be described simply as cat's eye, but as Cat's Eye Quartz, Cat's Eye Tourmaline and so on.

Colour change effect

Colour change gems are gems that appear to change their colour when viewed under two different sources of light. It is important to understand that it is actually not the gem that changes colour, but the way the brain interprets the signal that it receives. Two of the most famous gems that feature this effect are Alexandrite and colour change Garnet.

The sensation of colour change in gems therefore depends upon certain basic requirements:

1. A source of white light

2. Suitable modification to this light

3. The eye and brain to perceive and interpret the light

The change in body colours are caused by the removal, by the gem material, of certain wavelengths of visible light from the white light. The remaining light waves leaving the gemstone are added together and interpreted by the brain as a single colour.

The light which we see mostly appears to be white. The human brain perceives it as a single colour. However, we know through science that white light is made up of the individual colours of the spectrum, its components are combinations of red, orange, yellow, green, blue and violet light.

Lights from different sources have different combinations or balances of these component colours. For example, pure, bright sunlight, has very strong blue components. Light from electric lightbulbs (incandescent light) seems, to our eyes, to be similar to sunlight but is actually far richer in red wavelengths.

Exactly how is the colour change effect caused?

When incident light enters a gemstone, it is usually white light. As the light passes through the gem, the gem absorbs some of the component colours of the spectrum. The resulting mixture of light that is "transmitted" to the human eye has been modified by the gem. The remaining mixture of wavelengths is "added up" by the brain to perceive a single colour.

GEM CRYSTAL PROPERTIES

Alexandrite is a very rare gemstone that under different light sources will demonstrate different hues

Colour Change Garnet is both beautiful and rare

167

GEM CRYSTAL PROPERTIES

Gems that absorb different light sources and then display different results are referred to as "colour change" gems

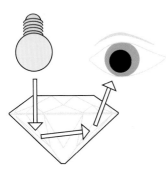

The lightbulb has more red waves than light from the sun

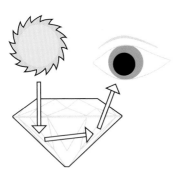

Sunlight features more blue waves.

This absorption of certain colours, or wavelengths, is called the "selective absorption of light". This selective absorption of light wavelengths is always consistent for an individual gemstone. It is this consistency to absorb specific wavelengths that causes our perception of the colour change effect when viewing an item under two different light sources.

The quality and value of a colour change gem is judged by:

1. The strength of the colour change seen

2. The distinctiveness and attractiveness of its colour under candescent light (e.g. sunlight)

3. The distinctiveness and attractiveness of its colour under incandescent light (e.g. most artificial light)

4. Clarity

5. Quality of the cut

6. The gem's size and carat weight

7. The gem's rarity in relation to its quality

Double refraction

Double Refraction is an optical "doubling" effect possessed by some gemstones. Gemstones that show double refraction are known as anisotropic gemstones. In these gems we see a "twin" image of features in the gem.

Double refraction is not valuable as an optical property to the jeweller or to the consumer – it largely goes unnoticed. However, to the gem dealer and gemmologist, double refraction is useful as an aid to identification.

Its two most useful applications are:

1. The distinguishing of Diamond from Moissanite – a very convincing Diamond simulant that shows distinct double refraction while Diamond does not.

2. The immediate identification of Zircon from other gems. Zircon has very strong and noticeable double refraction.

Double refraction has one very unusual side effect that greatly intrigued early man, and, indeed, today some people still find fascinating - pleochroism.

Pleochroism

Atoms in some gemstones are arranged in such a manner that light rays are split into two separate components. These two rays possess slightly different colours to each other. The effect to the eye is that a gem exhibits different colour tones when viewed from different angles. This property is known as "pleochroism".

Put simply pleochroism is a body colour effect, whereby different body colours are seen in different directions of the gemstone's body.

Examples of strongly pleochroic stones are Iolite, Tanolite¨, Tanzanite and Tourmaline.

Many gemstones are pleochroic, but the two component colours seen by the eyes are so similar that we tend not to think of them as being pleochroic even though they are.

Examples of weak to medium pleochroic stones are Ruby, Sapphire, Emerald and Chrysoberyl.

Some gemstones, due to their crystal structures, do not possess any pleochroism at all. This lack of pleochroism is extremely useful when making diagnostic tests on some gems. For example Ruby and Red Spinel share many similar characteristics and often the only way of distinguishing between the two are by pleochroic tests.

Notable examples of non-pleochroic stones are Spinels, Garnets and Diamonds.

GEM CRYSTAL PROPERTIES

The back facets of Moissanite. Clearly visible is the doubling of the facet lines, a feature that can never be seen in a Diamond

The back facets of a Diamond. No doubling of the facet lines is ever visible

"Doubled" facet edges and scratches seen through the gemstone

The above Tanzanite demonstrates strong pleochroism

FIRE, LUSTRE & BRILLIANCE

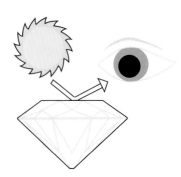

Lustre is the surface reflection of light

Due to their colour, Black Diamonds do not display the brilliance or fire usually associated with Diamonds - instead their colour accentuates an amazing lustre

In these earrings featuring Diamonds, it is the Black Diamond (circled) that displays the most visible lustre

Fire, lustre, brilliance and iridescence

These often-used terms to describe the visual appearance of the interaction between light and a gem are often misunderstood and even misused by some in the industry.

Put simply, reflection is the return by a surface of some of the light that falls upon that surface. Reflection from gem materials is never perfect. It depends upon the composition and condition of the reflecting surface.

Reflection in gemstones is divided into two categories

	Effects observed
1. External reflection	Lustre
2. Internal reflection	Brilliance
	Dispersion (fire)
	Iridescence
	Asterism & chatoyancy
	(See page 165)

Lustre

Lustre, defined by both gemmology and most dictionaries, is a "surface reflection effect". It is the amount of light that is reflected from a material's surface. The word "lustre" quantifies the reflective power of a material.

If nearly all of the light that falls upon a surface is reflected, resulting in a very bright reflection, the gem is said to have a "high lustre". It is similar to the reflection of the sun off a mirror.

If much of the light is absorbed by the material, resulting in a dull reflection, the material is said to have a "poor lustre". For example a brick would be said to have poor lustre.

The following terms are commonly used to describe the lustre of various gem materials:

Adamantine
Very bright, reflective, almost metallic lustre, as displayed by Diamond.

Sub-adamantine
Bright lustre, often from gemstones having high refractive indices such as Zircon, Ruby, Sapphire and Demantoid Garnet.

Vitreous

The lustre seen in polished glass, and in most transparent gemstones whose refractive indices fall within the middle range of values, for example Emerald and Tourmaline.

Resinous

Certain gem materials that are soft and have low refractive indices, like Amber, have a resinous lustre.

Silky

Some fibrous minerals such as Gypsum and Malachite have a silky lustre.

Metallic

This is the very high lustre shown by metals such as gold and silver, and by gem such as polished Hematite and Pyrite.

Pearly

Pearls are composed of crystalline layers from which light is reflected at and near the surface.

Brilliance

Brilliance is a combined internal and external reflection effect. Certain cutting angles allows the light to pass straight through the gem or to be deviated to the side. Accurate cutting to optimum angles will allow light to travel back towards the viewer when looking directly into the table facet.

Gems with low refractive indices (e.g. Quartz, Beryl, Iolite etc.) are not usually cut to show maximum brilliance as a very steep pavilion would be required. This would make the resulting gems too deep to be set into jewellery.

It is important to note that not all gems have the same optimal cut. Although it is true than many gems demonstrate optimal brilliance when cut to the same proportions as a perfectly "Round Brilliant Cut Diamond", other gem types benefit from either deeper or shallower pavilions. Optimising the cut (faceting) for each gem type is an art in itself. Gems that are not cut correctly, either through a lack of experience or due to the gemcutter aiming to maximise the carat weight, rather than extract maximum beauty, will mean that the gem will not display its optimum brilliance.

FIRE, LUSTRE & BRILLIANCE

Demantoid Garnet displays a bright sub-adamantine lustre

Malachite has a silky lustre

Amber has a resinous lustre

171

FIRE, LUSTRE & BRILLIANCE

Dispersion (Fire)

As light passes from one medium to another its individual colours or wavelengths are bent as they enter the new optical medium. Different wavelengths or colours are bent by different amounts.

The resulting effect to the eye is that the light no longer appears to be white, but appears as separate colours. As you move your head you see the colours change – this effect is known as "fire". Diamonds and Zircons are just two examples of gems that normally offer great fire. It is a desirable property and adds both beauty and value to a gemstone when it is present.

Iridescence

An important internal reflection effect caused by structural features is iridescence. Iridescence (play of colour) is a single colour, or a series of colours, produced by lightwaves suffering interference due to structural features or defects. Put simply, iridescence is a colour effect seen when light waves suffer interference, so that some colours are removed and others enhanced.

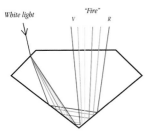

When a gem disperses different colours it is said to have "fire"

Different gemstones have a propensity to show different colours of iridescence. For example, iridescence in Opals (commonly called Opalescence) displays all colours while the iridescence in Pearls (commonly called the Orient) displays colours that are characteristically soft and delicate.

Opals often show an incredible amount of iridescence

Pearls have the ability to show a delightfully soft iridescence that provides an extra dimension to this gem of the sea

Steve Ashton, who is a TV presenter on Gems TV in the UK, has written the following section on mining techniques. To gain a better understanding of how gems are formed and then mined, all presenters on Gems TV have visited at least one gem mine on foreign soil.

In 2005, several of the UK presenters spent six weeks travelling the globe, visiting nine different countries and dozens of different villages and mines to bring back some stunning video footage. Here, Steve explains the basics of mining for gems.

Generally speaking, the gemstones you will see everyday on Gems TV are obtained from mother nature's treasure chest in one of two ways;

a) Host rock mining

b) Alluvial mining

a) Host rock mining

Mineral deposits can be found in different types of locations such as in underground caves (like Moonstone) inside mountains (like Tanzanite and Peridot) or embedded in other elements like Kimberlite (such as Diamonds) in the ground.

Got a craving for caving?

Some gemstones, such as Moonstone, can be harvested directly from underground caves. In the case of Moonstone from Tamil Nadu in Southern India, miners source this gem from mines and limestone caves spread out over a wide area near the village of Kangayam. Here the miners use Moonstone's characteristic shimmer or sheen to their best advantage. Shining flashlights on pegmatite feldspar veins, the illumination of light bounced back from iridescent Moonstone crystals quickly betrays their presence. The typical mining processes for collecting gems from these formations are similar to those used in ancient times - the pick axe and elbow grease.

MINING TECHNIQUES

Gems TV presenter filming at an alluvial mine

This boring technique is used in several countries to manually drill into the soil to hunt for gems

Steve Ashton sent underground in search of Moonstone

Environmentally friendly mining in Thailand

173

MINING TECHNIQUES

Steve Bennett meets a mine owner in Thailand

Gems TV presenter Matt McNamara shows a Sapphire mine returned to it's original beauty

Our team of buyers and presenters spend a lot of time in Tanzania

A Madagascan windlass mine from which several different gems were recovered

Mine every mountain......

Some of the most beautiful gems that you see on Gems TV come from digging into the side of a hill or mountain. Tanzanite is mined in this way. In the shadows of Mount Kilimanjaro in Northern Tanzania lie the Merelani foothills. Tanzanite is found in metamorphic rocks (these are rocks which have undergone a change in texture or composition as the result of heat and/or pressure) that belong to the Great Rift Valley.

Running at an angle of 41 degrees from the bowels of the earth to the surface, the deposit line (or strike zone) periodically folds over itself, creating richly coloured and concentrated pockets of Tanzanite.

To get to the Tanzanite, an "adit" is dug. This is an opening driven horizontally into the side of a mountain or hill for providing access to a mineral deposit.

Pipe mining

The mining of Diamonds can be used to describe the host rock principle very well.

Diamonds are mainly found in an area known as a primary deposit and occur near a "pipe". A pipe is a volcanic pathway that connects the earth's deep mantle to its surface. Diamonds are condensed carbon that succumb to extreme pressure and heat to form. They are carried upwards in the pipes amongst magma in volcanic eruptions. Because of the force of the eruption, the Diamond spends enough time to form but not long enough to burn up. The soil that surrounds these volcanic pipes comes in two distinct types, Kimberlite and Lamproite.

Since these eruptions occur mainly on a large scale, Diamond mines tend to be quite large. Initially, Kimberlite is dug from the surface of the pipe in rough, open-cast mines (big holes). Once the surface deposit has been exhausted, shafts are dug into the ground at the edge of the pipes and Kimberlite is extracted.

The way to get the diamond out of the "host rock" is by applying a little bit of science. Because Kimberlite is not very dense and Diamond is, essentially a "sieving" process is used (much like the pan mining techniques seen in good Western movies).

At the Cullinan mine in Pretoria, South Africa, they use a "sticky table", which is a table covered in grease that the Diamond rich Kimberlite stick to because of their density and the Kimberlite that contain no Diamonds, fall away.

When freed by erosion from the Kimberlite, Diamond crystals can be carried along by rivers. Riverbeds are dug away and the river silt is sieved. This technique is called "alluvial mining". "Marine mining" is the exploitation of sandy coastal strata by dredging. Finding Diamonds can thus be the result of large industrial operations, but also of small-scale methods or even manual labour.

b) Alluvial mining

Thousands and thousands of years ago, there were many more mountains than we see today. These mountains contained gemstones. Fortunately for gem lovers, Mother Nature did some of the mining hard work for us. Erosion of these "host rocks" meant that gems (such as Sapphires) were washed down into ancient riverbeds.

Much of the Sapphire you see on Gems TV is alluvially mined.

Typically, a miner will dig using either hand tools (on a small scale mine) or heavy industrial machinery. The earth is them taken to be washed. This is exactly how it sounds; the loose earth is blasted with water to get rid of the debris, leaving gemstones in the "wash". This wash is then trawled through to find the rough gemstones. It is an incredibly laborious and time consuming process that can from day to day, yield very little. It is extremely rare for miners to find an abundance of gemstones in any one day.

MINING TECHNIQUES

A Sapphire mine in Songea, Tanzania

Songea mine owner, Brad Mitchell scours the washed rough looking for Sapphires

Returning water to the river bed after mining in Songea

175

MINING TECHNIQUES

Sieving the washed gemstones

Mining for gems in Songea

Understandably, some of the mines that we visit are so secretive about their location that we can't always reveal their whereabouts

Work starts at sunrise at the Songea Sapphire Mine

History

The oldest known mine in the archeological record is the "Lion Cave" in Swaziland. At this site, which has a radiocarbon age of 43,000 years, men and women mined for the iron-containing mineral Hematite, which they presumably ground to produce the red pigment, ochre.

Sites of a similar age were found in the Netherlands and Hungary and may have been worked for flint for weapons and tools.

Another early mining operation was the Turquoise mine operated by the ancient Egyptians at Wady Maghareh on the Sinai Peninsula. Turquoise was also mined in pre-Columbian America in the Cerillos Mining District in New Mexico, where a mass of rock 200ft in depth and 300ft in width was removed with stone tools; the mine dump covers 20 acres.

Environmental mining

Gems TV strongly believes in only working with environmentally friendly mine owners.

For example, in Songea, in the Ruvuma river region of Southern Tanzania, the mine owner, Brad Mitchell, suffers from freelance miners digging on his mine. They destroy trees and excavate dozens of holes everyday in search of the wonderful Songea Sapphire. It is a condition of his license that he leaves the area exactly as he found it. Brad ensures every hole is filled, more trees are planted than are removed and that the landscape is left in an even better condition than when he arrived. This is the kind of person Gems TV deals with. Just one example of environmentally friendly gem mining, at the Bang Ka Ja mine in Thailand, the story is the same and, all over the world, Gems TV works with mines that are conscious of the environment. Many countries ensure conditions such as this are adhered to, sadly some do not.

FACETING & GEM CUTS

Cutting (also know as Lapidary) is the process whereby a rough stone is turned into a gemstone. The process makes a gem assume a certain shape, bringing out its lustre and colour, enabling it to be set into jewellery.

Apart from a polish, early gems were often set almost as they came out of the ground

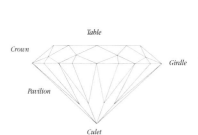

Unlike Diamonds, coloured gems possess variable optical properties and are not cut to a uniform ideal. A well-cut coloured gem exhibits even colour, an acceptable number of inclusions, good brilliance and shows the majority of carat weight when viewed from the top.

Broadly, the styles of gem cutting can be divided into faceted gems (gems with geometrically shaped flat polished faces) and non-faceted gems (those gems that do not have geometrically shaped flat polished faces such as Cabochons).

The cut of a gemstone largely depends on the shape of the gem rough (the shape of the raw gem as it comes from the earth). For perfect and beautiful rough coloured stones, the oval cut is generally the number one preference, as it maximizes beauty. Factors to consider when choosing to facet a gem in another shape include design aesthetics, inclusions and colour.

Round Brilliant cut

Gem cutters are considered "experts" once they have 2 years of experience and on average can facet 30 gems per day.

Round Brilliant cut

Round is from the Middle English word "rounden", which means "secret".

The Round Brilliant cut is also known as the Round cut, American Ideal cut or American Standard cut.

The standard number of facets of a Round Brilliant cut gemstone is 57.

Although no single inventor has officially been credited with the invention of the Round Brilliant cut, many sources do credit a Venetian cutter named Vincenzio Perruzzi and date the Brilliant's introduction to the 18th century.

The Russian mathematical genius Marcel Tolkowsky, a member of a large and powerful Diamond family, subsequently calculated the cuts necessary to create the ideal Diamond shape. As part of his PhD thesis in mathematics, Tolkowsky considered variables such as the index of refraction and covalent bond angles to describe what has become known as the Round Brilliant cut.

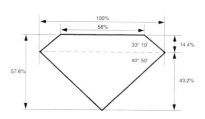

The above dimensions are the normal measurements for a Round Brilliant cut Diamond

177

FACETING & GEM CUTS

Tolkowsky's recommended cut height for a Round Brilliant is 58% that of the diameter of the Diamond, which breaks down to about 43% for the pavilion, and 14% for the height of the crown. This 58% is probably the most crucial dimension of the gem.

This cut is optically the most efficient. The Round Brilliant boasts one of the best recoveries for well shaped Diamond and gemstone rough; this translates into good value for consumers.

The Round Brilliant cut is designed to provide maximum optics for brilliance and scintillation, making the gem sparkle and dance in the light.

This cut was specially developed for Diamonds but is today common for all gem types.

Oval cut

Oval is from the Latin word "vum" meaning "egg".

The standard number of facets of an Oval cut gemstone is 69.

The Oval cut has an elliptical shape when viewed from the top.

For the Oval cut, the ratio of the length to the width should be approximately 2:1, although this does vary slightly depending on the optical properties of different gem types.

A well cut Oval gemstone can be nearly as bright as a Round Brilliant cut.

The Oval cut is a particularly beautiful shape and if well proportioned gives great scintillation and fire.

Baguette cut

Baguette is from the Italian word "bacchetta", meaning "rod or stick".

The approximate number of facets of a Baguette cut gemstone is 20.

The Baguette shaped gemstone is really only a special oblong shape.

Most oblong cuts are "step" cut, which means that the facets on the pavilion have been cut in steps, parallel to the edges, in the manner of a pyramid with its top chopped off. The base and table are square with triangular facets.

The Baguette cut best suits gem types that have rough in this shape such as Tourmaline.

To the Native American Navajo, the rectangle

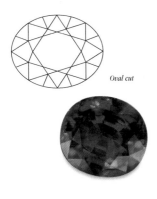
Oval cut

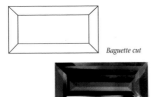
Baguette cut

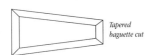
Tapered baguette cut

FACETING & GEM CUTS

symbolizes the female form, intelligence and divine contemplation.

Square cut

Square is from the Vulgar Latin word "exquadra" meaning "square shape".

The standard number of facets of a Square cut gemstone is 57.

The Square shaped gemstone is really only a special oblong shape where the sides are the same length.

Most oblong cuts are "step" cut, which means that the facets on the pavilion have been cut in steps, parallel to the edges, in the manner of a pyramid with its top chopped off.

Some believe this cut is a symbol for equality, fair mindedness, justice, order, satisfaction and truth.

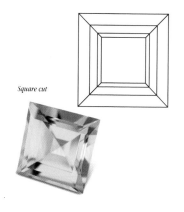

Square cut

Trilliant cut

The standard number of facets of a Trilliant cut gemstone is 43.

Trilliant cut gemstones are based on a triangular shape. Usually with truncated corners and displaying a variety of facet designs, this cut creates a spectacular wedge of brilliant fire.

The tips and culets of Trilliants are pointed and thin. Some jewellers only bezel-set Trilliants, though prongs that protect the tips work well and show more of the gem.

As you look down through the gem, the culet generally appears centred in the middle of the table showing the pavilion of the gem with an attention to symmetry. When you examine the gem in profile, the girdle and table facet are generally parallel. The pavilion's main facet usually extends from the culet perpendicularly until it intersects the girdle.

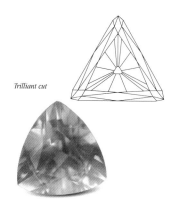

Trilliant cut

Because of their equilateral form, Trilliants return lots of light and colour. They are considered nearly as brilliant as Round cuts, so they are a great choice for customers who like brilliance but want something other than round. Variations include rounded-corner triangles, modified shield cuts and triangular step cuts.

There should be as few polishing marks as possible and the surface should appear glossy and reflective. Good polishing helps maximize brilliance and scintillation in Trilliants.

Trilliants work well with light-coloured gems – such as

FACETING & GEM CUTS

Opal in its natural rough state before any cuts are made

Diamonds, Aquamarines, Beryl's and White Sapphires – where cutters try to maximize brilliance.

Inversely, some cutters use Trilliants to effectively lighten and brighten the appearance of darker gems such as Tanzanite, Spessartite Garnet, Rhodolite Garnet and Amethyst.

First developed in Amsterdam, the exact design can vary depending on a particular gem's natural characteristics and the cutter's personal preferences. It may be a traditional triangular shape with pointed corners or a more rounded triangular shape with 25 facets on the crown, 19 facets on the pavilion and a polished girdle.

Did you know? Some twinned (a crystal growing within a crystal) Diamond rough is naturally triangular (called "Macle") and is ideal for Trilliants.

Pear cut

The standard number of facets of a Pear cut gemstone is 71.

A hybrid cut, combining the best of the Oval and the Marquise, it is shaped like a sparkling teardrop.

A nice Pear cut is generally one that is well cut with a polished girdle.

Although it varies depending on the optical properties of each gem type, Pear cuts should generally have a good depth such as 1.5:1 aspect ratio for a great look and a lively gem.

For rings, this cut compliments a hand with small or average length fingers. It is particularly beautiful for pendants and earrings.

Colour also shows fairly dramatically in a Pear cut gemstone.

Did you know? The world's largest cut Diamond (the Cullinan I mounted in the British Royal Sceptre) is a Pear cut.

Pear cut

Octagon cut

The standard number of facets of an Octagon cut gemstone is 53.

This is another "step" cut but with the four corners metered. The facets run in steps parallel to the gemstone circumference. This cut is differentiated from the Emerald cut by steps on the pavilion that are not equidistant.

Octagon cut

With this cut, colour plays a very important role in the beauty of the gemstone. Colour tends to show very dramatically in Octagon cut gemstones.

Emerald cut

The approximate number of facets of an Emerald cut gemstone is 50.

What does it look like? The Emerald cut looks like a rectangle from the top, with truncated corners. These can be beautiful gemstones with stepped facets; the sheen tends to display large flashes of these stepped angles on the pavilion of the gem.

Emerald cut

This is another "step cut" and it has rows of facets that resemble a staircase and usually are four-sided or elongated. It is known as a step cut because its concentric, broad, flat planes resemble stair steps.

The Emerald cut is differentiated from the Octagon cut by its equidistant steps on the pavilion.

The flat planes of the outside edges allow for a variety of shapes. Generally, the length-to-width ratio should be 1.5:1 to 1.75:1.

With this cut, colour plays a very important role in the beauty of the gemstone. Colour tends to show very dramatically in Emerald cut gemstones. The Emerald cut was developed specifically for Emeralds to reduce the amount of pressure exerted during cutting and to protect the gemstone for chipping. Today, modern cutting techniques make this less important and it is used for a wide variety of gem types.

Marquise cut

The standard number of facets of a Marquise cut gemstone is 57.

The Marquise cut is also known as the "Navette" shape and looks like a long oval that has been stretched out to a point at each end like a rugby ball viewed straight down from the top.

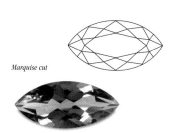

Marquise cut

The general ratio of length to width should be 2:1. It is important that the Marquise cut gem not be too shallow or light will pass through the back of the gem diminishing its brilliance and colour. However, as with all coloured gems, this can vary from type to type.

Marquise cut provides good brilliance and colour.

It is gorgeous when used as a solitaire or when enhanced by smaller gems.

Did you know? The Marquise cut was inspired by the

FACETING & GEM CUTS

fetching smile of the Marquise de Pompadour and commissioned by the Sun King, France's Louis XIV, who wanted a Diamond to match the smile.

Antique Cushion cut

Antique is from the Latin word "antquis", meaning "classic".

The approximate number of facets of an Antique Cushion cut gemstone is 64.

The Antique Cushion cut is also known as "The Old Miner" or "Old European" cut, because it looks like a cross between a deep cut with large facets that was common in the late 19th and the early 20th centuries and a modern Oval cut. As it looks somewhat like a sofa cushion, the word "Cushion" is typically used in combination with "Antique" but not exclusively.

Antique cushion cut

This shape is also sometimes referred to as the "Pillow" cut (for obvious reasons) or the "Candlelight" cut in reference to cuts designed prior to electric lights, when gems sparkled in the light provided by candles.

It has a marvellously romantic and classic look that stands out from other cuts.

Along with the Princess cut, the Antique Cushion cut maximizes a gem's lustre.

It is a primary cut first used on Ruby and Sapphire faceted in Ceylon (Sri Lanka).

Princess cut

The Princess cut generally has 76 facets.

The Princess cut, technically known as the "Square Modified Brilliant" cut, is a square version of the Round Brilliant cut with numerous sparkling facets.

Depth percentages of 70% to 78% are not uncommon.

The Princess cut is a "Brilliant Style" shape with sharp, uncut corners. The "Brilliant Style" refers to the vertical direction of the crown and pavilion facets.

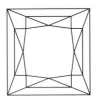

Princess cut

It is a relatively new cut and often finds its way into solitaire engagement rings. Flattering to a hand with long fingers, it is often embellished with triangular stones at its sides. Because of its design, this cut requires more weight to be directed toward the gem's depth in order to maximize brilliance.

The advantages of the Princess cut are not restricted purely to Diamonds; it is also used on many other

FACETING & GEM CUTS

gemstones.

Because of the extra faceting, and the effects this produces, Princess cuts are naturally more brilliant and sparkly.

The Princess cut generally works best with lighter coloured transparent gemstones.

Along with the Antique Cushion cut, the Princess cut maximizes a gem's lustre.

The Princess cut was designed for weight retention of octahedral Diamond crystals, helping to create more attractive Diamonds at more reasonable prices.

The Barion cut was the forerunner of the Princess cut and was invented about 30 years ago by Basil Watermeyer of Johannesburg. The Barion cut has been the subject of patents that have expired within the past ten years and this has led to the greater availability of similarly cut gemstones. The style now known as the "Princess" cut has become a generic style of cutting.

According to Harold Newman's "Illustrated Dictionary of Jewellery", the term Princess cut was previously applied to what is now known as the "Profile" cut developed by Arpad Nagy of London in 1961.

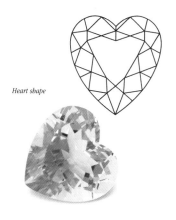

Heart shape

Heart shape

The standard number of facets of a Heart Shape cut gemstone is 59.

The Heart Shape is a pear-shaped gemstone or Diamond with a cleft at the top.

Generally, a Heart Shape's length to width ratio is slightly over 1:1, approximately 1.1:1 in favour of length, but usually not over 1.2:1.

The heart is the ultimate symbol of love.

Most Heart Shape cut gems are nearly round. This has the advantage of having a nearly round pavilion that provides beautiful brilliance.

Most Heart Shape cuts are purchased as single gems. Solitaire rings are set with hearts throughout the range of sizes. After necklaces and rings, most Heart Shape cuts are sold as matched pairs for stud earrings. The primary market for Hearts is for luxury jewellery. There is heavy interest in the Heart Shape cut in the Far East.

Hearts must be extremely well cut which makes them more expensive because excellent proportions result from a greater expenditure of rough. Understandably, noticeable increases in sales of Heart Shape cut gems

Gems TV's air conditioned and natural light cutting rooms are very different to the working conditions witnessed at some independent cutting houses

A Gems TV cutter preparing the initial cut on Amethyst

FACETING & GEM CUTS

The rough cut gem is fastened to a "Dob Stick" in order to be faceted

Over 50 facets will be added to this gem all by hand

The surface of the wheel is covered in Diamond dust to finish the faceting process

Gems TV presenter Lynn Garnett with Gems TV's highly skilled gem selectors who sort the faceted gems

occur around Valentine's Day.

As with all Fancy cuts, buyers of Hearts should look first at the overall make. The first question to ask is "do I find the gem pleasing to the eye?"

Generally, look for a balanced shape, avoiding extremes. Lobes should be rounded, and the cleft should be relatively sharp and distinct.

Briolette cut

From the French words "Brilliant" (brilliant or sparkling) and "Brignolette" (a small dried plum). A Briolette is a pear shaped gemstone covered with facets that comes to a pointed end.

The approximate number of facets of a Briolette cut gemstone is 84. The more facets the drop has, the more brilliant it is.

The Briolette cut is a drop-shaped gemstone with triangular or diamond shaped facets all the way around. There is no table, crown or pavilion. Considering the shape of the Briolette, it is the most difficult to cut. Because of the specific number of cuts to show the facets, the Briolette cut requires perfection from top to bottom.

A cutter can only cut and polish 5-10 Briolette gemstones per day.

The Briolette is a type of Rose cut, which dates back to the 14th century or earlier. No one knows for certain how old the Briolette cut actually is. There are rumours of Diamonds cut in India during the 12th century exhibiting this style of cutting. The Briolette is a relatively rare Diamond cut and far more common for coloured gemstones.

Briolette gems are found in antique and estate jewellery from the Victorian, Edwardian and Art Deco eras.

Briolette gems are increasing popular in fashion jewellery.

Briolette cuts are set in earrings, necklaces and pendants. They are also included in tiaras in antique or estate jewellery.

They are often used for earrings with a hanging wire or a simple precious metal cap, sometimes with a small Diamond accent. Briolettes have been featured in many industry publications and also in Vogue and Harper's Bazaar.

Most Diamond Briolettes are cut from white rough,

but coloured Diamond Briolettes, especially Fancy and Canary Yellows, are becoming more popular, followed by Cognacs and Champagnes. Again, it is very popular for coloured gemstones.

Every Briolette is unique, so look for beauty. Look for well-cut gemstones that have lots of brilliance. But as odd cut ones can also display brilliance, it is ultimately up to the individual.

FACETING & GEM CUTS

Briolette cut

Fancy cut

For those who want something really different, recent advances in cutting technology have produced a breathtaking range of innovative new shapes such as flowers, clover leaves, stars, triangles, kites and all manner of Fancy cuts.

Some of the new designs are variations on standard shapes, aimed at creating the illusion of a bigger, more perfect gemstone. Others play with the natural rough and still others are fashioned into revolutionary new shapes.

The important fact to remember is that this ever-widening choice of shapes and designs is being created to suit a variety of individual styles and tastes. No one cut is more beautiful than another. The magic of nature and the artistry of the cutter combine to make each a unique work of art.

Due to its bright transparent clarity, Rhodolite is often cut into Fancy cuts

Cabochon cut

The word Cabochon is derived from the old Norman French word "caboche", meaning head.

A Cabochon is a polished gemstone with a flat-bottom (or slightly rounded bottom) and a convex or rounded domed top. The traditional Cabochon is an Oval but Cabochons can also be fashioned into other shapes including Triangles and Rectangles.

Cabochons, commonly known as Cabs, are the oldest and most common form of gem cutting. Gems cut "en Cabochon" are shaped and polished, rather than cut. In antiquity, this was generally the only cutting option available other than using the gem with the natural facets of their crystal structure. Some of the most beautiful ancient jewellery was made with Cabochons, including astounding Royal East Indian jewellery and the breastplate of Aaron.

Cabochons are used for making jewellery, often carved as intaglios (a gem carved in negative relief) or cameos (a gem carved in relief), and are also used in

Cabochon cut

FACETING & GEM CUTS

Buff Top cut

Millennium cut

Concave cut

Mirror cut

crystal healing. Today, the Cabochon cut is applied to gems of limited transparency (Turquoise, Jade, Agate etc.) or as a result of predominate inclusions (relatively opaque Sapphires, Rubies or Emeralds) or for gems where the cut's curved surface accentuates special characteristics (iridescence, chatoyancy or the cat's eye effect, asterism or the star effect).

Buff Top cut

A Cabochon variant for transparent gems, the Buff Top cut mixes a Faceted cut with a Non-Faceted cut. This results in a gem with the typical domed top of a Cabochon and a faceted pavilion, giving the illusion of depth as the eye is drawn into the centre of the gem. The cut shows good brilliance and has a crown that is less easily abraded than those of faceted gems.

Millennium cut

Possessing an incredible 1,000 facets, the Millennium cut is so named as it was created by Rogerio Graca around 1999 as a unique and challenging symbol of the new millennium.

While sometimes confused with the Concave cut, the Millennium cut is easy to spot as it creates a gem packed full of facets.

One Millennium cut gem equates to approximately 18 times the amount of work of other cuts. Having 624 facets on the pavilion and 376 facets on the table, each facet has to be touched from one to four times during cutting and polishing.

The amount of time involved, combined with the design particularities (rough selection, keeping a degree of sharpness between each facet, making enough space for each facet etc.) and the need for precision cut machinery, eliminates the possibility of the Millennium cut ever becoming mainstream.

Concave cut

The Concave cut is a three dimensional conical shaped facet applied to the pavilion of the gem that creates depth as well as length and breadth. Instead of the facets being joined by an angle they are joined with a groove. This third dimension allows the gem to refract more light, thereby maximizing its brilliance. The Concave cut also distributes light more evenly, giving the gem a homogeneous interior glow.

While it is sometimes confused with the Millennium cut it can be easily distinguished by the lack of a standard number of facets and its application only to the pavilion.

While Doug Hoffman patented Concave cut technology in the early 1990's, his friend Richard Homer is credited as perfecting the technique of the Concave cut. While working towards a Geology Degree, Homer began cutting gems in 1974 to help pay his tuition. Since then, his designs have won 15 American Gem Trade Association (AGTA) Cutting Edge Awards.

Not all gems benefit from the Concave cut. Optimizing colour and light is always the first consideration in cutting gems, and although Diamonds and lighter toned gems increase up to 100% in brilliance when Concave cut, darker gems like Rubies can appear murkier and less attractive. Another disadvantage of the Concave cut is that it is significantly more expensive than traditionally cut gems. This is due to the higher weight loss and the additional labour required.

Mirror cut

The Mirror cut is characterized by an extraordinarily large table and thick girdle consisting of as much as 90% of the width of the gem. This makes the gem highly refractive and literally gives it the properties of a mirror, hence the name.

Sometimes referred to as the "Thin Stone", the Mirror cut was an early 16th century phenomenon that is making a comeback. It is a variety of the Round cut and appears in the names of some historic Diamonds including the "Mirror of Portugal" and the "Mirror of France".

FACETING & GEM CUTS

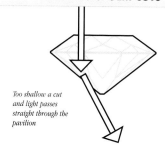

Too shallow a cut and light passes straight through the pavilion

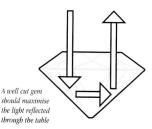

A well cut gem should maximise the light reflected through the table

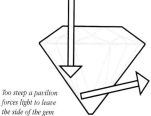

Too steep a pavilion forces light to leave the side of the gem

This Spinel gold ring features uncut gems

FACETING & GEM CUTS

*This particularly beautiful
Brazilian Kunzite is oval cut
and has 69 facets.*

Skilfully merging art and science, a variety of techniques are used to help gemstones reach their full potential. Critical as good cutting, treatments are an integral part of the modern gemstone industry. With its roots in antiquity, most of the treatments used simply facilitate the beautiful end results of the earth's natural processes. Below are some answers to common gemstone treatment and care questions. For more information on gemstone enhancements, treatments and care, please visit www.GemsTV.com.

Is the use of treatments globally accepted?

With close to 99% of the more popular gem types treated, all permanent treatments are universally accepted. As the majority of gemstones traded internationally have undergone some form of treatment, always assume treatment when purchasing gemstones.

Are all treatments permanent?

With the exception of Emeralds, whose beauty is enhanced by the application of colourless oils or polymers, Gems TV only knowingly accepts treatments that are permanent with normal wear. Our information sources for gem treatments includes university mineralogical, gemmological and geology departments, gem laboratories, trade associations, regulatory bodies, professional journals, books, the internet and individual experts.

Does treatment affect a gem's value?

For some varieties there is no difference between the value of treated and untreated gemstones. However, high quality unheated Rubies and Sapphires are extremely rare and command a much higher market price. When purchasing Rubies and Sapphires, please be aware that unheated material is almost non-existent, as a result, always purchase from a reliable supplier or have the seller's claim verified by a gemmologist.

GEMSTONE TREATMENTS

Are All Gemstones Treated?

No, the following list includes gemstones that are NOT treated:

Ambyglonite	Magnesite
Anatase	Manganotantalite
Andalusite	Marcasite
Anglesite	Mawsitsit
Apophyllite	Moldavite
Aragonite	Monazite
Axinite	Montebrasite
Barite	Moonstone
Bastnaesite	Natrolite
Bloodstone	Nuummit
Boracite	Obsidian
Brazilianite	Oligoclase
Burbankite	Pectolite
Bustamite	Pezzottaite
Calcite	Phenakite
Cassiterite	Pollucite
Celestite	Prehnite
Charoite	Pyrite
Chrysoprase	Pyroxmangite
Cinnabar	Remondite
Clinohumite	Rhodochrosite
Danburite	Scheelite
Datolite	Scolecite
Diospore	Sellaite
Diopside	Senarmontite
Dolomite	Shortite
Dumortierite	Siderite
Enstatite	Sillimanite
Eosphorite	Sinhalite
Epidote	Smithsonite
Euclase	Sphalerite
Eudialyte	Sphene
Fire Beryl™	Spinel
Gahnite	Staurolite
Garnet	Sugilite
Hauyne	Sunstone
Hematite	Tanolite™
Hemimorphite	Tremolite
Herderite	Tugtupite
Idocrase	Unakite
Iolite	Vesuvianite
Kornerupine	Villiaumite
Kyanite	Wilsonite
Larimar	Wulfenite

GEMSTONE TREATMENTS

Without heat treatment there would be no Tanzanite!

How do I care for my gemstone jewellery?

Caring for your gemstone jewellery (i.e. normal wear) is a matter of common sense and simple precaution.

Always remove your jewellery when engaging in activities that risk impact or exposure to chemicals or heat such as sports or housework.

Always put jewellery on after using cosmetics, hair spray or perfumes, not before.

Never remove your jewellery by pulling on the gems.

Never store your jewellery in heaps and always store your gem necklaces flat. The best way to store your gemstone jewellery is in the separate compartments of a jewellery box or in cloth pouches.

Carefully wipe jewellery with a soft lint free cloth after each wearing to remove oils and salts.

Once in a while, take the time to clean your jewellery. Always clean your jewellery with a cleaning solution or mechanical cleaner suitable for its gems.

How are some popular gemstones treated? Below are the treatments used for some popular gemstones.

Gemstone	Treatment & Explanation
AMETHYST	Heated. *Used to lighten colour and/or to remove smokiness, this treatment is only occasionally applied.*
APATITE	Heated. *Usually applied, this treatment improves appearance and/or deepens colour.*
AQUAMARINE	Heated. *Used to remove yellow components to produce a purer blue colour, this treatment is occasionally applied.*
CITRINE	Heated. *Usually applied, this treatment produces colour.*
DIAMOND (COLOUR ENHANCED)	Irradiated. The process known as Colour Enhancement involves using clean Diamonds and modifying their colour with a combination of electron bombardment and heat using safe electron-accelerator technology. This process exactly duplicates the natural exposure of Diamond crystals to radioactive elements during their formation. *Used to improve colour intensity or to produce unique colours, this treatment is always applied.*
EMERALD	Colourless Oil or Polymers. *Usually applied, this treatment improves appearance. Periodically, enquire if they need to be re-oiled.*
JADE	Dyed. *Rarely used, this treatment improves colour and uniformity.*
KUNZITE	Heated or Irradiated. *Commonly applied, this treatment improves and/or darkens colour.*
MORGANITE	Heated. *Commonly used, this treatment eliminates yellow overtones.*
PEARL (CULTURED)	Bleached, Dyed or Chemically Enhanced. *Occasionally used, these treatments improve colour and uniformity.*
RUBY & SAPPHIRE	Heated Occasionally With Additives. *Usually applied, this treatment produces, intensifies or lightens colour and/or improves colour uniformity and/or appearance. Examples of the additives used include Beryllium (a light element) to improve colour and Borax or Lead (i.e. glass) to improve appearance.*
TANZANITE	Heated. *Almost always applied, this treatment produces the colours for which this gem is known.*
TOPAZ (EXCEPT WHITE)	Irradiated, Heated or Coatings. *Used to improve colour intensity or to produce unique colours, this treatment is usually applied. Physical Vapour Deposition (PVD) coating involves the application of a bonded layer of fine titanium atoms (USA Patent Number 5,853,826 for Azotic Coating Technologies Inc.). When this oxide treatment falls within a certain thickness, optical interference produces a variety of colours.*
TOURMALINE	Heated or Irradiated. *Used to improve colour intensity, this treatment is commonly utilized for blue green colours and only rarely applied for other colour hues.*
ZIRCON (BLUE & WHITE)	Heated. *Used to improve colour, this treatment is always applied.*

THE GEM SUPPLY CHAIN

The supply chain in the coloured gem industry is extremely long – longer than the Diamond supply chain. It is not uncommon for a gemstone to pass through 7 and 10 pairs of hands from the mine to the consumer. By any industry standard, this is an extremely long and inefficient supply chain – although the price keeps going up, other than at the cutting and setting stages, there is no real "value add" being applied to the gem.

A busy gem trading hall full of brokers, agents and dealers

On its passage through so many pairs of hands, it is not uncommon for a coloured gemstone to increase in price by up to 1,000%! For example, this means a £200 Tanzanite gemstone from Tanzania may end up selling for £2,000 in the jewellers window and this does not even include the other jewellery components. Once you factor in labour, gold and Diamonds, our Tanzanite that started at £200 could end up retailing in a shop window for a whopping £4,000!

A gem dealer selling gems by their carat weight

The typical pairs of hands a coloured gemstone will pass through from the mine to consumer are highlighted below:

The supply chain - loose gem	Position sale prices (£ per Carat)
1. Miner	£100
2. Broker	£150
3. Cutters	£225
4. Wholesalers (Thailand)	£375
5. Wholesalers (USA/Europe)	£600
6. Retailer	£700
7. Consumer	£1,000
The final consumer pays 1000%	**£1,000**

At Gems TV, our aim is to remove as many of these stages as possible.

CARAT WEIGHT EXPLAINED

A 2.709 carat "one of a kind" Alexandrite ring sold on Gems TV for £2,497 in September 2005

Fifty six individual 12 point Alexandrites in a beautiful handcrafted bracelet sold on Gems TV for £897 in September 2005

Carat weight

The weight of a gem is measured in carats (ct). Unfortunately this is easily confused with the measurement for the purity of gold which is also a karat (k). The name "carat" dates back to ancient times, when gems were measured on scales against the "carob bean". The carob was used as they had a very consistent weight.

At the end of the 19th century, the carat weight measurement was internationally standardised at a fifth of a gram. Gemstones under 1ct are measured in points. A 50 point gemstone can also be referred to as a half a carat and a 25 point can be referred to as a quarter of a carat.

How does carat weight affect price?

Generally speaking, if you take two gemstones with different carat weights, but with similar cut, clarity and colour, the one with the higher carat weight will be valued higher. However, if the cut has been compromised in order to obtain maximum carat weight, a reduction in beauty might reduce the value of the gem.

With rare gemstones such as Alexandrite, Tanzanite, Ruby, Diamond and Sapphire, a 1ct gemstone in one piece is more valuable than say five 20 point gemstones of the same colour and clarity. Although the combined weight of the five gemstones is still 1ct, the rarity of a singular 1ct gem is much greater, thereby demanding a far higher price.

Take, for example, a 16ct Ruby sold at Sotheby's in New York in October 1988 for a staggering $3,630,000! If pricing was linear, that would make a similar 1ct Ruby worth $226,875!

The only exception where the combined weight of smaller gems might cost more than a singular gem of the same carat weight is where the cost of labour in applying all of facets to the individual gems outweighs the difference in gem price.

If you are buying a gem with a rounded carat weight, make sure that the quality of cut has not been compromised to achieve this rounded number.

JEWELLERY DESIGN

Mike Matthews, Vice President Product Development (UK), joined the Gems TV UK Design Team when he realised the potential of reaching many people with real gemstone jewellery. Bringing with him a wealth of jewellery design experience, Mike won the UK Jewellery Awards in 1999 and was runner up in a worldwide jewellery design competition set by Italian Vogue.

"Jewellery design is both an art form and surprisingly, a science. Inspiration and ideas can come from the most unexpected sources at the most unexpected times. This is one of the reasons I never go anywhere without a pad and pencil. The science part comes when you have to transform the idea into not only a beautiful looking, but also a practical and comfortable piece.

I always try and design jewellery that looks as stunning on as it does in a jewellery box, on the television or in a shop window. In my 22 years designing jewellery for many people all over the world, this has been the single most challenging part of my job. It's all very well seeing a piece on Gems TV and falling in love with it - what I must do is make sure it looks and feels as good when you first take it out the box and put it on. I try and make sure you will never want to take it off. As well as this there are many other factors that I have to take into account. Firstly, the gem I am working with can quite often heavily influence the look of the finished piece. For example, if I am working with Amethyst or Citrine (two of my favourite gems) I can really afford to push the boat out on the design front. Unusual cuts, exaggerated shapes, mixed metals - you name it. The reason being they are both affordable everyday gems. That's why I love them. Having said this, I always ensure that the gem is still the headline act.

If I am working at the other end of the scale, maybe with Paraiba Tourmaline, Alexandrite or AAAA Tanzanite, then the gem really does do the talking. This is where the important part is not what you put into the design, but what you leave out. As a designer I try and look at the shape of the main gemstone and design the jewellery to lead the eye

Mike Matthews designing more Gems TV jewellery

18K AAAA Tanzanite & Diamond White Gold Pendant and (below) the earlier design sketches

JEWELLERY DESIGN

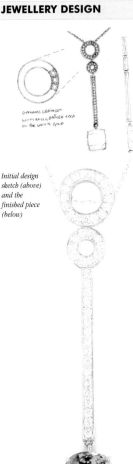

DIAMONDS GRAIN SET
WITH MILLGRAINED EDGE
IN THE WHITE GOLD

Initial design sketch (above) and the finished piece (below)

towards it - maybe using subtle diamonds or just the shape of the gold. When working with gems as rare and important as these, the ultimate sin for a jewellery designer is to direct attention away from the main gem.

Either way, I always work very closely with our highly skilled master craftsmen in Thailand, to make sure that all our designs are not only stunning, but also technically viable. This is the science part. We need to ensure that the gemstone will be secure in the particular design, that we take into account the weight of the piece so it is comfortable and unobtrusive, or in the case of earrings, that they hang from the ear correctly and are just weighty enough to retain a tactility whilst still being easy to wear.

Influences can come from diverse sources. For example, the way rock pools form by the sea, with their smooth organic shapes making the light play, right through to the noise of a sports car going through a tunnel. Both grab your attention, but in totally different ways. That's what well designed jewellery should do - grab your attention so you react in a way that makes you feel good.

The designer is the link between the gifts that nature gives us in the form of gemstones and the highly skilled artisans that make the designer's ideas a reality. It's an important job - and also one of the best."

Mike Matthews
Vice President Product Development (UK)
Gems TV (UK) Ltd

Our mission

Our mission is to make genuine gemstone jewellery affordable and available to everyone.

Focusing on the quality of the jewellery that we craft, we aim to provide value to our customers through the use of efficient processes, innovative, educational and entertaining sales channels, and effective customer service.

Who is Gems TV?

Gems TV is one of the worlds largest vertically integrated suppliers of high quality gemstone jewellery. By retailing our own handcrafted jewellery direct to consumers via DRTV (Direct Response Television) and the Internet, Gems TV has become a revolutionary industry leader.

Gems TV is a privately owned business with a jewellery workshop in Chanthaburi, Thailand and dedicated jewellery shopping channels broadcasting to over 10.7 million homes from Redditch, UK. We employ over 1,300 individuals, all of whom are passionate about the jewellery we produce.

Our vertically integrated business model removes complex traditional supply chains and allows us to provide the best value possible to our customers. Combined with our low cost operating environment, we make genuine high quality gemstone jewellery affordable and available to everyone.

JEWELLERY MAKING

The sign of quality gemset jewellery

We employ over 1,300 dedicated gem fanatics in Thailand

195

JEWELLERY MAKING

In the UK watch Gems TV 24 hours a day on Sky Guide 646, ntl channel 177 and Telewest channel 755

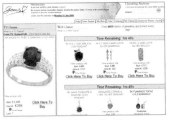

In Europe visit our website www.GemsTV.com

You can also watch Gems TV 24 hours a day on Sky Guide 660, ntl channel 179 and Telewest channel 756

In America and Asia visit our website www.Thaigem.com

Gems TV is truly a unique company created through the merger of Thaigem Holdings Limited, one of the world's leading gemstone and jewellery suppliers, and Eagle Road Studios Limited (ERS), a television shopping network and creators of "Snatch It ™", our proprietary reverse auction selling mechanism.

Established in the early eighties, Thaigem started as a traditional gemstone wholesaler in the gem-hub of Chanthaburi, Thailand. In 1998, Thaigem began to experiment with online sales which resulted in extremely rapid growth. By 2003, Thaigem had opened a state-of-the-art jewellery handcrafting workshop. Translating their expertise in gems into jewellery, Thaigem quickly capitalized on the benefits of vertical integration and soon became a major supplier of handcrafted jewellery to television shopping networks around the globe.

Commencing operations in 2004, ERS was the brainchild of the founders of Jungle.com and Software Warehouse PLC. ERS quickly grew into one of the UK's most successful television shopping networks by focusing on high levels of customer service. ERS owns and controls almost every aspect of their business, including a 23,400 square feet complex (housing two fully equipped TV studios, a dedicated sound studio, call centre and onsite warehouse), state-of-the-art broadcasting technology, two dedicated 24 hour digital TV channels, and proprietary sales and management software. ERS also developed and owns their "Snatch It ™" reverse auction selling mechanism. This dynamic mechanism is a captivating alternative to the stale, traditional "talking heads" approach to television shopping, offering viewers a truly interactive television shopping experience.

Launched on 8 October 2004, Gems TV was an overnight success and soon dwarfed the other business activities of Thaigem and ERS. On 12 June 2005, the two companies merged and now operate as one global organization under the name Gems TV Holdings Limited.

You can experience Gems TV, our handcrafted jewellery and engaging edutainment on Sky Guide (Channel 646 & 660), ntl (Channel 177 & 179), Telewest (Channel 755 & 756), www.GemsTV.com and www.Thaigem.com.

How do we buy gems?

First impressions might lead you to believe that Chanthaburi is typical of any provincial town in eastern Thailand. Silhouettes of Buddhist temples break through the ornate skyline of traditional Thai houses while the narrow streets below echo to the sound of market vendors selling fruits, vegetables, animals and… minerals. Make no mistake, inconspicuous Chanthaburi is the "Gem Capital" of Southeast Asia and home to the Gems TV workshop.

A town steeped in gem lore, Chanthaburi has been a centre of gem mining and cutting in Thailand for generations. Chanthaburi first gained its gemstone reputation as early as 1407 when the intrepid Chinese traveller Ma Huan wrote of a special place near Chanthaburi where hundreds of families sold bright clear Rubies. In 1868 the famous French explorer Henri Mouhot said, "precious stones of good quality are found in the mountains around Chanthaburi".

Several nearby mining areas flourished from the 19th century including Khao Ploi Waen, Bang Kha Ja, Nong Bon, Bo Rai and Ban Bo I Rem. At their peak in the late sixties, these mines yielded fine quality Sapphires, Rubies, Black & Gold Star Sapphires and Zircon, making Chanthaburi's gem market a hive of activity.

As Chanthaburi's mines neared depletion, the local industry developed extensive overseas supply networks for rough gems. Thanks to its skilled artisans, Chanthaburi continues to garner international recognition as a global headquarters for coloured gemstone production and trading. For the gem connoisseur, there is nowhere on Earth like Chanthaburi. The inventory of gems that find their way onto brokers' tables in its unique Gem Market reads like a who's who of the coloured gemstone world: Garnets, Rubies, Blue Sapphires, Fancy Sapphires, Tourmalines, Tsavorites and Zircons, to name but a few.

Known specifically for its expertise in processing Rubies and Sapphires, Chanthaburi is responsible for processing more than 80% of the world's supply of these gemstones. If you own Ruby or Sapphire jewellery, there is a very good chance your gems once visited Chanthaburi.

By nurturing contacts in the key gem markets of Madagascar, Sri Lanka, India, Brazil and East Africa, Gems TV has accumulated intimate knowledge of key gem producing and trading countries. This puts Gems

JEWELLERY MAKING

Nearly all designs are drawn by hand and not with computer systems

Head of Business Development Theo van Dort discusses jewellery design with one of our designers in Thailand

Attention to detail is critical when designing our handcrafted jewellery

197

JEWELLERY MAKING

Steve Bennett, the Managing Director of Gems TV Europe learning about colour matching

A large batch of gems being colour sorted

Only gems from one colour band are used in each design

Gems TV presenter Matt McNamara learns how Rubies are colour graded

TV in the unique position of being able to acquire certain rare gems that are often unattainable in the open market.

Our global contacts aside, the single biggest reason that we are able to offer such a large variety of gemstones is our location in Chanthaburi. Gems TV is positioned at the beginning of a supply chain that has traditionally seen gemstones suffer up to a one thousand percent mark-up on their journey to the consumer. As the biggest gem buyer in Chanthaburi, we often get a first look at any gemstones in the local market. This is one of the reasons our prices (and quality) consistently beat the competition.

Sourcing gems from over 40 countries, Gems TV currently stocks over 490 different gem varieties making our gemstone inventory one of the worlds most diverse.

Handcrafting jewellery: guided tour

The Gems TV jewellery workshop accommodates all aspects of both silver (925 Sterling) and gold (9K, 14K and 18K) handcrafted jewellery creation, including gem faceting, gem matching, design conceptualization, master model construction, wax injection, casting, jewellers (pre-finishing), gem setting, polishing & plating and quality assurance.

Cutting out the middlemen means that we continue the tradition of handcrafting high quality jewellery but on a larger scale. Due to the efficiencies of our business, we continuously sell our handcrafted jewellery direct to the public, at prices substantially below those that travel a convoluted route from bulk manufacturers to the eventual consumer.

Appreciating that people are individuals, we never produce huge numbers of one particular design, instead preferring to craft true "Limited Editions". With over 490 gemstone varieties to choose from, our artisans create over 70 new jewellery masterpieces everyday.

Gem cutting & gem matching

Completely reliant on the eyes and hands of skilled professionals, expert faceting and matching for size and colour is critical in ensuring that the key ingredients in a gorgeous handcrafted piece of jewellery, the gems themselves, really shine!

Before being set in jewellery, qualified professionals carefully examine each gem, separating them according to their clarity, colour, cut and carat weight. With satisfaction as our highest priority, Gems TV invests tremendous effort towards ensuring that only the highest quality gems are perfectly matched before being set into a stunning array of handcrafted jewellery designs.

JEWELLERY MAKING

We still use traditional methods to stretch gold

Design conceptualization

With a rich and varied colour palette, using hand drawing and computer aided design, our design team expertly creates beautiful designs to complement the gemstones we have unearthed from mother nature.

One of the design department's key responsibilities is to ensure that the designs are correctly communicated to the master model makers and in the process of finishing, checked for design correctness and manufacturing suitability.

Handmade jewellery

For smaller quantities, the jeweller literally starts with an amount of gold and then cuts, shapes, heats and stretches it into the final jewellery. For larger quantities, we make an original masterpiece and then cast the required quantity of pieces from the master, finishing them all by hand.

Many of the handcrafted pieces start from gold bars or grains. The jewellers are given the correct amount for the design and then alloy is added to create 9K, 14K or 18K gold. The first step is to soften the gold to make it easier to craft. To do this, the jeweller uses an atmosphere control melter to heat the gold to a temperature of 1,025°C.

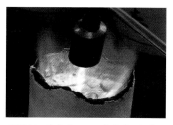

Gold being melted to form a one of a kind masterpiece

For some designs, rather than starting with nuggets of gold, the jeweller starts with a length of gold that is already shaped into a round rod. The equipment we use to stretch the gold to the correct thickness is traditional and the skills have been passed on many generations. Once the gold has been heated and cut into a rough state, the jeweller then starts to shape the body of the ring. This art is fascinating to watch, as within minutes you see a flat piece of gold transformed into jewellery by artisans whose only tools are their hammer and a wealth of experience.

The body of a ring starting to take shape

JEWELLERY MAKING

A craftsman removes the wax from the rubber mold

Wax molds are thoroughly checked before being cast

A tree of wax rings being put into the cylinder

Master model construction

When handcrafting larger quantities, we use a wax molding technique to construct the first step of the ring. The master model making workshop comprises two sections - silver model makers and wax carvers. Their expertise is diverse and includes everything from simple prong set and lightweight gemstone jewellery designs to artistically crafted masterpieces. These craftspeople are of critical importance, as their ability to turn a one dimensional drawing into a three dimensional master model is vital in ensuring that the finished jewellery exceeds all expectations. As with the old carpenters adage, measure twice cut once, all our master models must be exactingly precise, as any mistakes at this stage are going to appear in the finished jewellery.

Our designers, model makers and jewellery teams work closely together to ensure the very best results are achieved.

Wax injection

The wax injection department comprises of four sections: rubber mold making; wax injection; quality control & repair; and wax tree preparation. While the wax injection team carefully works with pre-set wax injection machines, the rubber mold makers understand the importance of correctly prepared rubber molds for improved wax injection. Down the line, the quality control team ensures wax pieces are cleaned and in proper condition for casting.

While all this sounds very complicated, the handcrafting process is actually very simple. From a drawing we produce either a silver or wax master model. Once we have a master model, we make a mold of these in rubber. We then use these rubber molds to make multiple wax copies. Once these have been checked to ensure they are perfect (remember, each of these will be a piece of handcrafted jewellery after casting, any mistakes here will show up in the finished design), the individual wax molds are placed on a tree ready for casting.

Casting

At the Gems TV jewellery workshop, the casting room includes the complete array of equipment for handcrafting jewellery, including investment preparation facilities, curing ovens, vacuum casting, a high water pressure investment cleaning area and waste water disposal facilities. With the right experts controlling this process, the very best results are achieved ensuring minimal complications for other processes further down the line. Again, like wax injection, the process itself is actually very simple. We simply put the tree of wax molds in a cylinder, pour in ceramic cement (i.e. investment powder), heat up the cylinders until the wax melts out, pour in the gold or silver in a vacuum to ensure every crevice is filled, wait till the metal sets, crack & clean away the investment and our handcrafted jewellery is well on its way to taking shape.

After casting, everything else is done by hand - the rings are carefully prepared for gem setting

Jewellers (pre-finishing)

Once removed from the casting tree, the pieces of jewellery, while starting to take shape, have a while to go before they look like the gorgeous handcrafted creations you see on Gems TV. Our jewellers carefully prepare and assemble the jewellery components ready for gem setting, all the while understanding the finishing needs for each individual design. In the case of bracelet assembly, the components are all assembled by hand with the only high technology employed being laser welding for superior strength. As with all stages involved in handcrafting jewellery, an imbedded quality control team approves every handcrafted piece before they are transferred to the next stage.

Gem setting

The gem setting team employs carefully selected gem-setters with abilities in both quality and quantity setting; true craftsmen and women, they handset an average of 150 gemstones per day per person. Gems TV have successfully produced a multitude of handcrafted jewellery designs featuring a wide variety of gemstones. Having a proven record with gemstone setting, Gems TV continuously ensures that the highest quality standards are met, while breaking new ground in both the types of setting and the gems within them.

Polishing & plating

At the polishing stage, we ensure that the best shine and finish are achieved but not at the expense of essential design details. This is done by careful separating individual polishing needs. When plating is required, plating specialists apply a carefully calculated

Rubies being set into a pendant

The last step before quality assurance is to polish the jewellery

201

JEWELLERY MAKING

Every single piece of our handcrafted jewellery is quality assured before leaving Thailand

Certificate of Authenticity

Item No: 60642

18K Paraiba Tourmaline White Gold Pendant

After quality control, your certificate of authenticity is produced

formula of rhodium or gold plating with an emphasis on both colour and brightness.

Quality assurance

Quality assurance at the Gems TV jewellery workshop encompasses two areas. The first being quality control teams that check each step of the handcrafting process and secondly, the final quality assurance after polishing. The successful implementation of quality control teams has helped minimize and eliminate problems downstream, and plays a key role in maximizing the quality of our handcrafted jewellery. The final product approval is done by quality assurance professionals with years of experience in the creation of high quality handcrafted jewellery. By working closely with quality control teams embedded in each department, they ensure quality standards always exceed expectations. This method ensures that suggestions and improvements are easily implemented throughout the creation of our handcrafted jewellery, where and whenever required.

Corporate citizenship

Employing over 1,200 in Thailand, our working conditions are equal or better than those of UK manufacturers. For those who have visited Thailand, you will know that it is the land of smiles. The smiles in our workshop are there for three good reasons: the working environment is of a high standard; the pay is good; and most importantly, the whole team is free to express themselves through the jewellery they create.

Gems TV is also at the forefront of education, sponsoring the Chanthaburi Polytechnic College's "Jewellery Production Course". This intensive tertiary course is made all that more practical by our workshop supervisors' regular guest lectures.

All our high quality handcrafted jewellery is presented in stylish and protective packaging

JEWELLERY SETTINGS

Most jewellery is crafted from individual components. The pieces are often created on the jewellers' bench and then skilfully joined. The components needed in most types of jewellery are incredibly simple. Even the most expensive tiffany-style Diamond ring features just three pieces - the band of the ring, the gallery that mounts the claws, and then finally the jewel itself.

With a few peripheral components such as earring-posts, chains, and hinges (often known as "findings"), these basic components are used to make everything from solitaire and gem-set rings, to earrings, necklaces, pendants and more complex pieces. While the claw setting is the most frequently seen method of setting gems and diamonds, there are a variety of other methods also used to set jewels in precious metals.

Claw setting - What does it look like?

Claw set

Also known as the Prong setting, the Claw setting has small metal claws with a vice-like grip that are bent over the girdle of the gem to ensure its secure and enduring position.

Typical Claw settings have 4 claws. Claw settings with 6 claws are also called the "Tiffany" setting because it was originally developed by the founder of Tiffany & Co. in 1886. Marquise and Trilliant cut gems can respectively have just two or three claws at the corners where the points of the jewels are nestled in specialized v-shaped claws.

The claws must always be equal.

The visible claw ends are often rounds, ovals, points, V-shapes (usually called "chevron"), flat and sometimes formed into ornamental shapes (usually called "enhanced prongs").

Why is this setting used?

As all gemstones are suitable for Claw setting, it is the most frequently used method of setting gems into jewellery because the claws are easier to adjust to the size of an individual gemstone.

Claw setting brilliantly shows off the gemstone, since the gemstone is positioned higher and is more easily seen.

Claw setting is especially popular for solitaire engagement rings and in bridal rings. When combined with Pave setting, Claw settings are considered to be the most suitable for women as this setting is more feminine, especially for designs with smaller shoulders

JEWELLERY SETTINGS

Bezel set

Pave set

and smaller gemstones.

Claw setting is best for earrings, necklaces, bracelets and rings.

The more claws, the more secure and safe your gemstones will be!

Bezel setting - What does it look like?

A Bezel setting is a crafted diskette of metal that holds the gemstone by its girdle to the ring, securely encircling the entire circumference of the gem. An age old technique that can appear very contoured and modern, it is labour intensive and must be crafted to precisely circumnavigate the outline of the gem.

Variations of the Bezel setting are the "Flush" or "Gypsy" settings. The surface of the ring has a window cut into it that exactly fits the size of the gem. Secured from underneath, the crown of the gem rises from the ring beautifully catching rays of light.

When the setting half surrounds the gemstone it is called a "Half-Bezel" or "Semi-Bezel".

A Bezel setting needs to be balanced and straight, from angle-to-angle. Gemstones cut with sides and angles are considered difficult, while Oval and Round are easier.

Bezels can have straight, scalloped edges and can be moulded into a gemstone of any shape.

Why is this setting used?

A Bezel setting protects the edges, the girdle and the pavilion of the gemstones.

Bezel setting adds height, dimension and a great modern look.

Bezel setting is best suited to people with active lifestyles. Bezel settings are considered the best for men because this style of setting looks masculine, especially when the designs have BIG shoulders and BIG gemstones.

Bezel setting is best for earrings, necklaces, bracelets and rings.

Pave setting - What does it look like?

Pronounced "pa vay", Pave setting is a Claw-like setting. They are so small they are barely visible. The claws are triangular in shape and are usually handmade.

The settings are created by use of tiny prongs that hold the jewels on both sides, or are crafted by scooping beads of precious metal out to hold the gems in place.

Why is this setting used?

Pave settings produce a carpet of brilliance across the entire surface of a piece of jewellery. The surface is encrusted, or quite literally "paved" in diamonds and gems, and the body of the jewellery is brought vibrantly to life.

Pave setting displays an illusionary bigger look using multiple gemstones.

Pave setting is usually combined with other gemstone settings to add more effect and beauty.

Pave settings are best for Diamonds. Pave setting is often used in conjunction with white gold, which further creates an effect of the whole piece of jewellery being crafted from Diamonds.

Pave setting is best for Round, Oval, Princess, Emerald, Square and Baguette cut gemstones.

Channel setting - What does it look like?

A setting technique whereby gemstones are held side-by-side with their girdles held between two long tracks of precious metal. When used with Square, Princess and Rectangular shaped jewels, the effect is breathtaking as no metal appears between the jewels - they appear to float in a tightly bejewelled chain within the jewellery.

The gemstones in Channel setting are set closely together so that no gold between the gems is necessary. This produces the maximum amount of light and brightness from the gemstones and allows the jewellery to keep looking bright for a long time.

In Channel setting it is very important gemstones with precisely cut pavilions are used, if not the gemstones will crack or be lost!

Why is this setting used?

Channel setting is quite often used in commercial jewellery designs. Often seen in eternity bands and tennis bracelets, gemstones are held side-by-side by their girdles between two long tracks of precious metal.

Channel setting is best for Diamonds and for Round,

Channel set

JEWELLERY SETTINGS

Bar set

Oval, Princess, Emerald, Square and Baguette cuts.

Channel setting is best for rings and bracelets.

Bar setting - What does it look like?

These are short bars that run like a railway track across a ring. Gemstones are individually set between these bars leaving the sides of the gemstones exposed to light.

An increasingly popular setting style, this technique maximizes the amount of light entering the gemstones creating superior brilliance and sparkle.

The Bar setting is a version of the Channel setting and can often combine a contemporary and classic look in one design.

Bar setting is best for Diamond rings and for Round, Oval, Princess, Emerald, Square and Baguette cuts.

A selection of settings for Fire Opal rings

Gold

Long considered the most precious of metals, gold is deeply woven into the very fabric of human culture. It captures our imagination and has inspired numerous legends and myths throughout the course of history. Gold has been treasured, hoarded, coveted and lavishly bestowed upon people, temples and objects of worship.

Responsible for creating global currencies, starting wars, toppling empires, causing mass migrations and more, gold has helped shape the course of human history - it is a metal that we are inextricably bound to.

Untarnishable and un-corrodible, it is the most malleable of metals, yet remains miraculously strong. While its rich lustre has long influenced the affairs of state and religion, its primary use remains within the realms of personal adornment.

Frequently featuring as an integral part of antique and modern jewellery's numerous different forms, purchasers should be aware of what gold varieties are on offer and why. The following will shed some light on this ancient metal's application in today's marketplace.

Gold purity

Pure gold is relatively soft and, as a consequence, has durability problems. Ornate pieces of jewellery can be bent, and expensive gemstones can be lost from their settings. This unacceptable tendency of pure gold has largely given rise to the modern gold we find in the jewellers' window today.

Virtually all gold featured in jewellery today is alloyed with secondary metals that enhance its everyday durability. These gold alloys are so frequent, that, in many countries many people find the colour of pure gold peculiar!

However, not all gold purities are the same. The different purities of gold alloys used by jewellers give consumers varying options regarding gold colour, affordability and durability.

Gold purity is measured in karats. While the term "karat" may sound identical to the term "carat", which is used to measure weight in gemstones, the two terms do not have the same meaning. Karat ratio in gold tells you the percentage or proportion of gold purity. Gold with a higher karat ratio, is comparatively more expensive gram for gram when compared to

Gems TV presenter Scott Worsfold holding over a kilo of pure gold at our workshops in Thailand

Gold nuggets being mixed with other alloys to produce 9k gold

A gent's ring with over 10 grammes of 9k yellow gold

PRECIOUS METALS

Yellow gold is still the most popular in Europe

Palladium is mixed with gold to create white gold

Traditional yellow gold remains hugely popular in Europe

Above ground stocks of gold in 2004

Central banks and supernational organisations hold just under 1/5th of all mined gold

gold with lower Karat ratios. Expressed as a ratio of 24 parts, the most frequently seen gold purities are:

22 karat:	91.6%	Pure gold
18 karat:	75%	Pure gold
14 karat:	58.5%	Pure gold
9 karat:	37.5%	Pure gold

Gold colours

Gold comes in a number of different colours offering consumers a wide choice when buying this lustrous precious metal:

Yellow gold: Displaying a timeless colour, yellow gold is the most popular gold colour. It is usually alloyed with copper and silver.

White gold: Harder than yellow gold with a bright lustrous white colour, white gold is most commonly alloyed with palladium. Palladium, a rare and expensive precious metal, increases the value of white gold to above that of yellow gold.

Rose gold: Mostly alloyed with copper, this increasingly popular gold type has a striking pink to reddish hue.

Gold sources

Gold is mined in only a handful of countries. In terms of output, the main sources are South Africa, USA, Australia, Canada, China, Russia, Peru and Indonesia.

Gold as an investment

Due to the popularity of gold, it has been used to both purchase goods and exchanged for goods for thousands of years. Even until the early 1900s, gold reserves formed the basis of the world monetary systems. Even today, a huge proportion of the world's gold, is held in government reserves. When you purchase gold jewellery, although you are not guaranteed that you will ever make a profit on your acquisition, you are assured that you have gained something with intrinsic value.

Silver

With a rich history stretching back some 5,000 years, like gold, silver occupies a hallowed place in our collective history. From the age-old Sumerian city of Ur, to the ancient Americas, to Greco-Roman culture and the ancient Far East, silver has been used by nearly all global cultures over the last two millennia.

Sharing much in common with its more glamourous counterpart gold, silver is also most frequently used for personal adornment.

PRECIOUS METALS

Silver purity

Like gold, pure silver or fine silver is relatively soft and malleable. As a result, painstakingly crafted jewellery and other objects can be easily damaged if created from pure silver. As a consequence, silver is commonly alloyed with secondary metals, usually copper, to create a more durable precious metal.

Silver is extremely popular and is mainly used for fashion jewellery

Sterling Silver is the standard for beautiful high-quality silver jewellery and other objects d'art. It's 92.5% pure silver and is alloyed with secondary metals for added strength and durability. Unlike gold, but like platinum, silver purities are expressed as units of 1,000 parts. The most regularly seen silver purities are:

958: 95.8% pure silver, also known as Britannia silver.

925: 92.5% pure silver, also known as Sterling silver.

Platinum

Sixty times rarer than gold, platinum is only found in a few locations worldwide - Russia's Ural Mountains, South Africa's Merensky Reef, and a few small mines in the USA. and Canada. Relatively new to the jewellery market, platinum is fast becoming incredibly popular and is already a bedrock of the contemporary jewellery landscape. Purer, stronger and denser than gold, platinum is considered by many to be the ultimate and most luxurious of all the precious metals.

Silver in its rough nugget form

Platinum purity

Platinum purity is expressed differently than gold. Instead of expressing purity in ratios of 24 parts, platinum standards are expressed as units of 1,000 parts. The most regular platinum purities seen are:

950:	95%	Pure platinum
900:	90%	Pure platinum
850:	85%	Pure platinum

British hallmarks for silver

Sterling silver   *Britannia silver*

HALLMARKING

A platinum engagement and wedding ring designed by Gems TV

The Assay Office scrape a sample of gold to test for purity

Technology is increasingly being used to back up the historical method of cupellation to confirm gold purity

Hallmarking is used in several countries around the globe to protect the public against fraud and traders against unfair competition.

Introduced in 1327, it represents one of the earliest forms of consumer protection. In the UK, a hallmark consists of three compulsory marks which give you the following information:

• Who presented the jewellery (i.e. sponsor or makers mark).

• What is its guaranteed standard of purity.

• What Assay Office tested and marked the jewellery.

It is a British legal requirement to hallmark all items that contain over 1 gramme of gold, whereas with silver it is a requirement to hallmark all items containing over 7.78 grammes.

Another way Gems TV goes just that little bit further in making your jewellery special is in the application of a date symbol at the Assay Office. In the past, it was a legal requirement to add a symbol to the hallmark to show the year that the item was hallmarked. Today, this requirement has been removed. However, Gems TV continues to have the additional mark added to the hallmark. The reason that we do this is that we believe it adds extra value to the piece in years to come.

Imagine the feeling your great grandchildren will have when looking at the hallmark and being able to use the Internet to identify the year the jewellery was marked.

Sponsor or maker

This shows the person or company responsible for sending the jewellery to the Assay Office. The sponsor may be the manufacturer, retailer, importer, etc. In our case you will find the marks "GTV", which shows it is a genuine Gems TV product.

Assay office mark

There are four British Assay Offices, Birmingham (Anchor), Edinburgh (Castle), London (Leopard's Head) and Sheffield (Rose):

Birmingham

Edinburgh

London

Sheffield

Standard marks

These show the standard of fineness, the purity of the precious metal, in parts per thousand.

9 karat

14 karat

18 karat

22 karat

HALLMARKING

The Assay Office sometimes use lasers

Gems TV jewellery receiving its official stamp

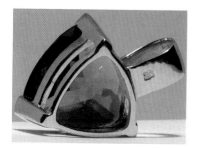

TOP 9 TIPS

Watch out for Diamond imitators such as Cubic Zirconia and Moissanite

A vivid coloured Chrome Diopside ring

9 Tips to buy gems and jewellery

One of the best ways to ensure that you are getting great value when collecting jewellery is to always purchase from Gems TV!

However, we do appreciate that if you are looking for a particular gemstone that for some reason we temporarily cannot source, you might want to use other jewellers in order to expand your collection. Here are our top nine tips to help you judge the value of your potential purchase.

1. Make sure it is the real thing!

"There is no fraud or deceit in the world which yields greater gain and profit than the counterfeiting gems." (Pliny the Elder in his Historia Naturalis, 1st Century AD).

The fraudulent selling of fake gems and fake gold is unfortunately as widespread today, as it was in the 1st century AD. Compounding the problem is the introduction of lab generated gems that are very difficult to distinguish from the real thing. There are many books written on the subject and the Internet is becoming a very useful tool in providing more information on identifying the real thing from the impostors.

Take Diamonds for example. We recommend that you only buy Diamond jewellery from reputable jewellers. Be aware that several man made substitutes such as Cubic Zirconia and Moissanite are very difficult to detect with the naked eye. The Gemmological Institute of America's website (www.gia.edu) offers good advise on spotting Cubic Zirconia and Moissanite.

2. Colour

Study the colour of the gem and if possible make comparisons to others. While vivid, saturated, deeper colours are generally more highly prized, colour preferences are ultimately up to personal taste. The best colour for any gemstone should be obvious from several metres away.

3. Carat & clarity

Larger gems are more highly prized than small ones and gems with fewer and smaller inclusions are generally more highly prized than those with more numerous and larger inclusions.

However, please remember that sometimes inclusions increase the value of a gemstone or are a common natural characteristic.

For example, fine inclusions that cause star or cat's eye effects increase the value of a gem and inclusions in Emeralds (see page 48) are a common feature that show the gem's natural relationship with the Earth.

TOP 9 TIPS

A 26ct Swiss Blue Topaz which has near perfect clarity

4. Cuts

Well cut gems of good symmetry, attractive design and fine polish are more prized than poorly cut gems. Regrettably, some gemstones, such as Ruby and Emerald, are often poorly cut in order to maximise weight at the expense of their appearance.

5. Rarity

Rare gems are more highly prized than more common varieties. However, if the gem is so rare that it is essentially unknown to the general public, its value suffers and it is relegated to the status of a "Collectors' Gem".

Gems such as Bracite, Cildrenite, and Simpsonite are extremely rare, attractive and durable, but don't command prices appropriate to their rarity, because there are currently few people who are aware of them.

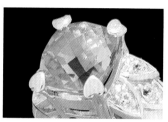

At Gems TV we believe that the quality of the cut is paramount

6. Historical connotations & origin

While there are exceptions, gemstones that are rich in history and folklore are generally more prized than those lacking historical connotations. When specifying an origin, Gems TV undertakes a series of checks based on our experience to ensure that a gemstone displays the characteristics indicative of the origin specified. While Gems TV does everything possible to ensure that the origins we specify are correct, gemstone origin is considered a matter of opinion.

Goshenite, whose siblings include the well known Emerald and Aquamarine, is a rare member of the Beryl family

TOP 9 TIPS

A brass bracelet gold plated and fraudulently sold as 18k gold

7. Is it real gold?

Plated gold is sometimes sold as real gold. If a street vendor offers you gold jewellery at a price that you feel is unbelievable, then it probably is! Remember that seeing 9K or 18K engraved on jewellery does not guarantee that it is real gold. If you are in a country where there is an official government stamp, such as the United Kingdom or Switzerland, then ensure that the correct stamp has been applied (see page 210).

Don't do a Barry! Even our Managing Director's assistant Barry has been caught out when buying gold. While on holiday he was offered a bracelet that was stamped 18k (see picture on the left) but when he had it checked back in the UK, it was found to be gold plated brass.

8. Guaranteeing weight

Check with the jeweller whether the weight of gold and the carat weight of the gems are an average or are guaranteed. If they are only an average, you should ask the salesperson "what is the range". In most countries, respectable jewellers will be aware of the range of tolerances used by their suppliers. If you are unsure about your gram and carat weight, ask the retailer to put into writing what they will guarantee.

9. Insurance

Don't assume that your jewellery collection is automatically insured by your household policy. It is always wise to take photos and catalogue all of your jewellery. Try and keep all your receipts and get as much written details as possible from the retailer. If your catalogue is a hard copy, make sure you take a photocopy and keep the second copy at a friend's house or as some collectors do, leave a copy with your family lawyer or solicitor. If your catalogue is a soft copy on your PC, make a copy of the data and keep it in a different location.

Certificate of Authenticity

Item No: 60676

18K Ceylon Padparadscha Sapphire
Gold Ring

MTGW: 2.067ct
Metal Type: 18K Yellow Gold
Approx Metal Weight: 2.74g
Gems Name(s): Ceylon Padparadscha Sapphire
Gem Shape(s): Oval
Gem Size(s): 4.5x3.5mm
Gem Piece(s): 7
Gem Weight(s): 2.067ct
Origin: Sri Lanka

• This certificate guarantees the authenticity and quality of this handcrafted jewellery.

• As gemstones are nature's creations, no two gemstones are absolutely identical. Therefore, the gem weight specified on this certificate is the Minimum Total Gem Weight (MTGW) used to create this jewellery design. Your specific handcrafted piece will most likely contain a higher gem weight.

• A permanent record of this certificate is retained for verification purposes.

• From mythology to gemmology, learn about more gemstones and jewellery, including their characteristics, history, legends and proper care at www.GemsTV.com.

Gems TV (UK) Ltd., PO Box 12016, Redditch, 097 9RI
Phone: 0845 63 88 663 Fax: 01527 406 136 Email: customercare@gemstv.com
Sky Guide 646 & 660, tel 177 & 179, Telewest 755 & 756 WWW.GEMSTV.COM

All Gems TV jewellery comes with a minimum total gem weight (MTGW) guarantee

Steve Bennett of Gems TV shares his views on getting jewellery valued....

JEWELLERY VALUATIONS

The Oxford Dictionary says that a valuation is an "estimation of a thing's worth".

As you will probably want to insure the jewellery you purchase from us for the cost of replacement and not the low price that you paid, it often means that you have to seek an independent valuation from a local jeweller.

Before seeking independent valuations please take the following points into consideration:

Basis for valuation

What is the basis of the valuation? It could be said that a valuation is really what someone is prepared to pay for something. For example, what is the value of the Mona Lisa? Is the value the same as the cost of the canvas and the paint or is it determined by the amount that someone will pay for it? We believe that valuations for jewellery should reflect the average cost you would have to pay to replace the item if lost or stolen.

It is my opinion that the ONLY way to achieve a true valuation is to ask a jeweller to make an exact replica of the piece of jewellery. Tell them "I want it as a gift for a friend who likes mine". Tell them it must be identical in carat weight, similar in colour, similar in clarity, cut, etc. also tell them that it must have the same gold weight.

Tell them "please put the price in writing and write down that you guarantee to honour the price for 30 days, in order for me to check that my friend is happy". What you now have in your hand is an independent valuation.

"I bought a Paraiba Tourmaline ring from yourselves for £999 and I have today received a certificate stating that the 18k ring is worth £9000! I'm speechless! The size of the stone came back as 6.373ct and I purchased it believing it to be a 4.359ct ring!!! WOW...what a brilliant return! This is the first valuation I have ever had done...and I'm so thrilled! Thank you again.

P.S. I had thought that the valuations that appear on Gems may have been exaggerated a little NOW I KNOW THEY ARE NOT!!!"

Julie,Staffs
May 2006

"I brought a Black Diamond Gold Ring last September paying £185. On receipt I was thrilled to pieces, the ring is so simple and so elegant, the Diamond is stunning and I cannot believe the lustre I get from it, this is often commented upon by colleagues... the valuation came back at £1,650. What a shocker! Hence it is now insured, especially as I never take the ring off. Thank you for offering such quality and stunning jewellery, I was never a buyer or wearer before I fell upon your channel on Sky and now I am totally hooked, as are my friends whom I rave about you to."

Tracy, Yorkshire
April 2006

JEWELLERY VALUATIONS

"I sent away for a valuation on my beautiful 9k white gold Padparadscha Sapphire ring and my 9k yellow gold Fancy Sapphire bracelet...The Padparadscha Sapphire ring, which had cost £99, was valued at £695!...Even better still, my Fancy Sapphire gold bracelet, which I bought in October for £77, was valued at £775! Wow! I have purchased many pieces from Gems TV since I discovered you in October 2005, some more expensive than others, and I must say that no matter how low priced an item is, it is always beautifully made and the quality of the gems is wonderful. Well done Gems, keep up the good work!"

Rachel, Gt Yarmouth
March 2006

"Hi there. I bought a Chinese Pearl necklace about a month ago for £65 and I am highly delighted. I haven't had it valued, but I was looking in a jeweller's window in Edinburgh last week and saw an almost identical one on sale for £350, so I was even more delighted.

Even the clasp was the same as mine - thank you! I have bought a lot from you over the past year, my latest purchase was on Sunday: Alexandrite earrings."

Linda, West Lothian
June 2006

Independent

On these pages you will read just a handful of the thousands of comments received by letter and email from delighted customers who have informed us that they have received valuations way beyond our start price (let alone the price they paid for it). However, we have also had others that have commented that their local jeweller had provided a valuation below that of their expectations. This comes as no surprise to us at Gems TV, as the question beckons "Is a local jeweller the right person to give a true independent opinion on a product that has been supplied by possibly their biggest competitor?"

As soon as they see our hallmark on an item, you can rest assured that they will not be feeling very independent.

Knowledge

Although most independent jewellers will have a good understanding of valuing gold, silver and Diamonds, many will not have even seen some of the gemstones that you can purchase from Gems TV

With a lack of understanding of how to value such items as Tanzanite and Alexandrite, you may struggle to get a valuation that has any real accuracy.

Comprehensive

To achieve a comprehensive valuation, in most cases, a jeweller would need to dismantle the jewellery to calculate an accurate carat weight of each gem and to check all of the gem's cuts which due to their being set in the jewellery are not visible to the naked eye. The Oxford dictionary describes the word assessment as "estimate the size, value or quality of", how would it be possible to asses the size or cut of a gem without removing it? To avoid the jeweller having to do this, feel free to show them your "certificate of authenticity" that we ship with all of our designs.

Fear of making a mistake

Like every profession, jewellers are fearful of making a professional mistake. If you tell a jeweller how little you paid for an item, they will find it very difficult to provide you with an unbiased judgement.

As Gems TV is a manufacturer of handcrafted jewellery that sells direct to the consumer, cutting out numerous middlemen, our customers are assured that they are buying jewellery at a fraction of what they would pay for similar high quality products via normal means.

A changing world

Because Gems TV is unique and because Gems TV has introduced a new cost-effective way of selling jewellery, many jewellers are unable to comprehend how we do it (especially those who are in direct competition with us). Whilst some independent jewellers thank us for increasing the awareness of coloured gemstones and therefore growing consumer demand, other short-sighted jewellers actively try to discredit our services and our products. Please bear this in mind when seeking valuations.

On page 223 we have details of valuers that have been recommended by our customers.

JEWELLERY VALUATIONS

"I recently went on a cruise and there was a promotional jeweller on board who gave a talk on gems you could buy on board duty free - they were all more expensive than Gems. He mentioned Tanzanite, which he said was the rarest gemstone you could buy, apart from Alexandrite, which most people would never ever see. He said only one person in a million would ever own Alexandrite and I was sitting there with an Alexandrite ring on my finger! I went to speak to him later and showed him my Alexandrite ring. He could not believe it and shook my hand as he had never seen an Alexandrite in all the years he had been in the jewellery business. He later sent me a bottle of champagne to my cabin saying what a pleasure it was to meet someone with an Alexandrite ring. I told him where I purchased it and the price I paid - he was amazed. Thank you Gems for making me one in a million and making me feel very special."

Lynne, Mid Glamorgan
January 2006

"I recently sent five rings away for valuation. The staff at the local jewellers were absolutely astounded when they saw the rings. I was equally astounded when the valuations came back. An Aquamarine solitaire in 18k gold I bought for £179 was valued at £950. If anyone has any doubts about the quality and value of the gems they snatch, this should reassure them."

Jan, Northampton
January 2006

217

BIRTHSTONE GEMS

Garnet

January's birthstone:

Sacred Garnet, the zodiac gem of Aquarius, is cited in the Holy Bible as the gemstone that delivered Noah and his ark to salvation. Garnets are believed to act as healing gems that both protect and strengthen the wearers' spiritual and emotional powers. Available in a myriad of rich tones from full-bodied reds and oranges to verdant greens, Garnet's warmth brings a welcome glow to the cold winter months.

Amethyst

February's birthstone:

Amethyst, the zodiac gem of Pisces, is said to be the preferred gemstone of St. Valentine. Favoured by queens and coveted by kings the intense lavender-purple hues of Amethyst are believed to possess magical properties that promote wisdom, courage, quickening of the wit and sharpening of the mind. Enduringly popular, Amethyst is a gemstone of legend whose lore is only surpassed by its beauty.

Aquamarine

March's birthstone:

Aquamarine, gemstone of the sea god Poseidon and the zodiac gem of Scorpio, has mesmerised all who gaze into its fathomless tones. The seafarers of old believed that when faced with tempestuous seas, casting offerings of Aquamarine into the ocean would placate Poseidon's anger. A gem of cleansing and purification, Aquamarine's scintillating colour and clarity are said to bring peace and happiness and aid the renewal of relationships.

Diamond

April's birthstone:

"Diamonds are Forever", sang Shirley Bassey, while Marilyn insisted they were "A Girl's Best Friend". Celebrated in song, Diamond has long reigned as the ultimate statement of ardour and affection. Believed to be the tears of the Gods, splinters from falling stars or the prodigy of lightning struck rocks, the myths and legends associated with Diamonds continue to transcend both cultures and continents.

BIRTHSTONE GEMS

May's birthstone:

The green fire of Emerald, zodiac gem of Cancer, has been associated with rejuvenation for more than 3,000 years. Venerated by Aztec high priests and coveted by the crown heads of Europe, Emerald occupies a hallowed place in gemstone history. Emeralds are believed to have powerful metaphysical properties affecting both the conscious and unconscious mind, strengthening memory and increasing psychic awareness.

June's birthstones:

Pearl, Moonstone and Alexandrite, signalling the start of summer, present a trilogy of gems that reflect the wonders of the sea, sky and earth. Cleopatra bewitched Marc Anthony with a love potion of ground salt water Pearls, while Moonstone's mystical iridescence captivated ancient civilisations who believed its play of light was due to spirits living within this celestial gem. Terrestrial Alexandrite continues to mesmerise all who lay eyes upon its extraordinary colour-change.

July's birthstone:

A symbol of kingship, passion and romance, Ruby's velvety crimson hues saw them named "Rajnapura" or "King of Gems" by the ancient Hindus. Mined for over 2,500 years, the ancient Burmese believed that Rubies generated mystical forces and were thus a powerful protector from harm. Gemstone to Capricorns, Rubies were also believed to contain prophetic powers, enabling wearers to predict the future based on changes in their colour intensity.

August's birthstone:

Peridot, the gemstone of Librans, were believed by the ancient Hawaiians to be the goddess Pele's tears, while biblical references to the gem include the high priest's breastplate. Ottoman Sultans gathered the world's largest collection of Peridot during their 600 year reign. Peridot was once believed to possess the power to protect the wearer from spells, promote tranquil sleep, provide foresight and give divine inspiration.

BIRTHSTONE GEMS

September's birthstone:

The zodiac gem to Taurus, Sapphire, "Gem of the Heavens", comes in every colour of the rainbow, from the traditional blues to a myriad of fancy colours. Sapphires are emotionally linked to calmness and loyalty, explaining their popularity in engagement rings. The guardians of innocence, Sapphires symbolise truth, sincerity and faithfulness, and are thought to bring peace, joy and wisdom to their owners.

October's birthstones:

Tourmaline and Opal bless those born in October with a cornucopia of colour. Described as the "Chameleon Gemstone", Tourmaline comes in an unparalleled kaleidoscope of colours. Many refer to Tourmaline as the "Muses' Gemstone", as they believe its imaginative colours contain inspirational powers. Opal's unique play of colour has intrigued civilisations since the dawn of time, with the ancient Arabs believing that Opals had fallen from heaven in flashes of lightning.

November's birthstones:

November babies can celebrate with a colourful pairing of two of the world's perennial favourites, Citrine and Topaz. Taking its name from the French word for lemon, the ancient Greeks and Romans believed Citrine's vibrant golden tones were symbolic of happiness. While Topaz, the zodiac gem of Sagittarius, was called the "Gem of the Sun" by the ancient Egyptians who believed it coloured by the golden glow of their sun god Ra.

December's birthstones:

From ancient traditions to contemporary fashion, cool blues and vivid purples are combined in the unmistakable beauty of Turquoise, Zircon and Tanzanite. While 7,000 year old Turquoise jewellery had been found in the tomb of an Egyptian Queen, it was a mere 1,000 years ago that the fire of Zircon mesmerised the ancient Khmer. A thousand times rarer than Diamonds and with a only decade of mining remaining, Tanzanite is the fashion gem of the millennium.

Although these gems are associated with wedding anniversaries, many people give them as gifts to celebrate all kinds of anniversaries.

1st
Gold
Jewellery

2nd
Garnet

3rd
Pearls

4th
Blue
Topaz

5th
Sapphire

6th
Amethyst

7th
Onyx

8th
Tourmaline

9th
Lapis Lazuli

10th
Diamond
Jewellery

11th
Turquoise

12th
Jade

14th
Opal

15th
Ruby

16th
Peridot

17th
Amethyst

18th
Cat's Eye
Beryl

19th
Garnet

20th
Emerald

21st
Iolite

22nd
Spinel

23rd
Imperial
Topaz

24th
Tanzanite

25th
Silver
Jubilee

30th
Pearl Jubilee

35th
Emerald

39th
Cat's Eye

40th
Ruby

45th
Sapphire

50th
Golden
Jubilee

52nd
Star Ruby

55th
Alexandrite

60th
Diamond
Jubilee

65th
Star
Sapphire

70th
Sapphire
Jubilee

75th
Diamond

ZODIAC GEMS

Originating in ancient India, below is a correlation of gems with the astrological signs.

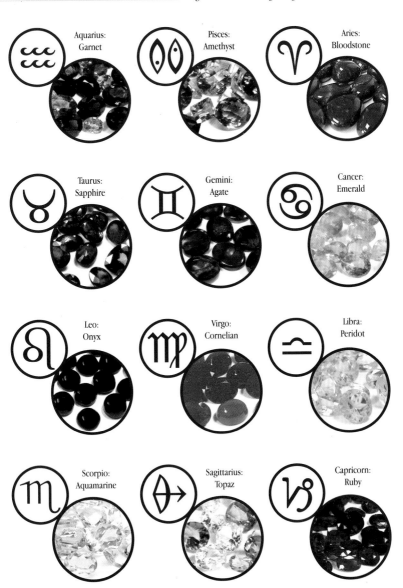

Aquarius: Garnet

Pisces: Amethyst

Aries: Bloodstone

Taurus: Sapphire

Gemini: Agate

Cancer: Emerald

Leo: Onyx

Virgo: Cornelian

Libra: Peridot

Scorpio: Aquamarine

Sagittarius: Topaz

Capricorn: Ruby

Gemmological Institute of America (GIA)
World Headquarters
The Robert Mouawad Campus
5345 Armada Drive
Carlsbad,
California 92008
USA
Tel: 760-603-4000

International Coloured Gemstone Association
19 West 21st Street,
Suite 705
New York,
N.Y. 10010-6805
USA
Tel: 212-620-0900

SafeGuard Quality Assurance Ltd
PO Box 8706
Newhall Street
Birmingham
B3 1FH
Tel: 0121 236 2122
Fax: 0121 236 2128

GAGTL Gem Testing Laboratory
27 Greville Street
London EC1N 8TN
Tel: + 44 207 404 3334
Fax: + 44 207 404 8843

Gemmological Association
27 Greville St
Saffron Hill Entrance
EC1N 8TN
Tel: +44 20 7404 3334
Fax: +44 20 7404 8843

USEFUL CONTACTS

While these independent valuers have been recommended to us individual customers, they are not endorsed by Gems TV. Gems TV have contacted the individual jewellers and they have given us permission to include their details. If you know of a valuer that offers an efficient and cost effective valuation, please email their details to valuations@GemsTV.com

Stanleys (Ring resizing)
113 Vyse Street, Birmingham B18 6LP
Tel: 0121 236 7806

A.J.R Jewellers
Dinnington, Sheffield S25 2PN
Tel: 01909 568452

Crystal Needs Valuations
P.O. Box 181, Ormskirk L39 0WZ
Tel: 07837 064 277

The Jewellery Store
Bank St, Galasheils, Scottish Borders TD1 1EL
Tel: 01896 757 777

Nicholson and Stanforth
2-3 Cross Street, Beverley,
East Yorkshire HU17 9AX
Tel: 01482 886097

Watling Goldsmiths of Lacock
15 East Street, Lacock SN15 2LF
Tel: 01249 730422

INDEX

A

AAAA Tanzanite..........132
African Cats Eye 139
Agate 8
Alexandrite 9
Almandine Garnet 62
Almandine Star
    Garnet 62
Almandine Spinel 127
Amber 13
Amethyst 15
Ametrine 18
Ammolite 20
Anapaite 155
Andalusite 21
Anglesite 155
Apatite..........................22
Apophyllite 155
Aquamarine 23
Aragonite 155
Aventurine 26
Axinite........................155
Azurite 155

B

Balas Ruby 127
Barite 155
Bastnaesite 155
Beryl 27
Bi-Coloured
    Tanzanite 132
Bi-Coloured
    Tourmaline 145
Bixbite..........................28
Black Opal 91
Bloodstone 155
Boracite 155
Boulder Opal 91
Blue Agate....................8
Blue Azurite 155
Blue John Fluorite 55
Blue Lace Agate 8
Blue Topaz 141
Brazilian Emerald........51
Burbankite 155
Bustamite 155

C

Cairngorm 106
Calcite 155
Californite....................69
Carnelian..................106
Cancrinite 155
Carletonite 155
Cassiterite 29
Cats Eye Alexandrite....9
Cats Eye Apatite 22
Cats Eye
    Chrysoberyl 31
Cats Eye Diopside 46
Cats Eye Moonstone....83
Celestite 155
Cerussite....................155
Ceylon Sapphire........114
Chalcedony..................30
Chalcedony Quartz ..106
Charoite 155
Chivor Colombian
    Emerald..................50
Chrome Diopside.......46
Chrysoberyl 31
Chrysocolla................32
Chrysoprase 33
Cinnabar....................155
Citrine..........................34
Cobalt Calcite 155
Cobalt Spinel 127
Colour Change
    Garnet 58
Colour Change
    Sapphire 117
Columbian Emerald 51
Cornelian 35
Coscuez Columbian
    Emerald..................51
Crazy Lace Agate..........8
Creedite 155
Crocidolite Cats Eye ..139
Crying Gemstone 45
Cryptocrystaline
    Quartz 105

D

Danburite 36

Datolite 155
Demantoid Garnet 58
Diamond......................37
Diopside 45
Disthene 78
Dolomite 155
Dumortierite..............155

E

Ekanite 155
Emerald 48
Enstatite 155
Epidote 155
Espirito Santo
    Aquamarine............23
Euclase 155
Eudialyte 155
Evening Emerald 48

F

Fancy Sapphire 116
Feldspar 173
Ferozah 150
Fire Agate 8
Fire Opal......................93
Firestone......................79
Flame Spinel..............127
Flint..............................30
Fluorite 55
Fosterite-Olivine 101

G

Gahnite Spinel 127
Garnet..........................58
Genthelvite 155
Gibeon Meteorite 155
Golden Beryl 27
Gomedha 58
Goshenite 155
Green Agate 8
Green Beryl 27
Greenstone..................72
Green Sapphire 117
Green Tourmaline 146
Golden Beryl 27

H

Hauyne 155

Heliodor 65
Hematite 155
Hemimorphite 155
Herderite......................67
Hessonite 59
Hexagonite 155
Hiddenite 68
Hollandine 60
Howlite 155
Hyacinth 154

I

Idocrase 69
Imperial Topaz 143
Inca Rose 107
Indian Agate 8
Indian Jade 72
Indicolite 146
Indicolite Tourmaline 146
Iolite 70

J

Jacinth........................154
Jade..............................72
Jadeite..........................72
Jargon Yellow Zircon 153
Jasper 73
Jelly Opal 93

K

Kanchanaburi
    Sapphire 114
Kornerupine................75
Krystallos 105
Kunene Spessartite......60
Kunzite 76
Kyanite 78

L

Labradorite 79
Lapis Lazuli..................80
Larimar 155
Layered Tektites 137
Lazurite 123
Leifite 155
Ligure 153
Leifite 155
Ligure 133
Limonite 155

M

Macrocrystalline
   Quartz 105
Madagascan
   Sapphire 114
Maderia Citrine............34
Magnesite 155
Malachite 82
Malaia Garnet 59
Mammoth Ivory 155
Mandarin Garnet 60
Manganotantalite 155
Marcasite....................104
Marha Rocha
   Aquamarine...........24
Matara Diamond........153
Mawsitsit....................155
Mecca Stone 35
Mellite........................155
Merelani Mint Garnet..60
Meteorite 138
Mexican Fire Opal 93
Milarite 155
Moldavite 138
Monazite 155
Montebrasite...............155
Mookite.......................155
Moonstone 83
Mottramite 82
Mozambique Garnet...61
Morganite 84
Moss Agate 8
Mother of Pearl............85
Mtorolite.....................33
Muzo Colombian
   Emerald...............50
Mystic Moonstone 83
Mystic Topaz 143

N

Nigerian Sapphire 115
Natrolite 155
Neon Apatite...............22
Neon Tourmaline 146
Nephrite 72
Noble Red Spinel 127
Nosean 123
Nuummit 155

O

Obsidian 88
Oligoclase 155
Onyx 89
Opal 90

P

Padparadscha
   Sapphire 117
Pakistani Emerald........51
Palin Sapphire 114
Parisite 155
Peacock Stone.............82
Pearl 95
Pectolite 155
Peridot 101
Petalite 155
Pezzottaite...................103
Phenakite 155
Pink Beryl 27
Pink Tourmaline 149
Pink Sapphire 119
Pink Topaz 141
Pollucite 155
Prase 33
Prasiolite 155
Prehnite 155
Purple Sapphire 119
Pyrite........................104
Pyrope Garnet 61
Pyroxmangite 155

Q

Quartz.......................105

R

Rainbow Moonstone ..83
Remondite 155
Rhodochrosite 107
Rhodolite Garnet 61
Rhodonite.................155
Rose Quartz 106
Rose Topaz 141
Rubellite 155
Rubicelle 125
Ruby 108
Russian Alexandrite 9

Rutile 155
Rutilated Quartz 106

S

Sadoine 35
Santa Maria
   Aquamarine...........24
Sapphire 112
Sard...........................155
Sardonyx....................155
Scapolite 121
Scheelite 155
Schefferite..................45
Senarmontite 155
Serandite....................155
Shortite 155
Siderite 155
Sillimanite.................122
Sinhalite 155
Smithsonite...............155
Smoky Quartz...........106
Snowflake Obsidian 88
Sodalite 123
Spectrolite 155
Spessartite Garnet 60
Sphalerite 155
Sphene 124
Spinel 125
Spodumene 155
Star Diopside 46
Star Moonstone 83
Star Garnet 62
Star Quartz 106
Star Sapphire 119
Starlite 154
Staurolite 155
Sugilite 155
Sunstone....................129

T

Tanolite™ 131
Tanzanite....................132
Tektite 138
Thaumasite 155
Tiger's Eye 139

Titanite 124
Titanium Cat's Eye
   Moonstone 83
Topaz.........................140
Tsavorite Garnet 62
Tourmaline 144
Tree Agate 8
Tremolite 155
Tri-Coloured
   Tourmaline 145
Tugtupite 155
Turquoise 150

U

Umba River Sapphire 115
Unakite 152
Uralian Emerald 52
Ureyite 155

V

Vermarine 155
Villaumite 155
Violan Diopside 46

W

Water Sapphire 70
Watermelon
   Tourmaline 145
Wemerite....................121
White Beryl..................27
White Sapphire..........119
White Schefferite 45
White Topaz 141
Willemite 155
Wood Agate..................8
Wulfenite 155

Y

Yellow Beryl 27
Yellow Sapphire 119

Z

Zambian Emerald........52
Zinc-Schefferite............45
Zircon 153

ACKNOWLEDGEMENTS

Gems TV would like to thank the following team members for their contribution to this guide:

(In alphabetical order)
Alex Sharp, Clive Bryant, Debby Cavill, Don Kogen, Dylan Bartlett, Emma Jeffares, Gavin Linsell, John Bennett, Jo Wheeler, Lee Roberts, Mary Baladad, Michelle Duggins, Mike Matthews, Steve Ashton and Steve Bennett.

Plus, thanks to all the Gems TV presenters and our skilled craftsmen at our workshops in Thailand. Many thanks also go to our customers who have allowed their valuations to be printed.

In the UK watch Gems TV 24 hours a day on Sky Guide 646, ntl channel 177 and Telewest channel 755

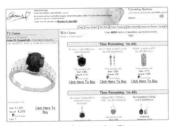

In Europe visit our website www.GemsTV.com

You can also watch Gems TV2 24 hours a day on Sky Guide 660, ntl channel 179 and Telewest channel 756